Modern Language

Approaches to Teaching
World Literature

Joseph Gibaldi, Series Editor

1. Joseph Gibaldi, ed. *Approaches to Teaching Chaucer's* Canterbury Tales. 1980.
2. Carole Slade, ed. *Approaches to Teaching Dante's* Divine Comedy. 1982.
3. Richard Bjornson, ed. *Approaches to Teaching Cervantes'* Don Quixote. 1984.
4. Jess B. Bessinger, Jr., and Robert F. Yeager, eds. *Approaches to Teaching* Beowulf. 1984.
5. Richard J. Dunn, ed. *Approaches to Teaching Dickens'* David Copperfield. 1984.
6. Steven G. Kellman, ed. *Approaches to Teaching Camus's* The Plague. 1985.
7. Yvonne Shafer, ed. *Approaches to Teaching Ibsen's* A Doll House. 1985.
8. Martin Bickman, ed. *Approaches to Teaching Melville's* Moby-Dick. 1985.
9. Miriam Youngerman Miller and Jane Chance, eds. *Approaches to Teaching* Sir Gawain and the Green Knight. 1986.
10. Galbraith M. Crump, ed. *Approaches to Teaching Milton's* Paradise Lost. 1986.
11. Spencer Hall, with Jonathan Ramsey, eds. *Approaches to Teaching Wordsworth's Poetry.* 1986.
12. Robert H. Ray, ed. *Approaches to Teaching Shakespeare's* King Lear. 1986.
13. Kostas Myrsiades, ed. *Approaches to Teaching Homer's* Iliad *and* Odyssey. 1987.
14. Douglas J. McMillan, ed. *Approaches to Teaching Goethe's* Faust. 1987.
15. Renée Waldinger, ed. *Approaches to Teaching Voltaire's* Candide. 1987.
16. Bernard Koloski, ed. *Approaches to Teaching Chopin's* The Awakening. 1988.
17. Kenneth M. Roemer, ed. *Approaches to Teaching Momaday's* The Way to Rainy Mountain. 1988.
18. Edward J. Rielly, ed. *Approaches to Teaching Swift's* Gulliver's Travels. 1988.
19. Jewel Spears Brooker, ed. *Approaches to Teaching Eliot's Poetry and Plays.* 1988.
20. Melvyn New, ed. *Approaches to Teaching Sterne's* Tristram Shandy. 1989.
21. Robert F. Gleckner and Mark L. Greenberg, eds. *Approaches to Teaching Blake's* Songs of Innocence and of Experience. 1989.
22. Susan J. Rosowski, ed. *Approaches to Teaching Cather's* My Ántonia. 1989.
23. Carey Kaplan and Ellen Cronan Rose, eds. *Approaches to Teaching Lessing's* The Golden Notebook. 1989.
24. Susan Resneck Parr and Pancho Savery, eds. *Approaches to Teaching Ellison's* Invisible Man. 1989.
25. Barry N. Olshen and Yael S. Feldman, eds. *Approaches to Teaching the Hebrew Bible as Literature in Translation.* 1989.
26. Robin Riley Fast and Christine Mack Gordon, eds. *Approaches to Teaching Dickinson's Poetry.* 1989.
27. Spencer Hall, ed. *Approaches to Teaching Shelley's Poetry.* 1990.

28. Sidney Gottlieb, ed. *Approaches to Teaching the Metaphysical Poets.* 1990.
29. Richard K. Emmerson, ed. *Approaches to Teaching Medieval English Drama.* 1990.
30. Kathleen Blake, ed. *Approaches to Teaching Eliot's* Middlemarch. 1990.
31. María Elena de Valdés and Mario J. Valdés, eds. *Approaches to Teaching García Márquez's* One Hundred Years of Solitude. 1990.
32. Donald D. Kummings, ed. *Approaches to Teaching Whitman's* Leaves of Grass. 1990.
33. Stephen C. Behrendt, ed. *Approaches to Teaching Shelley's* Frankenstein. 1990.
34. June Schlueter and Enoch Brater, eds. *Approaches to Teaching Beckett's* Waiting for Godot. 1991.
35. Walter H. Evert and Jack W. Rhodes, eds. *Approaches to Teaching Keats's Poetry.* 1991.
36. Frederick W. Shilstone, ed. *Approaches to Teaching Byron's Poetry.* 1991.
37. Bernth Lindfors, ed. *Approaches to Teaching Achebe's* Things Fall Apart. 1991.
38. Richard E. Matlak, ed. *Approaches to Teaching Coleridge's Poetry and Prose.* 1991.
39. Shirley Geok-lin Lim, ed. *Approaches to Teaching Kingston's* The Woman Warrior. 1991.
40. Maureen Fries and Jeanie Watson, eds. *Approaches to Teaching the Arthurian Tradition.* 1992.
41. Maurice Hunt, ed. *Approaches to Teaching Shakespeare's* The Tempest *and Other Late Romances.* 1992.
42. Diane Long Hoeveler and Beth Lau, eds. *Approaches to Teaching Brontë's* Jane Eyre. 1993.
43. Jeffrey B. Berlin, ed. *Approaches to Teaching Mann's* Death in Venice *and Other Short Fiction.* 1992.
44. Kathleen McCormick and Erwin R. Steinberg, eds. *Approaches to Teaching Joyce's* Ulysses. 1993.
45. Marcia McClintock Folsom, ed. *Approaches to Teaching Austen's* Pride and Prejudice. 1993.

Approaches to Teaching Brontë's *Jane Eyre*

Edited by

Diane Long Hoeveler

and

Beth Lau

The Modern Language Association of America
New York   1993

Library of Congress Cataloging-in-Publication Data

Approaches to teaching Brontë's Jane Eyre / edited by Diane Long
    Hoeveler and Beth Lau.
        p.   cm. — (Approaches to teaching world literature ; 42)
    Includes bibliographical references and index.
    ISBN 0-87352-705-4 (cloth) ISBN 0-87352-706-2 (pbk.)
    1. Brontë, Charlotte, 1816–1855. Jane Eyre. 2. Brontë,
Charlotte, 1816–1855 — Study and teaching. 3. Governesses in
literature. I. Hoeveler, Diane Long. II. Lau, Beth, 1951–.
III. Series.
PR4167.J5A66   1993
823'.8 — dc20   93-16427

Published by The Modern Language Association of America
10 Astor Place, New York, New York 10003-6981

Printed on recycled paper

CONTENTS

Preface to the Series   vii

Preface to the Volume   viii

PART ONE: MATERIALS   *Beth Lau*

Introduction   3
Editions   4
Biography   6
Background Studies   7
Critical Studies   9
Aids to Teaching   14
Bibliographies   15

PART TWO: APPROACHES

Introduction   *Diane Long Hoeveler*   19

Teaching the Times and the Life

Jane Eyre and *A Vindication of the Rights of Woman*   22
    James Diedrick

The Place of *Jane Eyre* in the Brontë Family Canon   29
    Janet H. Freeman

Jane Eyre and Biography   36
    Thomas L. Jeffers

Jane Eyre and the Governess in Nineteenth-Century Britain   43
    Mary Poovey

Teaching the Literary and Philosophical Traditions

Jane Eyre, Bertha, and the Female Gothic   49
    Tamar Heller

"Beauty and the Beast": Growing Up with Jane Eyre   56
    Phyllis C. Ralph

Jane Eyre and Christianity   62
    Susan VanZanten Gallagher

Jane Eyre: Charlotte Brontë's New Bible   69
    Keith A. Jenkins

Teaching Specific Contexts

Jane Eyre and Narrative Voice   76
    John O. Jordan

Fire and Light in *Jane Eyre*   82
    Mary Burgan

Contrast and Liminality: Structure and Antistructure
   in *Jane Eyre*   87
   Mark M. Hennelly, Jr.

Jane Eyre and Pictorial Representation   97
   Margaret Goscilo

Jane Eyre and Imperialism   104
   John Kucich

Jane Eyre and the Politics of Style   110
   Dennis W. Allen

Jane Eyre through the Body: Food, Sex, Discipline   116
   Diane Long Hoeveler

Jane Eyre as a Novel of Vindication   124
   Bernard J. Paris

Jane Eyre and Family Systems Therapy   130
   Jerome Bump

Rediscovering *Jane Eyre* through Its Adaptations   139
   Donna Marie Nudd

Taking a Walk; or, Setting Forth from Gateshead   148
   Robert L. Patten

A Kristevan Reading of the Marriage Plot in *Jane Eyre*   154
   David Rosenwasser

Contributors and Survey Participants   162

Works Cited
   Editions of *Jane Eyre*   163
   Books and Articles   163
   Films and Filmstrips   176
   Recordings   176

Index   177

PREFACE TO THE SERIES

In *The Art of Teaching* Gilbert Highet wrote, "Bad teaching wastes a great deal of effort, and spoils many lives which might have been full of energy and happiness." All too many teachers have failed in their work, Highet argued, simply "because they have not thought about it." We hope that the Approaches to Teaching World Literature series, sponsored by the Modern Language Association's Publications Committee, will not only improve the craft — as well as the art — of teaching but also encourage serious and continuing discussion of the aims and methods of teaching literature.

The principal objective of the series is to collect within each volume different points of view on teaching a specific literary work, a literary tradition, or a writer widely taught at the undergraduate level. The preparation of each volume begins with a wide-ranging survey of instructors, thus enabling us to include in the volume the philosophies and approaches, thoughts and methods of scores of experienced teachers. The result is a sourcebook of material, information, and ideas on teaching the subject of the volume to undergraduates.

The series is intended to serve nonspecialists as well as specialists, inexperienced as well as experienced teachers, graduate students who wish to learn effective ways of teaching as well as senior professors who wish to compare their own approaches with the approaches of colleagues in other schools. Of course, no volume in the series can ever substitute for erudition, intelligence, creativity, and sensitivity in teaching. We hope merely that each book will point readers in useful directions; at most each will offer only a first step in the long journey to successful teaching.

Joseph Gibaldi
Series Editor

PREFACE TO THE VOLUME

> Why was I always suffering, always browbeaten, always
> accused, for ever condemned? Why could I never please?
> Why was it useless to try to win any one's favour?
> — *Jane Eyre*

With these powerful and poignant words the adult narrator we know to
be Jane Rochester projects herself back into the psyche of the child Jane
Eyre, a move that recapitulates the task we all undertake as individuals
who seek to understand ourselves in the continuum of time and experience.
When the child's voice emerges as a distinct, hideously clear enunciation
of pain, we cannot help but assent to and identify with the tale it tells. *Jane
Eyre*, perhaps more than many other novels, repeatedly confronts both
instructors and students with opportunities for self-scrutiny. That is, students
who engage the text as it was meant to be read — viscerally and with passion
— end up discovering as much about themselves, their own memories of
childhood, their own struggles for autonomy, as they do about the cultural,
social, economic, religious, and literary backgrounds that constitute the
milieu of the novel.

Effective teachers of literature seek to do many things in an often limited
time period. We all hope to impart critical thinking skills to our students,
since the ability to analyze and synthesize data is crucial for survival in a
society based on documents of various complexity. And we seek to convey
information about the past so that our students will understand and appreciate the present. But, finally, when all the cognitive jargon is spent, we have
to admit that we chiefly hope to interest students in the work of literature
itself — its structure, its artistic values, its metaphors, its vision of possibilities. Success in opening up a work of literature for students in a classroom
brings us that sudden sense of transparency, when narrator, text, instructor,
and class all pursue a shared meaning, a shared perception, a shared understanding. To such an end is this volume offered.

Three dozen teacher-scholars contributed their expertise and experience
to this volume, either by writing an essay or completing a questionnaire
on teaching *Jane Eyre*. The first section of the volume, by Beth Lau, summarizes the suggestions contributed by those instructors; it also surveys the
vast terrain of primary and secondary sources available to teachers and
students of *Jane Eyre*. This "Materials" section is followed by twenty essays
on teaching various aspects of the text. These essays were selected for inclu-
sion in the book because they demonstrate the vitality and diversity of
current work on teaching Brontë's life and times and on the ideas developed

in her major novel. Whether you are intrigued by classroom drama or family systems psychotherapy, poststructuralist or post-Freudian approaches, you will find that these essays have something to offer both beginning and experienced teachers of *Jane Eyre*. Like the other volumes in this series, *Approaches to Teaching Brontë's* Jane Eyre hopes to illuminate the teaching of a work that deserves its place in the canon through its continued vigor and vision.

My coeditor, Beth Lau, and I wish to acknowledge our debt to MLA series editor Joseph Gibaldi, as well as to Alicia Mahaney Minsky, former assistant acquisitions editor, and Rebecca Lanning, assistant editor, for their guidance and encouragement. We are also indebted to the MLA's Publications Committee for sponsoring both the series and this volume and to the outside readers who generously gave of their time and expertise. Finally, we thank the Office of Research Support of Marquette University, in particular Thaddeus Burch, S.J., and Lynn Miner, for financial assistance with the preparation of this volume.

                                                          DLH

Part One

MATERIALS

Introduction

The survey on which this volume is based asked teachers of *Jane Eyre* to identify the editions of the novel they prefer and the background and critical works they have found most useful. In this account of the survey results, I occasionally supplement the respondents' suggestions with other helpful works, but what follows is necessarily a selective bibliography. For a more extensive review of *Jane Eyre* scholarship and criticism, one can consult the bibliographies listed at the end of this "Materials" section. Further references to books and articles on particular topics may also be found in individual essays on teaching various aspects of the novel.

I have not listed works for students and works for teachers separately, as some volumes in this series do, since a number of respondents said either that they assign no outside readings for students or that they recommend the same works for students as they do for teachers. Certainly the titles respondents most often cited as useful for teachers do not differ significantly from those cited as useful for students. I have noted, however, several works that seem particularly appropriate for student readers.

Editions

Paperback Editions of Jane Eyre

Survey respondents recommended six different paperback editions of *Jane Eyre*. Some teachers listed more than one edition, explaining that they use different texts in different courses. A few others remarked that they simply use whatever edition is cheapest and most easily available. The two most popular texts cited in the survey are the Penguin, edited by Q. D. Leavis, and the Norton Critical, prepared by Richard J. Dunn and now in a second edition.[1] The Penguin, which beat out the Norton by one vote, is clearly the favored volume for those who want the text of the novel without extensive additional materials. Respondents praised the Penguin for its low price, availability, "handy size," "decent binding," and helpful though unobtrusive explanatory notes. Leavis's introduction, which gives an overview of Charlotte Brontë's life and an analysis of central issues in the novel, was also commended. Besides the introduction and notes, the Penguin text includes a facsimile of the original title page of *Jane Eyre* as well as Brontë's preface to the second edition and note to the third edition. One oddity of this edition, especially striking for its juxtaposition with what has come to be regarded as a central feminist text, is that Q. D. Leavis is identified as "the widow of the distinguished literary critic, Dr. F. R. Leavis."

The Norton Critical Edition was valued for its reliable text, explanatory notes, and, most especially, its background and critical sections, which one respondent considered indispensable. Another teacher described the Norton edition as the "best available combination of text, background, and critical apparatus." For background material, the Norton second edition provides (in addition to facsimiles of Brontë's original title page and her dedication to Thackeray, her preface to the second edition, and her note to the third edition) several documents relating to the Cowan Bridge School for Clergymen's Daughters, selections from Brontë's juvenile writings, a sample of Brontë's letters, some contemporary reviews, and excerpts from Elizabeth Gaskell's biography of Brontë. The "Criticism" section reprints commentary on the novel by Virginia Woolf, Robert B. Heilman, Adrienne Rich, Sandra M. Gilbert, Helene Moglen, and Terry Eagleton (for more on these works, see the "Critical Studies" section below). The Norton Critical Edition generally is considered most appropriate for upper-division courses; several respondents said they used an alternative text for lower-division students.

Some instructors recommend the World's Classics text, edited by Margaret Smith, who, along with Jane Jack, also edited the standard Clarendon edition of *Jane Eyre*. Although the other editors mentioned here all follow the third edition, Smith uses as her copy text the first edition of the novel, which some teachers prefer as well. Smith's edition offers an introduction, explanatory notes, and a "Note on the Text" that describes the differences among the manuscript and various printed versions of the novel and states Smith's reasons for favoring the first edition. The World's Classics text, like the other editions previously cited, includes a facsimile of the original title page, the preface to the second edition, and the note to the third edition. Other reasons teachers mentioned for choosing the World's Classics edition were its low price, availability, and print size, which is somewhat larger than Penguin's.

The Norton Anthology of Literature by Women, edited by Sandra M. Gilbert and Susan Gubar and often used in women's literature courses, includes the entire text of *Jane Eyre*. The anthology contains a valuable introduction to nineteenth-century literature that surveys important historical and cultural developments of the period in both England and America. The headnote to *Jane Eyre* draws on points made about the novel in Gilbert and Gubar's extremely influential work *The Madwoman in the Attic* (see "Critical Studies," below). *The Norton Anthology of Literature by Women* also features selected bibliographies for each of the writers included in the volume.

Survey respondents named two other teaching editions. The Signet Classics (New American Library) edition has the distinction of being the cheapest of the recommended paperbacks. One respondent listed Mark Schorer's Riverside edition, but this text is now out of print. If the volume is available in one's campus library, however, it might still be used for the purpose this teacher mentioned: she assigns Schorer's introduction "to show students how far we've come since he wrote it."

Critical Editions of Brontë's Writing

Teachers of *Jane Eyre* may find it helpful to consult scholarly editions of the novel and of Brontë's other works. As stated above, the standard edition of *Jane Eyre* is the Clarendon, edited by Jack and Smith, reprinted with corrections in 1975. The introduction describes the novel's composition and publication history and explains the choice of copy text (the first edition). Textual notes record variants from the manuscript and the second and third editions. The volume also provides extensive explanatory notes and five appendixes covering such topics as the chronology of events in the novel, factual bases for some episodes, Brontë's spelling, and "Opinions of the Press" (those printed at the end of the third edition of *Jane Eyre*).

Clarendon has issued critical editions of all the Brontë novels, which are becoming the new standard texts. Anne Brontë's *The Tenant of Wildfell Hall* (1991), edited by Herbert Rosengarten, is the final Brontë novel to appear in the Clarendon series. Charlotte's *The Professor* (1987), *Shirley* (1979), and *Villette* (1984) are all edited by Herbert Rosengarten and Margaret Smith.

Christine Alexander is preparing a modern critical edition of Brontë's juvenilia (*An Edition of the Early Writings of Charlotte Brontë*). Three volumes — *The Glass Town Saga, 1826–1832*; *The Rise of Angria, 1833–1834*; and *The Rise of Angria, 1834–1835* — have been published, and another volume is projected. Alexander's edition will supersede Fannie E. Ratchford's *The Brontës' Web of Childhood*, Ratchford and William C. DeVane's *Legends of Angria*, and T. J. Wise and J. A. Symington's *The Miscellaneous and Unpublished Writings of Charlotte and Patrick Branwell Brontë*. Alexander's *The Early Writings of Charlotte Brontë*, which provides an extensive discussion and summary of the juvenilia, is useful especially in lieu of a complete edition of these writings. Several modern editions of particular Angrian tales also exist. Among the most popular are *Five Novelettes* (ed. Gérin), *"The Secret" and "Lily Hart": Two Tales by Charlotte Brontë* (ed. Holtz), and *Something about Arthur* (ed. Alexander).

The standard edition of Brontë's letters is still the incomplete and inaccurate *The Brontës: Their Lives, Friendships and Correspondence*, in four volumes, edited by Wise and Symington. The most complete and reliable edition of her poetry is *The Poems of Charlotte Brontë: A New Text and Commentary*, edited by Victor A. Neufeldt.

Biography

The lives of the Brontës have held a persistent fascination for readers of English literature, and biographical studies have always loomed large in Brontë scholarship. Elizabeth Gaskell's 1857 *The Life of Charlotte Brontë*, a work that initiated the interest in and study of Brontë's remarkable, tragic life, is still considered a classic biography. Many survey respondents recommend it to students and draw on it for their own work. The standard biography, and the one most often cited by respondents, is Winifred Gérin's 1967 *Charlotte Brontë: The Evolution of Genius*. Gérin's detailed study provides a comprehensive account of the events and circumstances of Brontë's life, although some teachers prefer the feminist perspective of Margot Peters's *Unquiet Soul: A Biography of Charlotte Brontë*. In the preface to *Charlotte Brontë: The Self Conceived*, Helene Moglen explains that her book intentionally eschews conventional goals of objectivity and thoroughness in favor of a more speculative, psychological approach that seeks to get at the heart of Brontë's personality and creative genius. Moglen's first chapter, "Survival," recounts and analyzes Brontë's life through 1845. Subsequent chapters are devoted to each of the four novels, and a brief conclusion treats Brontë's relationship with Arthur Bell Nichols, her marriage, and her death. Appearing too recently to figure in the surveys is Rebecca Fraser's *The Brontës:*

Charlotte Brontë and Her Family. Fraser draws on new material and insights that have surfaced since Gérin's biography, including the Seton-Gordon papers, Brontë's marriage settlement, and the feminist revolution in literary criticism. Reviews appearing thus far have been mixed, however, and it is unlikely that Fraser's work will become the new standard biography.

Survey respondents recommend several other biographical studies. Margaret Lane's *The Brontë Story: A Reconsideration of Mrs. Gaskell's* Life of Charlotte Brontë is, as the subtitle suggests, based on Gaskell's volume, but Lane updates the earlier work with new information that has come to light since the mid–nineteenth century. Gérin's two pamphlets for the Writers and Their Work series, *The Brontës: The Formative Years* and *The Brontës: The Creative Work*, can be a helpful introduction for students. For introductory works that contain biographical chapters as well as criticism of Brontë's writing, respondents mention Margaret Howard Blom's *Charlotte Brontë*, Tom Winnifrith's *The Brontës*, and Pauline Nestor's *Charlotte Brontë*.

A number of pictorial biographies were cited as useful reference works. Phyllis Bentley's *The Brontës and Their World*, Brian Wilks's *The Brontës*, and Arthur Pollard and Simon McBride's *The Landscape of the Brontës* all provide many illustrations and photographs of people, objects, buildings, and landscapes associated with the Brontës' lives and fiction. Francis B. Pinion's *A Brontë Companion: Literary Assessment, Background, and Reference* also contains illustrations, along with biographical sketches of each of the Brontës and other reference and critical material. (For more references to and discussion of biographical studies, see the essays by Thomas L. Jeffers and Janet H. Freeman in this volume.)

Background Studies

The background material most often assigned to students is that provided in the Norton Critical Edition of *Jane Eyre*. A variety of other works, however, may be instructive for teachers and students of the novel. Two studies that elude easy categorization are Winnifrith's *The Brontës and Their Background: Romance and Reality* and Pinion's *A Brontë Companion*. Winnifrith's book covers topics such as the history and current condition of Brontë texts (seriously flawed in the early 1970s, when Winnifrith was writing), the Brontës' religious beliefs and attitudes toward sex and social class, their readings, and contemporary reviews of the Brontë novels. The Pinion work contains, in addition to the biographical sketch mentioned above, commentary on all Brontë's writing (including poems, juvenilia, and letters), a section entitled "People and Places in the Novels," a "Glossary of Unusual Words," a select bibliography, and several appendixes, one of which features biblical and literary allusions in Brontë's novels and another that catalogs Brontë films.

Miriam Allott's *The Brontës: The Critical Heritage* collects contemporary reviews of *Jane Eyre*, and Allott's introduction usefully summarizes and analyzes the reception of each Brontë novel. Early and later Victorian responses to *Jane Eyre* may also be found in Allott's *Charlotte Brontë: Jane Eyre and Villette: A Casebook*. The Norton Critical Edition reprints the remarks of some of Brontë's contemporaries, and Winnifrith's *The Brontës and Their Background* has a chapter called "Reviews and Reviewers."

Two classic and still often cited studies of the Victorian period are Walter E. Houghton's *The Victorian Frame of Mind, 1830–1870* and Richard D. Altick's *Victorian People and Ideas.* Elaine Showalter, in *A Literature of Their Own*, provides a social history of women writers in Victorian England. In *The Female Malady: Women, Madness, and Culture in England, 1830–1980*, Showalter includes a discussion of *Jane Eyre* in her study of attitudes toward and treatment of mental illness in the nineteenth century. M. Jeanne Peterson's "The Victorian Governess: Status Incongruence in Family and Society" has become a classic essay on the governess figure. (For a further discussion of the governess in *Jane Eyre* and the Victorian period generally, see Mary Poovey's essay in this volume.)

Teachers often assign works setting forth some of the insights and methods of feminist literary criticism in conjunction with *Jane Eyre*. In this category, survey respondents cite Virginia Woolf's *A Room of One's Own*, Patricia Meyer Spacks's *The Female Imagination* (especially the chapter "Growing Up Female"), and the first two chapters of Gilbert and Gubar's *The Madwoman in the Attic*.

Respondents suggest a number of books on Victorian fiction that, while not treating *Jane Eyre* directly, may be valuable as background sources. Jerome H. Buckley's *The Victorian Temper* has a chapter entitled "The Pattern of Conversion," and the scope of his *Season of Youth* is readily apparent from its subtitle, *The Bildungsroman from Dickens to Golding*. The titles of A. O. J. Cockshut's *Man and Woman: A Study of Love and the Novel, 1740–1940* and Ioan Williams's *The Realist Novel in England: A Study in Development* are also self-explanatory. One teacher says that he occasionally assigns J. Hillis Miller's *The Form of Victorian Fiction* because, "while reductive, it is useful for undergraduates in search of answers."

Two histories of the English novel that include sections on Brontë and *Jane Eyre* are Lionel Stevenson's *The English Novel: A Panorama* and Walter Allen's *The English Novel: A Short Critical History.* Allen's volume, however, may offend some readers by its frequent disparaging remarks about Brontë and her writing. Like the Schorer introduction to the Riverside *Jane Eyre*, mentioned above, the work may serve to illustrate how far criticism has evolved since the 1950s. One final reference work that teachers should be aware of is C. Ruth Sabol and Todd K. Bender's *Concordance to Brontë's Jane Eyre.*

Critical Studies

The critical work survey respondents cited most often is, far and away, Gilbert and Gubar's *The Madwoman in the Attic*. The interpretation of *Jane Eyre* set forth in chapter 10, "A Dialogue of Self and Soul: Plain Jane's Progress," made something of a revolution in Brontë studies, and it has been largely responsible for placing feminist readings at the forefront of approaches to the novel. Among Gilbert and Gubar's most original points are their emphasis on Jane's anger toward and rebellion against a repressive patriarchal society and their interpretation of Bertha Mason Rochester as a double who acts out Jane's aggression and passion.

After *Madwoman*, the most popular feminist readings among survey respondents were Rich's "Jane Eyre: The Temptations of a Motherless Woman," first published in *Ms.* magazine in 1973 and reprinted in Rich's *On Lies, Secrets, and Silence* and the Norton Critical Edition of *Jane Eyre*; Showalter's analysis of the novel in *A Literature of Their Own* (112–22); and Moglen's chapter "*Jane Eyre*: The Creation of a Feminist Myth" in *Charlotte Brontë: The Self Conceived* (part of the chapter is also reprinted in the Norton Critical Edition).

Other feminist studies that teachers found useful are Harriet Bjork's *The Language of Truth: Charlotte Brontë, the Woman Question, and the Novel*; Patricia Beer's *Reader, I Married Him: A Study of the Women Characters of Jane Austen, Charlotte Brontë, Elizabeth Gaskell, and George Eliot*; Barbara Rigney's *Madness and Sexual Politics in the Feminist Novel*; Pauline Nestor's *Female Friendships and Communities: Charlotte Brontë, George Eliot, Elizabeth Gaskell*; and two essays, Maurianne Adams's "*Jane Eyre*: Woman's Estate" and Nancy Pell's "Resistance, Rebellion, and Marriage: The Economics of *Jane Eyre*."

Among general studies of the novel, Robert B. Martin's perceptive and balanced *The Accents of Persuasion: Charlotte Brontë's Novels* was most often cited. Other popular general readings are Virginia Woolf's essay "*Jane Eyre* and *Wuthering Heights*" in *The Common Reader* (reprinted in the Norton Critical Edition); Kathleen Tillotson's *Novels of the Eighteen-Forties*; Inga-Stina Ewbank's *Their Proper Sphere: A Study of the Brontë Sisters as Early-Victorian Female Novelists*; W. A. Craik's *The Brontë Novels*; Earl Knies's *The Art of Charlotte Brontë*; and Karen Chase's *Eros and Psyche: The Representation of Personality in Charlotte Brontë, Charles Dickens, and George Eliot*.

Respondents commended John Maynard's *Charlotte Brontë and Sexuality* as an insightful psychological study. An earlier, decidedly nonfeminist view of Brontë's attitude toward sexuality as reflected in *Jane Eyre* is developed by Richard Chase in "The Brontës; or, Myth Domesticated." Chase's is another interpretation that may be useful as an illustration of changes in

Brontë criticism over the past forty years: one teacher assigns Chase's essay "to present an earlier view that might inspire a heated discussion." Other psychological works are Barbara Hannah's *Striving towards Wholeness*, a Jungian interpretation; Karen Ann Butery's "Jane Eyre's Flight from Decision" and "The Contributions of Horneyan Psychology to the Study of Literature"; Charles Burkhart's *Charlotte Brontë: A Psychosexual Study of Her Novels*; and Robert Keefe's *Charlotte Brontë's World of Death*, which regards the deaths of Brontë's mother, sisters, and brother as the central, shaping events of Brontë's life. Two other essays concerned with her response to loss as reflected in her fiction are Adams's "Family Disintegration and Creative Reintegration: The Case of Charlotte Brontë and *Jane Eyre*" and Susan D. Bernstein's "Madam Mope: The Bereaved Child in Brontë's *Jane Eyre*." (Bernard J. Paris's and Jerome Bump's essays in this volume also describe psychological approaches to the novel.)

Most interpretations of *Jane Eyre* focus on the novel's protagonist, but Brontë's male characters have been examined as well. F. A. C. Wilson ("The Primrose Wreath: The Heroes of the Brontë Novels"), Gail B. Griffin ("The Humanization of Edward Rochester"), and John Maynard (*Charlotte Brontë and Sexuality* 110–14) see Rochester as a complex personality who grows by abandoning the false notions of masculinity and femininity that society has taught him and by becoming a more androgynous and thus a more fully human being. Paul Pickrel ("*Jane Eyre*: The Apocalypse of the Body") diagnoses Rochester as a man suffering from depersonalization who puts up a series of false fronts to impress others and "regain autonomy, to reclaim or reoccupy himself" (165; on Rochester's personality, see also Bump's essay in this volume). Showalter explains the appeal of brutish men like Rochester for Brontë and other women of her time in *A Literature of Their Own* (133–52). Dianne F. Sadoff (*Monsters of Affection: Dickens, Eliot, and Brontë on Fatherhood*) regards Brontë's male characters as father figures, whereas Jane Miller (*Women Writing about Men*) considers them chiefly brother figures.

Terry Eagleton has written a classic Marxist interpretation of *Jane Eyre* (*Myths of Power*; reprinted in part in the Norton Critical Edition). Jina Politi's "*Jane Eyre* Class-ified" examines class issues in the novel, and both Gayatri Spivak ("Three Women's Texts and a Critique of Imperialism") and Nancy Armstrong (*Desire and Domestic Fiction: A Political History of the Novel*) investigate Brontë's attitude toward imperialism. (For more on political and class issues in *Jane Eyre*, see the essays by Dennis W. Allen, John Kucich, and Diane Long Hoeveler in this volume.)

A number of critics have studied formal elements of the novel. Imagery is analyzed by Robert B. Heilman, "Charlotte Brontë, Reason, and the Moon"; David Lodge, "Fire and Eyre: Charlotte Brontë's War of Earthly Elements"; Nina Auerbach, "Charlotte Brontë: The Two Countries"; and Cynthia Linder, *Romantic Imagery in the Novels of Charlotte Brontë*. Enid Duthie (*The Brontës and Nature*) classifies and analyzes the many nature images in Brontë's writing. Judith Williams (*Perception and Expression in the Novels of Charlotte Brontë*) studies "curtained enclosures, shrines, and stages" in *Jane Eyre* (19); she also traces the development of Jane's spiritual and imaginative perception, that is, her ability to see clearly and accept the truth. Peter Bellis's "In the Window-Seat: Vision and Power in *Jane Eyre*" also analyzes modes of perception in the novel. Using Lacanian theory, Bellis distinguishes between a penetrating male gaze and the marginal female outlook that ultimately dominates as Rochester is blinded and Jane sees for him, herself unobserved. (On imagery, see the essays by Mary Burgan and Mark M. Hennelly, Jr., in this volume.)

Related to visual imagery are the paintings Jane Eyre executes in the novel. Barbara T. Gates, in " 'Visionary Woe' and Its Revisions: Another Look at Jane Eyre's Pictures," synthesizes much previous commentary on the three surrealistic paintings Jane shows to Rochester. Pickrel takes up the subject in "*Jane Eyre*: The Apocalypse of the Body" (173–77), and Millgate ("Narrative Distance in *Jane Eyre*: The Relevance of the Pictures") comments on all Jane's paintings, from her landscapes at Lowood to her verbal portraits of nature for her blind husband at the novel's end, as emblems of Jane's emotional development.

Various stylistic features are examined by Karl Kroeber, *Styles in Fictional Structure: The Art of Jane Austen, Charlotte Brontë, and George Eliot*; Margot Peters, *Charlotte Brontë: Style in the Novel*; Garrett Stewart, "Teaching Prose Fiction: Some 'Instructive' Styles"; and Doreen Roberts, "*Jane Eyre* and 'The Warped System of Things.' " Knies, in *The Art of Charlotte Brontë*, argues for the significance of the first-person narrator in *Jane Eyre*. Narrative patterns in the novel are also the subject of Peter Allan Dale's "Charlotte Brontë's 'Tale Half-Told': The Disruption of Narrative Structure in *Jane Eyre*"; Rosemarie Bodenheimer's "*Jane Eyre* in Search of Her Story"; and Rachel Blau DuPlessis's "Endings and Contradictions." (See the essays by Dennis W. Allen and John O. Jordan in this volume for further discussion of style and narrative issues.)

Although many critical studies point out conflicts in *Jane Eyre* between reason and passion, id and superego, activity and passivity, and so forth, two popular essays specifically concerned with this topic are R. E. Hughes's "*Jane Eyre*: The Unbaptized Dionysos" and Richard Benvenuto's "The Child of Nature, the Child of Grace, and the Unresolved Conflict in *Jane Eyre*." (In this volume, Mark M. Hennelly, Jr., and David Rosenwasser each treat oppositions or central contrasts in the novel.)

Brontë's religious attitudes are considered by Barbara Hardy, *The Appropriate Form: An Essay on the Novel*; Winnifrith, *The Brontës and Their Background*; Thomas Vargish, *The Providential Aesthetic in Victorian Fiction*; and Dale, "Charlotte Brontë's 'Tale Half-Told.' " (The essays by Keith A. Jenkins and Susan VanZanten Gallagher in this book address religious issues in *Jane Eyre*. See also the discussion of source studies below.)

Brontë's use of fairy tales in the novel has attracted much critical attention. Recommended works on this topic are Paula Sullivan, "Fairy Tale Elements in *Jane Eyre*"; Robert K. Martin, "*Jane Eyre* and the World of Faery"; Keefe, *Charlotte Brontë's World of Death* (113–22); Karen E. Rowe, "'Fairy Born and Human Bred': Jane Eyre's Education in Romance"; and Phyllis C. Ralph, *Victorian Transformations: Fairy Tales, Adolescence, and the Novel of Female Development* (see also the essay by Ralph in this volume).

Heilman's ground-breaking "Charlotte Brontë's 'New' Gothic" reexamines Gothic elements in the novel as symbols of psychological states rather than as stock melodramatic conventions. My research indicates that Heilman's essay has been more frequently reprinted than any other essay ever written on *Jane Eyre*. Ruth Yeazell ("More True than Real: Jane Eyre's 'Mysterious Summons'") develops an argument similar to Heilman's about supernatural events in the novel. An important recent work that analyzes *Jane Eyre* as a female Gothic novel is Eugenia C. DeLamotte's *Perils of the Night: A Feminist Study of Nineteenth-Century Gothic*. (The female Gothic genre in relation to *Jane Eyre* is also studied by Tamar Heller in the "Approaches" section of this volume.) Jerome Beaty ("*Jane Eyre* and Genre") asserts that *Jane Eyre* largely follows the conventions of the governess novel popular at the time.

Aspects of Romanticism in Brontë's novel are analyzed by Richard Dunn ("The Natural Heart: Jane Eyre's Romanticism") and Donald D. Stone (*The Romantic Impulse in Victorian Fiction*). Both Gérin, in "Byron's Influence on the Brontës," and Moglen discuss the influence of Byron and Byronism on Brontë's fiction. The first chapter of Duthie's *The Brontës and Nature* considers the influence of Scott, Byron, Wordsworth, and Coleridge on Brontë's attitude toward nature. (On Romanticism and *Jane Eyre*, see James Diedrick's essay "*Jane Eyre* and *A Vindication of the Rights of Woman*" in this volume.)

A number of other studies consider literary sources of *Jane Eyre*. As previously mentioned, Pinion's *A Brontë Companion* contains an appendix listing allusions to the Bible and other literary works in Brontë's novels. The Clarendon edition of *The Professor* (ed. Smith and Rosengarten) also has valuable indexes of quotations from and allusions to the Bible and other books and writers in all the novels. (On the Bible and *Jane Eyre*, see Keith A. Jenkins's essay in this volume.) The legacy of John Bunyan's *The Pilgrim's Progress* for Brontë is examined by Millgate ("Jane Eyre's Progress") and Barry Qualls (*The Secular Pilgrims of Victorian Fiction: The Novel as Book of Life*). Florence Swinton Dry's *The Sources of* Jane Eyre focuses on Walter Scott and Charles Dickens, and Lawrence J. Dessner's *The Homely Web of Truth: A Study of Charlotte Brontë's Novels* includes the chapters "Literary Culture" and "George Sand and Walter Scott." Winnifrith discusses a variety of eighteenth- and nineteenth-century texts Brontë may have read ("The Brontës and Their Books," in *The Brontës and Their Background*), and

Duthie (*The Foreign Vision of Charlotte Brontë*) considers the ways in which French authors affected Brontë's outlook and prose style. Finally, Tillotson (*Novels of the Eighteen-Forties*) argues for the influence of Patrick, Emily, and Anne Brontë's writing on *Jane Eyre*.

Since Brontë's novel is commonly taught in courses on Victorian fiction, teachers and students may be interested in works that compare *Jane Eyre* with other fiction of the period. Several works already mentioned discuss Brontë in the context of other nineteenth-century writers. Besides the items just listed in the discussion of influences, useful works include those by Stevenson, Allen, Beer, Showalter (*Literature*), Gilbert and Gubar (*Madwoman*), Nestor (*Female Friendships*), Kroeber, Sadoff, Karen Chase, Vargish (on Brontë, Dickens, and Eliot), and Butery ("Contributions," on *Jane Eyre, Daniel Deronda, Jude the Obscure*, and *Portrait of a Lady*). In addition, several works not previously cited compare *Jane Eyre* with novels by other Victorian writers, especially those by Dickens. Q. D. Leavis, in a note to the Penguin edition of *Jane Eyre* (485–86) and in appendix B to the *David Copperfield* chapter of *Dickens the Novelist* (Leavis and Leavis), examines the depictions of childhood in *Oliver Twist, Jane Eyre*, and *David Copperfield* and considers the influence each novel may have had on the one that came after it. Appendix A of *Dickens the Novelist* compares the relationship between David Copperfield and his child-wife, Dora, to the relationships between St. John Rivers and Rosamond Oliver in *Jane Eyre* and Lydgate and Rosamund Vincy in George Eliot's *Middlemarch*. Ronald Berman, in "The Innocent Observer," and L. R. Leavis, in "*David Copperfield* and *Jane Eyre*," also draw parallels between *David Copperfield* and Brontë's novel. Helen von Schmidt, in "The Dark Abyss, the Broad Expanse," explores, as her subtitle explains, versions of the self in *Jane Eyre* and *Great Expectations*. Both Schmidt and L. R. Leavis regard Dickens as the superior novelist. Finally, Beth Kalikoff's "The Falling Woman in Three Victorian Novels" finds similar patterns in the treatment of women exposed to temptation, in *Jane Eyre, Mary Barton*, and *The Mill on the Floss*. (In this volume, essays by Bernard J. Paris, Robert L. Patten, and David Rosenwasser link *Jane Eyre* with other nineteenth-century novels.)

Jean Rhys's *Wide Sargasso Sea*, which sympathetically narrates Bertha Mason Rochester's life and feelings, is often taught in conjunction with *Jane Eyre*. Critics who have compared these two novels include Michael Thorpe (" 'The Other Side': *Wide Sargasso Sea* and *Jane Eyre*"), Elizabeth Baer ("The Sisterhood of Jane Eyre and Antoinette Cosway"), Spivak, and Joyce Carol Oates ("Romance and Anti-romance: From Brontë's *Jane Eyre* to Rhys's *Wide Sargasso Sea*").

In the "Biography" section above, I list four works appropriate for undergraduates as introductions to Brontë's life. The same books—Gérin's *The Brontës: The Creative Work*, Blom's *Charlotte Brontë*, Winnifrith's *The Brontës*, and Nestor's *Charlotte Brontë*—also contain critical commentary on *Jane Eyre* and therefore serve as useful introductions to interpretation of the novel.

Collections of essays, such as the popular compilation in the 1987 Norton Critical Edition of *Jane Eyre*, are valuable resources for students and teachers who wish to survey influential readings of Brontë's work. The 1971 Norton Critical Edition includes, besides the Woolf and Heilman pieces retained in the 1987 edition, essays by Richard Chase, G. Armour Craig, Robert B. Martin, Barbara Hardy, and Sylvère Monod that some teachers may still wish to consult and assign to students. Another frequently read volume is Ian Gregor's *The Brontës: A Collection of Critical Essays*, which reprints essays by Heilman and Lodge and introduces one previously unpublished essay by Mark Kinkead-Weekes. Judith O'Neill's *Critics on Charlotte and Emily Brontë* contains, in addition to some nineteenth-century reviews, essays by Tillotson, Heilman, and David Cecil. Harold Bloom has edited two volumes in the Chelsea House series that offer criticism on *Jane Eyre*. *Modern Critical Interpretations: Charlotte Brontë's* Jane Eyre collects pieces by Craik, Hardy, Eagleton, Moglen, Gilbert and Gubar, Bodenheimer, and Margaret Homans. *Modern Critical Views: The Brontës* features essays by Raymond Williams, Bodenheimer, and Ewbank. Both volumes also have introductions by Bloom. Finally, Allott's *Charlotte Brontë* comprises essays on *Jane Eyre* by M. H. Scargill, Tillotson, Heilman, and David Crompton.

Aids to Teaching

Many teachers find the various film adaptations of *Jane Eyre* helpful for generating class discussion (see Donna Marie Nudd's essay in this volume). The two most popular *Jane Eyre* films are the 1944 black-and-white version, directed by Robert Stevenson and starring Joan Fontaine and Orson Welles, and the 1970 Delbert Mann version, in color, starring Susannah York and George C. Scott, which was first shown in the United States on television but released in England and Europe as a feature film. These movies have been analyzed and compared with Brontë's novel in several fine essays. Sumiko Higashi ("*Jane Eyre*: Charlotte Brontë vs. the Hollywood Myth of Romance") points out various ways in which the 1944 Stevenson film departs from the novel and transforms Jane's story of courage and independence into a conventional Cinderella plot, with Rochester rather than Jane as the central character. Both Michael Riley ("Gothic Melodrama and Spiritual Romance: Vision and Fidelity in Two Versions of *Jane Eyre*") and Kate Ellis and Ann Kaplan ("Feminism in Brontë's Novel and Its Film Versions") compare the 1944 Stevenson and 1970 Mann films and conclude that the Mann version is clearly superior, though Ellis and Kaplan note some shortcomings in Mann's work.

Two other film versions of *Jane Eyre* available on video are the 1983 BBC production, starring Zelah Clarke and Timothy Dalton, and an hour-long 1952 Westinghouse Studio One production starring Katharine Bard and Kevin McCarthy. Pinion lists several other movie adaptations of *Jane Eyre* in an appendix to *A Brontë Companion*, and Nudd provides a bibliography of stage and film adaptations later in this volume.

Other audiovisual aids mentioned by survey respondents are *The Yorkshire of the Brontë Sisters*, a fifteen-minute video depicting Brontë country; a fifteen-minute sound filmstrip called *Austen, the Brontës, and George Eliot* (one of two filmstrips in a package entitled *The Nineteenth-Century Novel*); and a four-hour video entitled *The Brontës of Haworth*. All three are available from Films for the Humanities. *The Brontës: Fantasy and Reality* (Guidance-Harcourt) consists of two color filmstrips and two LPs. An audio-tape of Vineta Colby lecturing on *Jane Eyre* is distributed by Gould Media, and Caedmon offers a three-record "abridgement of the novel," with Claire Bloom reading the part of Jane and Anthony Quayle that of Rochester. One teacher finds the movie *The Elephant Man* useful for discussing nineteenth-century attitudes.

Picture books on the Brontës and the Yorkshire countryside can give students a sense of the people and places evoked in *Jane Eyre*. Bentley's *The Brontës and Their World*, Wilks's *The Brontës*, and Pollard and McBride's *The Landscape of the Brontës*, all mentioned above in the biography section, are appropriate resources. Another work cited in the survey is *Literary Landscapes of the British Isles: A Narrative Atlas*, by David Daiches and John Flower. Some teachers show their own slides of Haworth and the Yorkshire moors.

Margaret Goscilo's essay in the "Approaches" section of this volume describes a slide presentation Goscilo has developed of Thomas Bewick prints, Brontë drawings, and various nineteenth-century paintings that have interesting parallels to *Jane Eyre*. Goscilo also provides a list of published sources for the reproductions she uses in her presentation.

Bibliographies

Although it is somewhat dated, Rosengarten's bibliographical essay "The Brontës" remains a helpful introductory survey of primary and secondary materials. Anne Passel has published *Charlotte and Emily Brontë: An Annotated Bibliography*, which lists primary and secondary works for Charlotte and Emily Brontë and for the Brontë family (jointly authored writings). The secondary works are organized into separate sections on nineteenth-century reviews, criticism of each novel and other writings, general criticism of the writer, and biographies. Rebecca W. Crump's three-volume *Charlotte and Emily Brontë: A Reference Guide* is a fully annotated bibliography of writings on the Brontës from 1846 to 1983. Alexander's *Bibliography of the Manuscripts of Charlotte Brontë* is a valuable listing of all known manuscripts of Brontë's writings, excluding letters.

Teachers may also wish to consult some of the annual bibliographies that include books and articles on Brontë. The *MLA International Bibliography*, a comprehensive, briefly annotated listing, is carried by nearly all college and university libraries. *Brontë Society Transactions* publishes an annual annotated bibliography of works by and about the Brontës. The summer issue of *Victorian Studies* contains a bibliography of the year's noteworthy publications on the Victorian period and includes a section on Brontë. Entries are not annotated, but references to reviews are provided for the books listed.

Brontë is featured in a number of bibliographies devoted to women writers. One such work is the *Bibliography of Women and Literature*, edited by Florence Boos with Lynn Miller, a revision and expansion of listings that originally appeared annually in the journal *Women and Literature*. Volume 1 covers 1974 to 1978, volume 2 covers 1979 to 1981, and the forthcoming volume 3 is devoted to the years 1981 to 1985. Another recent work that I have used in undergraduate teaching is Narda Lacey Schwartz's two-volume *Articles on Women Writers: A Bibliography*.

NOTE

[1] Unless otherwise indicated, all quotations from *Jane Eyre* in this volume are from the 1987 Norton Critical Edition, edited by Richard J. Dunn.

Part Two

APPROACHES

Introduction

Shortly after Jane Eyre arrives at Lowood, she asks Helen Burns about the teachers at the illustrious educational institution. Helen offers some cursory remarks on the other instructors and then describes Miss Temple as the ideal teacher:

> Miss Temple has generally something to say which is newer than my own reflections: her language is singularly agreeable to me, and the information she communicates is often just what I wished to gain.
>
> (49; ch. 6)

Jane Eyre, like many Victorian novels, is infused with images of instruction, with portraits of both students and teachers. Unlike many other literary heroines, however, Jane had the experience of being a teacher, just as her creator, Charlotte Brontë, did. But to say that Jane thrived on teaching— that she was a Miss Temple—would be to misread the dismay she barely concealed as she faced the daunting task of teaching "the ranks of the British peasantry" (343; ch. 34). And to say that teaching *Jane Eyre* to today's students is a pure joy would be to underestimate the challenges involved. Taught more frequently than any of Brontë's other novels, *Jane Eyre* presents distinct problems for the contemporary undergraduate instructor, not the least of which is the work's sheer length. But the instructors who responded to the questionnaire on the novel also discussed the advantages of teaching *Jane Eyre*. Almost all of them spend from two to three weeks on the novel, and most supplement the text with pertinent background material. Ideally, the language, images, issues, and ideologies that emerge from *Jane Eyre* will be, to paraphrase Helen Burns, just the information students wish to gain.

The essays that follow are arranged by contextual and textual concerns into three sections, moving generally from questions "outside" the text to questions "inside" it. The first section focuses on the historical milieu, the Brontë corpus, and biography, topics we believe are prerequisites to any thorough reading and teaching of *Jane Eyre*. The opening essay, by James Diedrick, situates *Jane Eyre* within the linguistic traditions that the novel both subverts and valorizes. Teaching the novel in relation to Mary Wollstone-craft's *Vindication of the Rights of Woman*, Diedrick asks his students to confront and question notions of "masculinity" and "femininity" as those concepts were ideologically constructed by the early feminist movement. Janet H. Freeman's essay places *Jane Eyre* within the context of the other novels written by Brontë and her sisters. Freeman teaches students to recognize both the emergence of Jane's unique voice and the Brontë sisters' novelistic dialogue about the nature and role of women in nineteenth-century British society. The essay by Thomas L. Jeffers discusses biographies of Brontë as well as the methods and practice of biography as a genre. Jeffers provides ideas for journal writing, explaining how students can mimic Brontë and transform their own lives into texts. In the final essay in this section, Mary Poovey investigates the figure of the governess in the novel. By subordinating the social and economic dimensions of the occupation, Poovey argues, Brontë makes the governess into a symbol for class and sexual anxieties about middle-class British women during the "hungry 1840s."

The essays in the second section explore the literary and philosophical traditions that inform the meaning and structure of *Jane Eyre*. Tamar Heller's essay examines ways of teaching the novel within the tradition of the female Gothic, which Heller usefully contrasts with its modern aberrant form, the Harlequin romance. The essay also presents a new approach to the role and meaning of Bertha in the novel. According to Phyllis C. Ralph, *Jane Eyre* is representative of the fairy-tale genre. Relying primarily on comparisons with the Beauty and the Beast story, Ralph's essay describes *Jane Eyre* as a variant of the adolescent female fantasy about gaining identity and status through love and the successful mastery of various trials. Religious issues in the novel, specifically its engagement with nineteenth-century Christianity and the Bible, are the focus of the final two essays in this section. Susan VanZanten Gallagher explores the novel's relation to the Evangelical, Calvinist, Methodist, and Church of England traditions, concluding that Brontë's work should be taught as a "Christian feminist bildungsroman." In his essay, Keith A. Jenkins explains how he teaches Brontë's biblical references as a process of textual transmutation in which the novel becomes a radically antipatriarchal revision of the Bible.

The essays in the final section — "Teaching Specific Contexts" — all address discrete issues in teaching the novel, through an analysis of a specific aspect of the work, a critical theory, or a unique pedagogical strategy. The first essay in the group, John O. Jordan's *"Jane Eyre* and Narrative Voice," asks the deceptively simple question "Who is the narrator of *Jane Eyre?*" His answer introduces methods of examining narratology and "identity" in the novel. In addition to narrative voice, imagery has traditionally been a central teaching focus for *Jane Eyre*. Mary Burgan's essay "Fire and Light in *Jane Eyre*" presents a new-historicist approach to this familiar topic. In another essay about imagery — specifically, the force of contrast in the novel — Mark M. Hennelly, Jr., suggests ideas for teaching what he calls "structure and antistructure."

Also related to the topic of imagery, Margaret Goscilo's essay explores pictorial representation as a way of understanding the novel's zeitgeist, the Brontë biography, and Brontë's creative process. Goscilo usefully describes a slide presentation she has developed to acquaint students with Romantic and Victorian iconography that illuminates Jane's own paintings and the Bewick engravings that figure prominently in the novel. John Kucich's essay *"Jane Eyre* and Imperialism" discusses methods for teaching the novel's imperialistic subtext and the marginalization of Bertha as "other." Relying on the theories of Jean Baudrillard, Dennis W. Allen directs students' attention to descriptions of objects and interiors as reflections of the ideological assumptions of industrial capitalism.

Diane Long Hoeveler's essay uses a modified Foucauldian approach to discuss Jane's pattern of eating and starvation and its connection with Jane's convoluted sexuality and the system of "disciplinary practices" that dominate the novel. The two essays that follow neatly complement each other in their focus on psychological themes. Bernard J. Paris argues that the novel ostensibly conforms to what he calls the "vindication" and the "education" paradigms in Victorian texts. By analyzing the rhetorical representation of Jane, however, Paris penetrates the plot contrivances that seem to portray Jane as both vindicated and educated. Jerome Bump relies on the fairly new school of family systems therapy to teach *Jane Eyre* in a course on the family in the Victorian novel. He details a variety of methods adapted from John Bradshaw's writings on the "inner child" that encourage students to demonstrate a personal and reflective involvement with the novel.

Three other imaginative approaches to *Jane Eyre* are described in the final essays in the volume. Donna Marie Nudd's valuable essay looks at the novel through its various stage and film adaptations. In her Performance of Literature course, Nudd uses Robert Stevenson's film version to explore ways in which film adapts and distorts novelistic conventions. Nudd's essay also includes a list of adaptations of the *Jane Eyre* story and suggests paper topics on three different stage versions of the novel. The two essays that conclude the volume focus on Brontë's work within the context of the Victorian novel. Robert L. Patten's essay recommends interrogating the text and examining the novel's opening chapter as the confluence of genre, narrative, and setting. Patten also touches on similar strategies used by Austen and Dickens. David Rosenwasser adapts the theories of Julia Kristeva to explore the marriage plot in *Jane Eyre, Pride and Prejudice, Jude the Obscure,* and *The Mill on the Floss.*

In teaching *Jane Eyre,* we are in some ways teaching ourselves, our best imaginings of our own pasts, presents, and self-created futures. Brontë, by radically reshaping her life and depicting her most extravagant fantasies, transmuted her own experiences as a woman and a teacher and in the process provided future teachers with a text that continues to intrigue and to generate new approaches.

TEACHING THE TIMES
AND THE LIFE

Jane Eyre and A Vindication
of the Rights of Woman

James Diedrick

In chapter 12 of *Jane Eyre*, when Jane reflects on the sense of confinement she had felt ten years earlier as she assumed her governess duties at Thornfield Hall, it seems almost as if the spirit of Mary Wollstonecraft has taken control of her pen:

> Women are supposed to be very calm generally: but women feel just as men feel; they need exercise for their faculties and a field for their efforts as much as their brothers do; they suffer from too rigid a restraint, too absolute a stagnation, precisely as men would suffer; and it is narrow-minded in their more privileged fellow-creatures to say that they ought to confine themselves to making puddings and knitting stockings, to playing on the piano and embroidering bags. It is thoughtless to condemn them, or laugh at them, if they seek to do more or learn more than custom has pronounced necessary for their sex. (96; ch. 12)

Recent criticism has been sensitive to the ways in which the novel embodies its narrator's rebellion against confining custom (Gilbert and Gubar, *Madwoman*; Moglen; Rich). No attempt has been made, however, to link the language of passages such as this one, and indeed the terms of the novel's feminism in general, to a tradition of feminist discourse that originated fifty-five years before *Jane Eyre* appeared, when Wollstonecraft published *A Vindication of the Rights of Woman* (1792). Wollstonecraft was not the first eighteenth-century woman writer to analyze the causes and lament the consequences of sexual inequality, of course. Both Mary Wortley Montagu and Catharine Macaulay had earlier attributed women's inferior social status to nurture rather than nature, and both had enumerated the many social benefits that would result from granting women a wider sphere of influence. Much of the argument in *A Vindication*, in fact, is indebted to Macaulay's *Letters on Education*, which Wollstonecraft reviewed for the *Analytical Review* in 1790. Wollstonecraft's essay is more philosophical in approach than a mere treatise on educational reform would be and far more ambitious in its analysis of culturally determined gender differences than the work of Montagu or Macaulay is. It is a radical critique of prevailing social structures, inspired by the egalitarian ideals of the French Revolution.

Wollstonecraft's radicalism, both in her personal life and in her writing, contributed to the precipitous fall of her reputation following her death. The tide of anti-Jacobin sentiment that swept across England once the war against France began had something to do with this decline; so did the posthumous publication, by William Godwin, of some of Wollstonecraft's works and his own scrupulously honest *A Memoir of the Author of* A Vindication of the Rights of Woman. The critical backlash changed feminist discourse for the next half century. The polemical zeal with which Wollstonecraft had engaged the "women's issue" gave way, in her successors, to more indirect critiques of sexual inequality. Writers like Fanny Burney, Maria Edgeworth, Jane Austen, and, later, the Brontës addressed some of the same concerns that *A Vindication* did but in oblique, fictional terms. Indeed, *Jane Eyre* can be read and taught as a fictional counterpart to Wollstonecraft's manifesto, with the heroine dramatizing women's struggles against the very social constraints Wollstonecraft forcefully analyzes in her essay. Pairing these two works in women's literature courses or in period or historical surveys can help illuminate the early history of feminism, the role fiction played in this history, and some of the ways in which feminism was transformed in the wake of Romanticism.[1]

Wollstonecraft's provocative radicalism is apparent from the first pages of *A Vindication*. In her introduction, she says that all who view women with a "philosophic eye" must, like her, wish that women "may every day grow more and more masculine" (8). By "masculine" Wollstonecraft of course means "rational," and central to her argument is the demonstration that the cultivation of reason in women has been systematically suppressed by cultural conditioning, with pervasively degrading results. Like Jane Eyre in the passage quoted above, Wollstonecraft flatly rejects the traditional "separation of virtues" doctrine that assumes different mental and moral capacities in men and in women. This doctrine received its fullest eighteenth-century expression in Rousseau's *Emile*, which views women primarily as creatures of sensibility, not reason, who are thus necessarily subject to the instruction and guidance of men: "Researches into abstract and speculative truths, the principles and axioms of science, in short, every thing which tends to generalize our ideas, is not the proper province of women . . ." (349). Much of *A Vindication* is a direct challenge to Rousseau's presumptions; apart from physical differences, Wollstonecraft insists, every distinction between men and women is culturally determined: "[N]ot only the virtue, but the *knowledge* of the two sexes should be the same in nature, if not in degree, and . . . women, considered not only as moral, but rational creatures, ought to endeavour to acquire human virtues (or perfections) by the *same* means as men . . ." (39). An effective way to engage students in exploring the many affinities between *A Vindication* and *Jane Eyre* (as well as some crucial differences) is to have them consider the extent to which Jane herself, in the course of her story, fulfills Wollstonecraft's wish that women "may every day grow more and more masculine." This approach provides many opportunities for discussion and writing, as the following paragraphs reveal.

In a brilliant rhetorical move, Wollstonecraft acquits God of the charges of misogyny she levels against her culture and enlists his authority in seeking to transcend it. She locates one culturally enshrined source of this misogyny in *Paradise Lost*. Eve tells Adam, "God is thy Law, thou mine: to know no more / Is woman's happiest knowledge and her praise" (4.637–38), and Adam, when he looks at Eve "in delight / Both of her Beauty and submissive Charms / Smil'd with superior Love" (4.497–99). For her part, Wollstonecraft says that if men wish women to be more than "the brutes who are dependent on the reason of man," men must let women "attain conscious dignity by feeling themselves only dependent on God" (36). Expressing thanks, she writes, "[God] gave me sufficient strength of mind to dare to exert my own reason, till, becoming dependent only on him for the support of my virtue, I view, with indignation, the mistaken notions that enslave my sex" (37). For Wollstonecraft, God becomes nearly synonymous with the exercise of reason and individual conscience. In the quasi-providential world of *Jane Eyre*, God seems to intervene in Jane's life repeatedly, whether to aid her in her quest for fulfillment (the fairy that suggests she advertise for a governess position, the voice of Rochester calling her back to him after Bertha's death) or to protect her moral integrity. But this spirit comes more and more to resemble Jane's own higher reason. When Rochester urges Jane to stay with him despite his marriage to Bertha, the voice of feeling within her asks, "Who in the world cares for *you*? or who will be injured by what you do?" A deeper voice answers, "*I* care for myself. The more solitary, the more friendless, the more unsustained I am, the more I will respect myself. I will keep the law given by God . . ." (279; ch. 27). In both texts, God empowers women to exercise their own moral judgment apart from male expectations.

But *Jane Eyre* contains other evocations of God as well. The patriarchal God who guides Brocklehurst and St. John is both socially determined and determining. Brocklehurst has appropriated God for the purposes of social control and class oppression. Although extreme, his practice reflects a historical reality: the subordination of the emotional and spiritual energies of Methodism to the utilitarian needs of nineteenth-century English society (Thompson 37). St. John is more complicated; he is not a hypocrite, but his belief in Pauline theology makes him fear his own sexuality and view female sexuality as a threat to his purity of vision. One result is his attempt to succeed where Brocklehurst failed and render Jane submissive; his selective praise of her as "docile, diligent, disinterested, faithful, constant" expresses his desire to subdue her to his needs (355; ch. 34). But by the time she confronts St. John, she has in one important sense achieved Wollstonecraft's wish. When he proposes that she accompany him to India as his wife, her reason tells her, "He prizes me as a soldier would a good weapon; and that is all" (356; ch. 34).

The eloquent indignation with which Jane rejects St. John's marriage proposal ("I scorn your idea of love . . . and I scorn you when you offer it" [359; ch. 34]) points to another crucial link between Wollstonecraft's essay and Brontë's novel. Both writers recognize that by restricting the definition of the feminine to those qualities St. John ascribes to Jane, society seeks to prevent women from fully exercising their reason and their developing virtue. Like Jane, Wollstonecraft is well aware that "women are supposed to be very calm generally": "Gentleness, docility, and a spaniel-like affection are . . . recommended as the cardinal virtues of the sex . . . ." (34). Yet the effect of this kind of cultural conditioning is pernicious, since "women are not allowed to have sufficient strength of mind to acquire what really deserves the name of virtue" (19). Instead, Wollstonecraft argues:

> Women are told from their infancy, and taught by the example of their mothers, that a little knowledge of human weakness, justly termed cunning, softness of temper, *outward* obedience, and a scrupulous attention to a puerile kind of propriety, will obtain for them the protection of man; and should they be beautiful, every thing else is needless, for, at least, twenty years of their lives.   (19)

Both Adèle Varens and Blanche Ingram are products, or rather victims, of this kind of teaching. When Jane first meets her, Adèle is a coquette in training, while Blanche flaunts her mastery of the art: "Whenever I marry . . . I am resolved my husband shall not be a rival, but a foil to me. I will suffer no competitor near the throne; I shall exact an undivided homage; his devotions shall not be shared between me and the shape he sees in his mirror" (158; ch. 17).

Rather than submit to these subterfuges of the enslaved, Wollstonecraft counsels rebellion against the conditions that give rise to them. Though else-where she is all too eager to denigrate the passions, Wollstonecraft consis-tently validates women's anger and indignation when they are expressions of reason in revolt against injustice, when they are "spurs to action, and open the mind" (30). Jane Eyre, whose last name hints at the ire that often overwhelms her as a child but becomes her ally as she matures, is repeatedly admonished, by the people and institutions she encounters, to suppress her rage, but this same anger helps her to escape from Gateshead, reform Lowood, and stand up to both Rochester and St. John. Her fury at St. John for demanding that she sacrifice all her desires to his missionary ambition enables her to see him clearly for the first time: "The veil fell from his hard-ness and despotism. Having felt in him the presence of these qualities, I felt his imperfection, and took courage. I was with an equal—one with whom I might argue—one whom, if I saw good, I might resist" (358; ch. 34).

In their treatment of anger, Wollstonecraft and Brontë both demonstrate that reason and passion are not necessarily antithetical. But elsewhere in her essay, Wollstonecraft mercilessly opposes the two. One of the most troublesome aspects of A Vindication, and a likely source of student resis-tance to other aspects of Wollstonecraft's argument, is her persistent deroga-tion of feelings in general and love and sexual passion in particular. As she frames her argument, those feelings are the enemies of reason and virtue. Her prescription to married couples makes this clear: "[A] master and mistress of a family ought not to continue to love each other with passion. I mean to say, that they ought not to indulge those emotions which disturb the order of society, and engross the thoughts that should be otherwise em-ployed" (30). Here Wollstonecraft sounds like no one so much as St. John, whose own sexual feelings threaten his religious ambition. Significantly, Wollstonecraft's treatment of feelings in A Vindication is not consistent with her own personal attitudes. Her letters to Gilbert Imlay and William Godwin suggest that she saw no contradiction between reason and feeling, intelligence and femininity (Letters). Reading some of these letters to stu-dents who are struggling with the severe, ascetic voice of A Vindication may help humanize the woman behind the rhetorical persona. So may a reminder that exaggeration, designed to counter Rousseau's distorted con-ception of women, is one of Wollstonecraft's strategies in the essay. Accord-ing to Rousseau, not only are women primarily creatures of feeling rather than reason, they are also fundamentally sexual beings: "[A] male is only a male now and again, the female is always a female . . . ; everything reminds her of her sex" (324). He also implies that women are constitu-tionally predisposed to please men—that their coquettishness is innate. Women educated in these assumptions, Wollstonecraft argues, become vic-tims of sensibility, victims of sexuality: "Their senses are inflamed, and their understandings neglected, consequently they become the prey of their senses, delicately termed sensibility, and are blown about by every momentary gust of feeling" (61). In resisting these assumptions, as Mary Poovey has shown, Wollstonecraft virtually denies women any sexual feelings at all ("*A Vindication*" 348).

Not so with Brontë. By the time she came to write *Jane Eyre*, the Romantic movement had elevated the expression and exploration of feelings to a culturally privileged position. Describing Austen's limits as a novelist, Brontë also defines her own province: "What sees keenly, speaks aptly, moves flexibly, it suits her to study; but what throbs fast and full, though hidden, what the blood rushes through, what is the unseen seat of life and the sentient target of death — that Miss Austen ignores" (*Jane Eyre*, ed. Leavis, 10). Virtually the entire realm of the nonrational is valorized in *Jane Eyre* — dreams, visions, the supernatural, all forms of desire, including sexual desire. Jane is frank and unapologetic in expressing her attraction to Rochester: "I looked, and had an acute pleasure in looking, — a precious, yet poignant pleasure; pure gold, with a steelly point of agony . . ." (153; ch. 17). Unlike Wollstonecraft, she does not oppose sexuality and virtue. In her characterization of St. John, in fact, Brontë dramatizes the destructive consequences of the kind of sexual repression Wollstonecraft implicitly advocates. Jane's marriage to a chastened Rochester may in one sense represent a "domestication" of sexuality but not its disavowal.

In teaching *A Vindication of the Rights of Woman* alongside *Jane Eyre*, I point students toward not only the striking parallels but also the differences between the two texts. This approach can help students better understand the two works and the cultural conditions that influenced them. In the essays my students write about the extent to which Jane becomes "more and more masculine," I ask them to explain how Wollstonecraft defines "masculine"; to examine both writers' treatment of reason and feeling; to analyze Jane's development and relationships throughout the course of the narrative; and to pay particular attention to the penultimate chapter of the novel, where Jane becomes Rochester's "prop and guide" in an ironic reversal of Adam and Eve's departure from Eden in *Paradise Lost*. I also encourage them to consider some "prewriting" questions, each of which could form the basis of a separate essay, before they develop a thesis: When and for what reasons do Wollstonecraft and Jane Eyre evoke the name of God? What is the connection between feeling and reason in Jane's relationship to Rochester? to St. John? How would you compare Wollstonecraft's and St. John's attitudes toward sexuality? What is the role of anger in Jane's life, and how does it relate to Wollstonecraft's critique of "gentleness"? In what ways are Adèle Varens and Blanche Ingram products of the kind of feminine education Wollstonecraft decries? These questions involve students in the two writers' struggles with questions that continue to concern us all. Reader, consider them.[2]

NOTES

[1] For those who teach these two works in the context of feminist history and theory, the Norton Critical Editions of both *A Vindication of the Rights of Woman* and *Jane Eyre* are the texts of choice: Carol Poston's 1988 edition of *A Vindication* provides essential secondary materials under the headings "Backgrounds," "The Wollstonecraft Debate," and "Criticism." Richard Dunn's 1987 edition of *Jane Eyre* contains excerpts from important feminist essays on the novel by Adrienne Rich, Sandra M. Gilbert, and Helene Moglen. Two anthologies containing excerpts from *A Vindication* are also worth consideration. *The Norton Anthology of English Literature* (ed. Abrams et al.), volume 2, contains the introduction, chapter 2, and selections from chapter 4. *The Norton Anthology of Literature by Women: The Tradition in English* (ed. Gilbert and Gubar) reprints the introduction, chapter 2, and chapter 13 (this anthology also contains the entire text of *Jane Eyre*).

[2] Several students who studied *A Vindication of the Rights of Woman* and *Jane Eyre* with me offered helpful suggestions about the writing of this essay. I would like to thank Kay Courter, Michelle Kroupa, Clinton Nelson, and LeeAnne Richardson for their contributions.

The Place of *Jane Eyre*
in the Brontë Family Canon

Janet H. Freeman

Jane Eyre is a pleasure to teach. That little girl in chapter 2, who suffers unjustly but fights back bravely, is immediately appealing, and once you are on her side, turning the pages is easy. My students tell me repeatedly that they like *Jane Eyre* because they like Jane Eyre. They say they can "identify" with her, and since I do, too, we have something to build on right from the start. Together, we are hooked. The question is, hooked on what? I think it is on Jane Eyre the storyteller, whose voice in my ear seems to have an almost irresistible authority. That authority is my subject here — what it developed from, in Charlotte Brontë's early writing; what it developed in response to, in the writing of her sisters; and what it developed into, in the novels Brontë went on to write.

Many others before me have remarked on what Margaret Blom calls the "compelling surge of Jane's first person narration" (104), but my students want to hear about the responses of readers like themselves, who know nothing of Currer Bell, who have never read *Jane Eyre* before, and who could not put it down. My four favorite examples happen to be men, all of them well past their student days: Mr. Williams and Mr. Smith of Smith, Elder, and Company, Publishers, who read *Jane Eyre* in manuscript form (Smith staying up late into a Sunday night before he finished it); William Makepeace Thackeray, who wrote to Williams, "I wish you had not sent me *Jane Eyre*. It interested me so much that I have lost (or won if you like) a whole day in reading it" (Allott, *Brontës* 70); and Patrick Brontë, who, according to Elizabeth Gaskell's account (324–25), knew nothing of the creation of *Jane Eyre* until his daughter placed the published version in his hands. The incident, well worth reading aloud, concludes with Brontë joining his daughters for tea somewhat later in the day: "Girls," he said to them, "do you know Charlotte has been writing a book, and it is much better than likely?" (325).

We are not told whether Patrick Brontë and the others identified themselves with the cruelly treated orphan child talking back to her oppressors or with her adult self, the storyteller who has compelled so many to read on; but it is important, I think, to assent to the power of that narrator, to endorse and share the experience of first-time readers of *Jane Eyre*. Jane Eyre speaks directly to such readers, in a voice that seems to have no antecedents or history, that moves unmediated, unaccompanied into the reader's imagination, that strikes at the desire for both autonomy and intimacy. This clarity, often described in absolute terms like *timeless* and *universal*, needs to be acknowledged. Then, of course, it needs to be examined.

My own most careful reading of *Jane Eyre*, toward which my teaching of the novel always seems to lean, is also a response to the story as told. It traces the gradual development of Jane's ability to tell about her experience in her own way. "What does Bessie say I have done?" are her first words (5; ch. 1), but that dependency does not last. Later, Jane promises Mrs. Reed that she will tell anyone who asks her the "exact tale" (31; ch. 4) of her wretched life at Gateshead, a vow she eventually keeps by addressing her reader with a confidentiality she shares with no one else, not even her devoted husband. Thus is the hook forged.

This reading of *Jane Eyre* derives from numerous details in the narrative, especially the many times Jane Eyre is asked to identify herself as she journeys from place to place. (Teachers might have students find out how often she responds to the question, Who are you? or how often she is made to listen to someone else's answer.) It is also bound by those details. It assumes that the text is autonomous, as if the text had generated itself somehow: "The inevitable outcome of *Jane Eyre* is *Jane Eyre*" (Freeman 698). At the same time, the narrator of *Jane Eyre* has acquired a history of sorts. Her fluency is no longer unaccountable, springing out of nowhere and requiring no explanation. That move — from accepting Jane Eyre's narrative voice as absolute, an ontological given, to seeing it as developing from the moment the child first talks back to John Reed and his mother — is an example of my preferred approach to the teaching of *Jane Eyre*. Assenting to Jane Eyre's authority over her own story, I also wish to demystify it, to find ways to explain it from outside as well as inside the text. I attempt to define Jane Eyre not as Brontë's creative miracle but as her achievement.

My most recent readings of *Jane Eyre* have been with undergraduates who were participating in a seminar I called The Brontë Family. When I asked them what reading *Jane Eyre* was like in the context of *Wuthering Heights*, *Agnes Grey*, *The Tenant of Wildfell Hall*, Charlotte Brontë's other novels, and a modicum of biographical materials (principally Phyllis Bentley's *The Brontës*, a short book with many fine pictures and a lively text), they surprised me by emphasizing biography — that much of *Jane Eyre* was, as one of them put it, "taken from life." Students recalled how the three sisters had gone out as governesses (assigned reading was M. Jeanne Peterson's essay on the Victorian governess), how all three had grown up in a village parsonage with no mother to stand between them and the parson — thus explaining to the students' satisfaction both the pious portions of the novel and the biblical allusions — and how Emily and Charlotte and their two older sisters before them had been sent off to the Cowan Bridge School (read Lowood).

Students might have noticed (alas they did not) that Brontë began to commit *Jane Eyre* to paper while keeping her temporarily blinded and immobilized father company in Manchester, as he slowly recovered from cataract surgery — a circumstance of some interest if we consider Rochester's condition when Jane agrees to marry him. Or they might have recalled the conversation Gaskell says took place in the parsonage, when Brontë

> told her sisters that they were wrong—even morally wrong—in making their heroines beautiful as a matter of course. They replied that it was impossible to make a heroine interesting in any other terms. Her reply was, "I will prove to you that you are wrong; I will show you a heroine as plain and as small as myself, who shall be as interesting as any of yours." (Gaskell 308)

Jane Eyre as the product of daughterly duty on the one hand and sibling disagreement on the other is an instructive picture.

A significant part of the "life" my students think *Jane Eyre* was taken from must have been purely imaginary—those other heroines imagined by Charlotte Brontë's sisters, for example. Anne Brontë's *Agnes Grey* is a story of tribulation followed by happiness, the tribulation of a young girl going off to a strange place as a governess and the happiness of finding at last the perfect husband, at which point the story is finished. But Agnes Grey is not another Jane Eyre: in fact, the differences between the two mean much more than the similarities do.

Agnes Grey is (naturally) anything but plain, and she is the darling of her loving family. She has to work hard to persuade them to let her leave the parsonage where she was born and go out into the world—that is, into the Bloomfield family, whose unruly children she is expected to govern without recourse to punishment. I will not retell the story of how little Agnes, her greatest skill the ability to persevere in silence, attracts the attention of the curate Mr. Weston; but her silence is worth pausing over. It is Agnes Grey's only strength as well as her only solace: "For their sakes at home," she confides to the reader, "I smothered my pride and suppressed my indignation" (57). Eventually that suppression, a sure sign of her moral supremacy, pays off. Mr. Weston proposes marriage, Agnes answers his fervent "You love me then?" with the single word "Yes," and the book is all but over (163).

Students of *Jane Eyre* may benefit from hearing descriptions of, and readings from, Anne Brontë's novel, because when Jane Eyre talks back to Mrs. Reed—and all her other oppressors, in their turn—it is as if she were also talking back to Agnes Grey. Her urgency, that is, has more than one motive, more than one context. She might also, especially when resisting Rochester's entreaties, be talking back to Emily Brontë's Catherine Earnshaw. Consider, for example, the question of soul: "Whatever our souls are made of," the young Catherine says to Nelly Dean, speaking of herself and Heathcliff, "his and mine are the same" (72). "Nelly," she continues in probably the most quoted passage in *Wuthering Heights*, "I *am* Heathcliff—he is always, always in my mind—not as a pleasure, any more than I am always a pleasure to myself—but as my own being" (74). This sameness is unthinkable to

Jane Eyre, whose decision to leave Rochester (and his wife) is made possible because, as she tells her reader, "[M]entally, I still possessed my soul, and with it the certainty of ultimate safety" (279; ch. 27). Much later, that soul possession makes possible the summons and response, one soul to the other, that brings Jane Eyre back to the repentant Rochester: "[P]erhaps your soul wandered from its cell to comfort mine," he suggests, awestruck at the possibility (394; ch. 38). Jane listens to him, turns to her readers, and, in a fine example of how narration can bind reader to narrator, tells us that yes, the words Rochester heard "whispering on the wind" were the words she herself, many miles away, had uttered. But though she confides the whole story to us, Jane Eyre keeps Rochester in the dark. Her soul remains very much her own.

Catherine Earnshaw, her soul fatally mingled with Heathcliff's; Agnes Grey, her only weapon sheer self-restraint; and Jane Eyre, plain, outspoken, her soul intact: these three heroines appeared on the literary scene within weeks of one another. We can bring them together in the mind—and in the classroom—as a way of extending and complicating that sisterly discussion about the morality of beauty. Jane Eyre really did not appear out of nowhere: she has her own sisters, whom she resists.

Among these sisters are heroines few of my students have ever heard of— Mina Laury, for instance, or Elizabeth Hastings, or poor Caroline Vernon. These creatures dwell in the "burning clime" of Angria, the imaginary kingdom Charlotte and Branwell Brontë created and sustained for over ten years, long before the composition of *Jane Eyre* (this early writing is well described in Blom 37–60). Thoroughly objectified, Charlotte Brontë's earliest heroines are invariably beauties, lovely to look at and delicious to possess, and one by one they helplessly give themselves away to masterful, irresistible men. Furthermore, they are never granted the authority of first-person narration.

"Caroline Vernon," the last of Brontë's extant Angrian narratives, was written in 1839. Its plot is all too predictable. Caroline, the illegitimate daughter of the earl of Northangerland and Louisa Dance, an opera singer and ballet dancer, has been the ward of the earl's son-in-law, the duke of Zamorna, since her early childhood. Both duke and earl are men accustomed to obedience from their subordinates—soldiers, politicians, servants, wives, mistresses—and they disagree about Caroline, who is now approaching womanhood. The earl, her father, banishes her to Paris, though the duke, her "guardian," wants her to stay with him. Caroline's Parisian initiation into the ways of the world only intensifies her illicit longing for the duke. (That longing is the subtext of extensive arguments between earl and duke, protector-father and protector-seducer.) When she runs away to join Zamorna, the die is cast. He sees it much more clearly than does she. Notice who gets to talk:

"I like to look at your dark eyes & your pretty face — " Miss Vernon
started & deeply coloured — never before had Zamorna called her face
pretty — "Yes" said he "it is exquisitely pretty — & those soft features
& dusky curls are beyond the imitation of a pencil — You blush because
I praise you — did you never guess before that I took a pleasure in
watching you — in holding your little hand, & in playing with your
simplicity — which has sported many a time, Caroline, on the brink
of an abyss you never thought of?" Miss Vernon sat speechless — She
darkly saw or rather felt the end to which all this tended, but all was
fever & delirium round her — The Duke spoke again — in a single blunt
& almost coarse sentence compressing what yet remained to be said,
"If I were a bearded Turk, Caroline, I would take you to my
Harem" — His deep voice, as he uttered this — his high-featured face,
& dark large eye, beaming bright with a spark from the depths of
Gehenna, struck Caroline Vernon with a thrill of nameless dread —
(352–53)

Caroline Vernon has nothing to say for herself as she succumbs to the
duke's words and flashing eyes: "I have a little retreat, my fairy, somewhere
near the heart of my own Kingdom," he tells her. "I call it my treasure-
house, & what I deposit there has always hitherto been safe" (353). Entering
into that haven, Caroline Vernon disappears from the story. A week or so
later, Zamorna leaves her and returns home to his embittered wife. The
earl of Northangerland, angry indeed at the loss of his jewel, warns: "Before
you die, you shall curse the day that you robbed me of my daughter" (358).
Whether that prediction ever comes to pass remains untold.

Admirers of Jane Eyre's ability to take charge of her own history need
to realize how fully Brontë had imagined its negation. Jane Eyre's willingness
to fight back, independent spirit, and eloquence on her own behalf follow
Caroline Vernon's surrender and the surrender of many others like her. Jane
Eyre's vital energy, though it may seem instantaneous, was earned in a
lengthy and arduous school.

None of those Angrian beauties, of course, was meant to be known to
us: their stories were shared with Branwell, and perhaps Emily and Anne,
but with no one else. When Charlotte Brontë decided to write fiction for
publication, her hero was no Zamorna and her hero's eventual wife neither
"a beautiful girl nor a lady of rank" but, rather, a teacher of "needlework,
or netting, or lace-mending, or some such flimsy art" (*The Professor* [ed.
Lane] xi, 89). One remembers Jane Eyre's words about women who confine
themselves to "knitting stockings" and "embroidering bags" (96; ch. 12).
Furthermore, this teacher has to learn to speak English. Frances Evans
Henri's command of that language is much improved by the end of *The Professor*, when she has become the wife of the professor William Crimsworth,

the mother of his son Victor, and the immediate predecessor of Jane Eyre (see Rodolff); but her husband is still the one who tells their story.

Speech, as an indicator of power, continues to inform my understanding — and my teaching — of Brontë's fiction. Giving a heroine the right to speak in her own voice was a decision Brontë made only twice in her life, and the first of those speakers was Jane Eyre (Ratchford 171). When you hear Jane Eyre's first words with that fact in mind, the ground shifts a little under your feet: Brontë had at last discovered a heroine with something of her own to say. The sudden appearance of *Jane Eyre* before the Victorian reading public, like its appearance on an undergraduate reading list, is therefore misleading. Brontë's search had taken years.

Jane Eyre's sudden success, however, did not lead to *Jane Eyre II*. Before ending a discussion of the novel, I ask what it is, exactly, that marks the moment when Jane Eyre has said enough. For me, it is when we are sufficiently convinced that married life with Rochester leaves nothing (except writing one's autobiography) to be desired. At the same time, the conclusion of *Jane Eyre* may not be as absolute as it seems. If Jane Eyre succeeds in speaking for herself, surely her creator shares that empowerment. The first page of *Shirley* captures Currer Bell's new authority. No longer the invisible editor of Jane Eyre Rochester's autobiography, she comes to us in her own voice:

> If you think . . . that anything like a romance is preparing for you, reader, you never were more mistaken. Do you anticipate sentiment, and poetry, and reverie? Do you expect passion, and stimulus, and melodrama? Calm your expectations; reduce them to a lowly standard. Something real, cool, and solid lies before you; something unromantic as Monday morning, when all who have work wake with the consciousness that they must rise and betake themselves thereto.
>
> (39 [Penguin ed.])

We know Jane Eyre's personal revelations are over once the narrator of *Shirley* — who now openly refers to herself as a novelist, that is, one who has "work" — begins to set us straight about what we ought to expect. That correction first took place in 1849, but it is still relevant. *Shirley*, as "unromantic as Monday morning," has two heroines, not just one, and two heroes for them eventually to marry. Not one of these four is given the novel's last word: that privilege firmly belongs (in a chapter ironically titled "The Winding-Up") to the novelist herself. Even a return to first-person narration, a little over three years later in *Villette*, is nothing like a return to *Jane Eyre*: no one would confuse Lucy Snowe's opening evocation of life with her "handsome, tall, well-made" godmother Mrs. Bretton and Mrs. Bretton's only son, the golden-haired Graham of the "good teeth" and "health without flaw" (61), with Jane Eyre's opening evocation of life at Gateshead, home of the corpulent Mrs. Reed, her two fussy daughters, and her only son, John, of the "dim and bleared eye and flabby cheeks" (7; ch. 1). Here are Lucy's own words:

> When I was a girl I went to Bretton [home of the Brettons] about twice a year, and well I liked the visit. The house and its inmates specially suited me. The large peaceful rooms, the well-arranged furniture, the clear wide windows, the balcony outside, looking down on a fine antique street, where Sundays and holidays seemed always to abide — so quiet was its atmosphere, so clean its pavement — these things pleased me well. (61)

Forty chapters later, "pierced deeper than [she] could endure, made now to feel what defied suppression," Lucy Snowe cries out, "My heart will break!" (580), and throws away for good the quietude she appropriated in chapter 1. The tracing of that long evolution is utterly unlike Jane Eyre's development. Lucy Snowe's narrative is equivocal, unreliable, and devious — no suggestion, here, that the "plain truth" (96; ch. 12) of what Rochester calls Jane Eyre's "unpolluted memory" (119; ch. 14) will suffice. Ambiguous, intense, and problematic, *Villette* is in my view the most fascinating of Brontë's novels. It is also her last.

Charlotte Brontë died much too soon. She is remembered most widely as the author of *Jane Eyre*, a story that after almost 150 years continues to grab its readers by the throat. But *Jane Eyre* is only a part of Brontë's complex but all too short history as a daughter, a sister, a great, unflagging artist. To read it well, we need to place it there, where it belongs.

Jane Eyre and Biography

Thomas L. Jeffers

How can the biographical record about Charlotte Brontë help us understand *Jane Eyre*? Brontë's contemporaries were at once absorbed in the question, wondering who "Currer Bell" was and, when they knew, pondering what connections might exist between her and her governess heroine. A century and a half later, readers are still asking. I suggest here ways of exploiting such curiosity for pedagogic purposes, to instigate both class discussion, which is naturally a public affair, and personal journal writing, which may either be a kind of secret between teacher and student or remain the latter's own property.

In a course on Victorian fiction, one week into the two I devote to Brontë's novel, I give the students a weekend to read at least the first sixteen chapters of Elizabeth Gaskell's *Life*, which carries them through the sensational publication of *Jane Eyre*. Gaskell trusted the documents: though a number of Brontë's letters, notably those to her radical friend Mary Taylor, had been destroyed, a great many, especially those to her conservative friend Ellen Nussey, remained. They would help the biographer examine her own text with her "whole power and heart, so that every line should go to its great purpose of making [Brontë] known and valued as one who had gone through such a terrible life with a brave and faithful heart" — one whose "circumstances made her faults, while her virtues were her own" (Wise and Symington, *Brontës* 4: 218–19, 211). But, of course, writing her friend's life wasn't so simple even for Gaskell. She felt obliged to suppress what she had found out about Brontë's passionate love for Constantin Héger, her teacher at the school in Brussels where Charlotte and Emily had gone to perfect their French and thus enable themselves to set up their own "school for young ladies" in Haworth. To be sure, there was no evidence that Brontë had ever been sexually indiscreet with Héger: clearly, at great cost to her physical and mental health, she had resisted that temptation, but readers might still be shocked that a young Englishwoman would even have *noticed* the temptation. Meanwhile, her brother, Branwell, at even greater cost to *his* physical and mental health, had been less virtuous; he had become the lover of Lydia Robinson, the mother of the children he had been hired to tutor. This event, too, Gaskell needed to erase, especially in the revised second edition, for fear of Lydia Robinson's threat of libel. By Victorian standards of reticence, sex was too serious to talk about. Gaskell's suppressions were but one reason why, in an age that had become more tolerant, Brontë's life would have to be rewritten. Every document would be opened, and new theses — some psychological, some political, all broadly feminist — would supplement Gaskell's ethical-theological interpretation.

Winifred Gérin's (1967) and Margot Peters's (1975) biographies are the best modern ones, but because its spirit is closer to the world that formed

Brontë, I prefer Gaskell's — in spite of its suppressions. To involve students in the *contest* of interpretation, I apprise them, when we first discuss the *Life*, of the contradictory responses the book provoked. The masculinist Charles Kingsley praised it for giving "the picture of a valiant woman made perfect by sufferings," an individual for whom "a simple, virtuous, practical home life is consistent with high imaginative genius" (Wise and Symington, *Brontës* 4: 223, 222) — a response that obscures all the rage and restlessness that, save in the matter of Héger, Gaskell had so candidly foregrounded. Mary Taylor's comments were more in line with what we are likely to feel today; she thanked Gaskell for her "true picture of a melancholy life," which, "[t]hough not so gloomy as the truth, . . . is perhaps as much so as people will accept without calling it exaggerated." But Taylor wondered why neither of the first two reviews had thought "it a strange or wrong state of things that a woman of first-rate talents, industry, and integrity should live all her life in a walking nightmare of 'poverty and self-suppression'" (Wise and Symington, *Brontës* 4: 225).

To grasp the "melancholy," in both its Romantic and its clinical sense, Gaskell knew that the reader had to feel the northern milieu in which Brontë spent all but about thirty months of her life. The first two chapters marvelously evoke the "dun and purple moors," by turns so sublime and so monotonous (55). No other biography so scrupulously describes the early-nineteenth-century neighborhood of Keighley and Haworth or offers an anthropological account of Yorkshire, stretching back to the days of Edward III; through the seventeenth century, when it was a Puritan stronghold; into the days of the Brontës, when the factories around Haworth, which in 1841 had a population of 6,300, had begun to smudge the air. Calling the inhabitants a people of "strange eccentricity," with a "wild strength of will" and an "even . . . unnatural power of crime," Gaskell makes the West Riding sound like the Wild West of North American legend. Among such a "lawless, yet [she concedes] not unkindly population" did the Brontë children, so soon motherless, cling fervently to one another (67). The social particulars of their early lives — the conditions of their father's pastoral work, the character and tasks of the servants, the companions and teachers at the school for clergymen's daughters to which they were sent — and those of their later lives as governesses, and again as pupils in Brussels, are all rendered with the sharpness of detail we would expect from the author of *North and South*. As Brontë's contemporary, Gaskell had an advantage that twentieth-century biographers, for all their study of old maps and school registries, cannot overcome. Appreciation of these minutely drawn images is important, since they are precisely the type offered in Brontë's novel. I thus encourage students to read *Jane Eyre* not just as a kind of autobiography (Jane's own, or Brontë's through Jane) but as a *history* of a representative figure — petite bourgeoise on the make, entangled woman breaking free — at that time, in that place. And to promote such historical understanding, I ask students to depict an episode in their own lives — setting it forth with a concreteness emulative of Brontë's. A densely circumstanced account of one's own history ought to place one in an excellent position to appreciate another's; it can at least help close the gap between the sublime (certainly Brontë) and the ridiculous (perhaps oneself).

Since *Jane Eyre*, like *David Copperfield* and *Great Expectations*, is an "autobiography" not merely of the first-person narrator but to some extent of the author who stands behind her — a proposition implying no lack of aesthetic control in the author, or of critical interest for us — then in addition to seeking connections between characters, scenes, and symbols within the narrative itself, students and teachers may look *behind* the text to discern the not-quite-written, "raw" experience in Brontë's life that informed it. The task would be like trying to picture in our minds the line and texture of Jane's watercolor drawings — the lurid Turner-cum-Martin depictions of icebergs, shipwreck, drowned sailors, mystic women, and veiled faces that Jane describes and Rochester praises but that obviously can't be replicated in words (110; ch. 13). Jane both hides behind and reveals herself through those watercolors, just as the young Charlotte and her siblings, when performing their plays, were urged by their father to hide and reveal — to "speak boldly from under cover of the mask" (Gaskell 94). Jane is Brontë's persona, her mask, and, with all the rudeness the living usually show the dead, we can step up close to the text and peer, as through the fissures for eyes and mouth, at the face beneath.

Brontë's contemporaries, whether they visited her at Haworth or gawked at her in London, were indeed obsessed by the possible resemblances between the writer and the heroine that had made her famous, and Gaskell's biography supplied them with much of the data they hungered for: Jane as orphan was modeled on Brontë as half orphan; Lowood and Brocklehurst were like Cowan Bridge and William Carus Wilson, the treasurer and secretary of that school; Helen Burns corresponded to Charlotte's sister Elizabeth; Jane's sufferings as a governess, and her ambitions for a better life, had their source in the Brontë sisters' experiences; and so on. One can find a brief summary of these parallels in Judith Thurman's essay.

Most students, however, are impatient with the *where*, *what*, and *who* of dryasdust source hunting. They wish to know *why* Brontë needed to write a novel based to a large degree on her own life, and they are impressed most strongly by the contrast between the novel's ending, in which Jane is a reasonably happy wife and mother, and Brontë's condition in 1847 — her brother a disgrace; her sisters struggling, like her, just to be published; Héger inaccessible in Brussels; and Zamorna, the swart, brave-as-Wellington, sinful-as-Byron, Rochester-like hero of her juvenile daydreams, hermeticized in those tiny-printed, hand-stitched Angrian chronicles. The marriage plot of *Jane Eyre* is not, of course, a conventional one; Jane's spiritual and fiscal independence made it in fact startlingly new. Yet it does have a Cinderella ending, and Thackeray guessed one reason why:

The poor little woman of genius! the fiery little eager brave tremulous homely-faced creature! I can read a great deal of her life as I fancy in her book, and see that rather than have fame, rather than any other earthly good or mayhap heavenly one she wants some Tomkins or another to love her and be in love with. But you see she is a little bit of a creature without a penny worth of good looks, thirty years old I should think, buried in the country, and eating up her own heart there, and no Tomkins will come.   (3: 233)

Thackeray is referring to the greater, grimmer *Villette*, but we can read back through his comments to *Jane Eyre*. He wasn't speaking merely from a masculine point of view, though in fact most of Brontë's masculine acquaintance noticed how "plain" she looked and how much her plainness seemed to bother her (Brontë often *said* that it distressed her). If she had been "beautiful," then some Zamorna, some Tomkins, would have given her the love she craved. Very well. The drive for wish fulfillment underlay the abundant juvenilia, which, as Q. D. Leavis says with only slight exaggeration, are "utterly without promise" (9).

While the erotically charged Cinderella tale cannot by itself account for the achievement of *Jane Eyre*, it may explain why some ninth graders continue to read it avidly. Twelfth graders or college students, on the contrary, should be alert to a psychosocial ambition in Jane, which, however meshed with eros, is still separable from it. In the journals my students keep throughout the term, I urge them to offer at least one Harlequin-romance entry — an exercise in frank self-indulgence. I ask them next not to explode their fantasies (that would be crushingly easy) but, with frank self-criticism, to adapt them to socioeconomic probabilities. The outcome is usually more Angrian than a mature sensibility desires, but their work approximates (a little) the synthesis of romance and realism of *Jane Eyre*.

Such writing enables students to approach the novel with a regard for the economic conditions of Brontë's time. For Jane, it is clear, expresses her author's desire to define herself not as Everybody, who was aspiringly middle class and female in early Victorian England, but as Somebody — a woman free to enjoy the same pleasures, take the same chances, glean the same prestige as men. The locus classicus is the discourse that opens chapter 12, with its references to "the busy world, towns, regions full of life [Jane] had heard of but never seen" and to the tale of imagined "incident, life, fire, feeling" she "narrated continuously" to herself (95–96). The terms are pretty vague, and of course Jane realizes that, in *her* social circumstances, the only choice is between different forms of servitude — being a governess in a home or being a teacher in a school. But with brains and a tongue, she is not helpless: her quick way of asserting and defending herself in happy repartee with Rochester shows her to be the new woman in prototype, a precursor to Clara Middleton in Meredith's *The Egoist*. Declaring that he can make whatever cross-caste marriage he wants, Rochester *calls* her his "equal," a person as smart and lively as himself, but speech and action alike betray his deep, lingering sultanism (222; ch. 23). If they can't marry in England, he will "keep" her in France. Her recoil from that suggestion is not just sexual priggishness, as many readers (mostly male) have thought; it is psychological self-affirmation — a refusal to enter a liaison in which, as his references to his prior mistresses suggest, she would be socially "inferior" and, in the end, powerless.

In any case, Brontë has to "punish" Rochester for having even thought about degrading Jane and for having earlier degraded himself by marrying Bertha for her £30,000. The deliberate humiliation of Bertha that some critics see remains, it seems to me, deeply subtextual. According to a surface reading of the text, Rochester was not to blame for her alcoholism or promiscuity; the accusing finger points, if anywhere, to the genes within ("her excesses [sexual and alcoholic] had prematurely developed the germs of insanity" inherited from her mother [270; ch. 27]) and to the patriarchy without, which is ill-equipped to find better outlets for her energy and intelligence. The external enemy is the one we can vengefully attack, and Rochester looks like its exemplar. In propria persona, Brontë would surely disapprove of vengeance, especially in the form of symbolic castration. She is all for reconciliation, a Christian via media between Brocklehurst's or Rivers's Calvinistic imperialism and Helen's pansalvationism. But if not quite everybody is to be saved, and if some are after all to be damned, by God and by the novelist, then who is who? The question is too hard for Brontë, and though she gives Rivers, the white man in India, the heroic last lines, she stays focused on her heroine's progress, which is not just spiritual but social and economic: Jane gains something like level footing with the upper class, thanks both to her share in Rochester's worldly goods and to the £20,000 inheritance from her uncle, three-fourths of which she has generously shared with her Rivers cousins. Now she can leave governessing children, "making puddings and knitting stockings" (96; ch. 12), to less fortunate women and quietly raise a family with her one-armed, purblind, domesticated Zamorna.

From this account of a woman's progress, the teacher can return to biography, asking specifically about Brontë's feminism and prompting students to write about it, in their journals or in research papers. As the modern biographies show, her radical feminism — on the conscious level, at least — differed from the twentieth-century model. She had drunk deeply of her father's petit-clerical opinions, which bristled with an aristocracy-aping distrust of revolutionary movements from below and an almost medieval expectation of divine compensations from above. Brontë was no Brocklehurst, of course: she believed in decrying evil when she saw it and then urging its eradication. But she knew that the elimination of some wrongs might well require generations, especially those involving immemorial abuses against women. For the moment, she was simply grateful that the patriarchal system had opened enough to let her peculiar gifts exhibit themselves. Others, if they had the talent, could surely make their own way. She said in praise of what she took to be John Stuart Mill's (actually Harriet Taylor's) feminist essay:

> [I]f there be a natural unfitness in women for men's employment there is no need to make laws on the subject; leave all careers open; let them try; those who ought to succeed will succeed, or, at least, will have a fair chance; the incapable will fall back into their right place.
>
> (Wise and Symington, *Brontës* 3: 278)

There is, as Margot Peters remarks, something "coldly Darwinian" about such a statement (*Unquiet Soul* 340); it reminds us of the concentration-camp atmosphere at Lowood, where, in a panic of noncooperation, the older girls bully the younger out of their share of food.

But such an interpretation of Brontë's remarks reflects our late-twentieth-century outrage. Approaching *Jane Eyre* biographically should alert us to the fact that, in a Victorian context, Brontë was perhaps less radical than Mary Taylor, Harriet Martineau, or Harriet Taylor. She was, however, sufficiently bitter about the subjection of women, first, to let her own rebellion cry out in the novel, through Jane's asseverations of comparable worth and through the plot's vindicatory gestures against her oppressors; and second, to analyze, in what we might still call real life (her correspondence with friends), *la condition féminine* politically and economically and to suggest the meliorative steps that at midcentury had a chance of succeeding. "It is true enough," she wrote to her editor W. S. Williams,

> that the present market for female labour is quite overstocked, but where or how could another be opened? Many say that the professions now filled only by men should be open to women also; but are not their present occupants and candidates more than numerous enough to answer every demand? Is there any room for female lawyers, female doctors, female engravers, for more female artists, more authoresses? One can see where the evil lies, but who can point out the remedy?

She was willing to wait while "philosophers and legislators [pondered] over the better ordering of the social system." Meanwhile, let women struggle to find what work they can: Williams's daughters would be better off marrying poor men, working to help their husbands and their children, than making "mercenary marriages" (Wise and Symington, *Brontës* 2: 215–16, 221).

A final note about work—Jane's, Brontë's, and ours. On learning of her inheritance, Jane quits her job teaching ignorant but educable village girls at Marsh End and thereby rejects one of the few kinds of employment

Victorian women were allowed to pursue. One cheer for her honesty: she won't pretend to have a vocation she doesn't feel. She would rather be a self-sacrificing wife and mother who, unlike most, *knows* she once had a few other choices, especially after receiving her uncle's bequest. But the major alternative, which Jane can turn to even in what we take to be a full household, is *writing* — the production, for instance, of this autobiographical novel, through which she can clarify the history not just of herself but (mutatis mutandis) of the "Reader," male or female, whom she addresses at the famous beginning of the final chapter. As Gaskell, George Eliot, the Brontë sisters, and their "sillier" counterparts were in these decades discovering, writing could be as prestigious and occasionally as lucrative a pursuit for a woman as for a man. Brontë may be excused from the charge that she didn't better dramatize that alternative for her female contemporaries: after all, as she was writing *Jane Eyre*, she could boast of nothing in the way of literary commerce. The sisters' *Poems*, published at their own expense, had sold but two copies, and the manuscript for *The Professor* had been rejected, as it must have seemed to Charlotte, by every press in Christendom. But a path had been pointed to. She herself would go on to write two more novels, and her readers, if they do not themselves aspire to publish their own stories, can still through her example think of writing as a means of clarification, not forever in the self-stimulating, fantastical mode of the Angrian chronicles but, as I have suggested, ultimately in the life-situated, social-historical mode of (auto)biography.

Jane Eyre and the Governess in Nineteenth-Century Britain

Mary Poovey

Focusing on Brontë's treatment of Jane Eyre as a governess provides a useful way to teach students how a literary text engages with and illuminates social issues that seem to lie outside the text. Specifically, placing Brontë's representation of the governess in the context of mid-nineteenth-century anxieties about this figure casts light on some of the contradictions inherent in the Victorian ideology of womanhood. Such a pedagogical tack can help students to conceptualize history as something more complex than an inert backdrop to literary texts and to think of literature as a participant in the construction of social meanings instead of a mirror that simply reflects the world outside its pages.

From sources like M. Jeanne Peterson's essay, students can recognize the significance of Brontë's portrayal of the governess. It is important, for example, to know that private teaching was almost the only occupation considered sufficiently "genteel" for middle-class women, because this form of work most closely approximated that of the wife and mother. Moreover, in the 1840s the number of middle-class women who sought work outside the home rose substantially. The increase was the result partly of the economic vicissitudes of the "hungry 1840s," which produced both agricultural distress and middle-class bankruptcies (Checkland 197–98), partly of the discrepancy between the numbers of marriageable women and men, and partly of the tendency, which was becoming more widespread, for middle-class men to defer marriage until they had attained a level of economic prosperity (Banks, chs. 3–6). As more unmarried middle-class women competed aggressively for the available governess positions, the hardships of teaching intensified, for overcrowding drove wages down and encouraged employers to place ever-stricter demands on the women who sought this work.

Equally important is the extent to which the attention governesses received from contemporaries exceeded the actual social problem they represented. The 1851 census lists 25,000 governesses, for example, but at the same time there were 750,000 domestic servants, whose working conditions and wages were often more debilitating. While this latter group drew only scant notice, however, the governess was the subject, in the 1840s and 1850s, of so many articles and novels that her plight came to seem like the fate that awaited any middle-class woman who failed to marry. The society's concern for private teachers was out of proportion to the numbers of women who actually suffered from their employment but it suggests that the governess played a key symbolic role for middle-class English men and women. In identifying this role, students should grasp both why Brontë treats Jane's position as anomalous and why the marriage that concludes the novel raises as many questions as it lays to rest.

In Brontë's novel, Jane's tenure as a governess constitutes the final stage of the move, painfully inaugurated at Lowood Institution, toward financial independence. Although Jane calls it a "new servitude" (75; ch. 10), her private-teaching position represents a crucial phase in the formation of what Brontë figures as Jane's personal autonomy. This independent spirit, in turn, lays the groundwork for Jane's final achievement: it is the basis of Rochester's attraction to her as well as the trait that enables Jane first to leave and then to return to him. Despite the obvious importance Brontë attaches to Jane's position as a governess, however, and the central role she assigns it in Jane's character development and in the plot, she never gives it the kind of narrative attention it seems to warrant. Indeed, almost as soon as Jane becomes a governess, Brontë marginalizes the work. Although she depicts several encounters between Jane and her pupil, Adèle, Brontë does not describe the instruction that takes place. Even the globes and the needlework that make brief appearances in the scenes at Lowood are absent at Thornfield, and the "accomplishments" of piano playing and drawing that were the intended outcome of Jane's training are displayed by Jane for others, not by Adèle. Even more significant than the marginalization of governessing is Brontë's representation of Jane's work primarily in psychological, not economic or social, terms. Jane seeks the work because she has no one to support her, for example, but Brontë makes it clear that Jane's socially anomalous status is a function of her personality and not of her position as a governess. Brontë also reduces the economic exchange that being a governess entails to an index of the "peculiarities" of Jane's employer (91; ch. 11). Rochester forgets Jane's salary at one point, then doubles it, and later halves it. By the time Blanche Ingram ridicules the "anathematised race" of governesses in front of Jane (155; ch. 17), then, Brontë has effectively elevated her heroine above this "race" by subordinating Jane's poverty to her personality and to the place her character has earned her in Rochester's affections. "Your station," Rochester exclaims, "is in my heart" (231; ch. 24). The individualistic and psychological vocabulary Rochester uses here pervades Brontë's portrayal of their relationship: "You are my sympathy," Rochester cries to Jane at one point (277; ch. 27). "I have something in my brain and heart . . . ," Jane tells the reader, "that assimilates me mentally to him" (154; ch. 17).

Students may well wonder why Brontë makes Jane a governess only to give this occupation so little attention. In response to this question, teachers can point out that, as suggested here, Brontë subordinates the social and economic dimensions of this position to the psychological trope of "character"; the class can then discuss the symbolic role the governess played for Brontë's contemporaries and specifically the anxieties this figure aroused. In *Jane Eyre*, these tensions surface decisively but indirectly, in passages to which I will return in a moment. To clarify the threat that occasioned such apprehensions, however, I find it helpful to direct students to contemporaries' views of the governess's plight.

Midcentury representations reveal that the governess was a source of particular concern for two reasons. In the first place, she challenged assumptions about the role gender should play in stabilizing the "natural" hierarchy of class. Especially in the depressed decade of the 1840s, women became both the focus, on the part of working-class men, of worries about competition for scarce jobs and the solution, advanced by middle-class men, for the social and political discontent hard times fostered. If only women would remain in the home, men of all classes argued, work would be available to men who needed it and the family income and morality would alike be restored. The increasing numbers of would-be governesses seemed to threaten this state of affairs, both because any working women challenged the notion that women would always be content to remain at home, where their labor was unpaid, and because the widespread perception that more middle- *and* lower-class women were entering the ranks of governess tended to obliterate the distinction between "genteel" work, which middle-class ladies could perform, and other kinds of work, which were thought to be suited to working-class women. Thus the governess brought the economic realities of the 1840s into sharp relief in a form that might undermine the "natural" distinctions that ought to anchor social relations and morality.

In the second place, the governess also called into question the morality that contemporaries claimed was natural to women. The passion that was feared to lurk in the governess was often represented only indirectly, as a "craving for pleasures," for example, or as "nervous irritability, dejection [and] loss of energy" ("Hints" 574), but references to the governess's "twisted coil of passion and levity," as well as suggestions that she was, in some ways, like the two most notorious exemplars of female sexuality — the lunatic and the prostitute — make the nature of the anxieties about this figure clear (Poovey, *Uneven Developments* 130–31). What the Victorians feared was that the governess might not be able to control her own sexuality — much less the sexual temptations to which her young charges were exposed or those that she, as a young unmarried woman, was thought to pose to the family's male members.

In making Jane a governess, Brontë therefore associates with her heroine traits that were not generally valued in women. Most students will recognize that the imaginative power of Brontë's characterization invests these qualities with considerable attractiveness. Brontë's novel also creates the opposite effect, which may be less obvious to students: at the same time that economic independence and sexual desire acquire value because they are associated with Jane, the issues of class and of sexual transgression associated with the role of governess inject into the novel the anxieties such transgressions evoked among Brontë's readers. Indeed, Brontë's treatment of Jane highlights an additional threat posed by the governess — one that could not be contained by returning women to their "proper" place in the home. This threat emerges, paradoxically, when Jane abandons her position as governess. In the scenes immediately after she leaves Thornfield Hall, which repay close reading in class, Jane seems to pit one of the governess's dangerous traits — her economic independence — against the other — her sexual susceptibility. Yet the state in which she finds herself — "absolutely destitute," "objectless and lost" (283, 284; ch. 28) — returns the disturbing side of both characteristics to the forefront of the narrative. Mistaken for an "eccentric sort of lady," a thief, and a figure too "sinister" to be named (289; ch. 28), Jane at this moment embodies the qualities the nineteenth-century British found most unsettling, and she demonstrates that these traits imperil not only society but the governess herself. Behind her apparent independence lurks dependence on the whims of the market; behind her sexual energy lies the potential for abandonment — or worse.

Students will observe that Brontë gives the narrative a happy ending when she restores Jane to Rochester. By this point, moreover, Jane is financially independent, not through her own labor but through the more acceptable route of inherited wealth. Her sexual vulnerability has also been neutralized by the injuries that have made Rochester dependent on her. Yet students may realize that this "solution" to the governess's plight is no more an effective counter to the tensions this figure provoked than is Jane's flight from Thornfield Hall a negation of the governess's threat. The fact that the cultural associations linked to the governess persist even though Jane no longer functions in this role underscores what the Victorian ideology of womanhood was meant to cover over: the ideal woman — the wife and mother — was as dependent as the women from whom she ought to differ.

To help students understand this concept, teachers might solicit opinions about what an ideal Victorian mother was meant to be. With some assistance, students should see that, theoretically, the governess was unlike the ideal middle-class mother. That the governess had to be taught and paid to perform services the mother automatically did for free emphasized the power of maternal instinct, which, as a noncompetitive, unselfish form of love, was considered the bedrock of womanly nature and the basis for social morality. The notion that women naturally gave love and service without pay was, in turn, central to the representation of domesticity as desirable; this representation, along with the disincentive to work outside the home that it enforced, was instrumental to fostering the image of women as moral and not economic agents, antidotes to the evils of competition. Finally, a sphere of relative freedom from economic necessity was crucial to establishing some boundary to the market economy; the wife, protected and fulfilled by maternal instinct, was proof that the commodification of labor, the alienation of human relations, the frustrations and disappointments inflicted by economic vicissitudes, stopped at the door of the home. From this complex ideological picture, students can see that laments about the governess's plight in the 1840s belonged to a discourse about the relations between motherhood, gender, class, and labor.

The problem was that governesses — especially in such numbers and in such visibly desperate straits — gave the lie to the economic and domestic representations that underwrote this ideology. Not only did the governess's plight bring the uncertainties of the marketplace into the middle-class home, thereby destroying the separation of spheres, but the very existence of so many governesses meant that, whatever middle-class women might want, not all of them could be (legitimate) mothers because they could not all be wives. Thus, even though mid-Victorian writers offered the unpaid mother as the norm, motherhood had to be rhetorically constructed *as* the norm in defiance of real social conditions. Brontë's novel reveals that the figure from whom the middle-class mother had to be distinguished was not just the working-class woman but the middle-class governess as well, for the governess was both what a woman who should be a mother might actually become and the woman who had to be paid for doing what the mother should want to do for free. The governess was the figure who ought to ensure that a boundary existed between classes of women, but she could not, precisely because she was like the woman from whom she ought to have differed.

When Brontë restores the traits associated with the governess to her heroine on her departure from Thornfield Hall and when she rewards Jane with marriage to Rochester, she exposes the contradictions inherent in this ideological configuration. Most obviously, Jane's marriage collapses the boundary between the governess and the mother. Even earlier, however, Jane has been inscribed in a series of women that undermines the uniqueness of the wife and mother. Among these women are the lunatic Bertha and Céline Varens, the French opera dancer and mother of Adèle. Rochester's intention in describing these women to Jane is to insist on her difference from them, but she immediately sees what Rochester will not — that if Jane assents to his proposal to remain with him, she will become "the successor of these poor girls" (274; ch. 27). Even her departure from Thornfield Hall cannot sever her connection with these women; because Jane returns to Rochester before she knows that Bertha is dead, she is placing herself in the very series she wanted to disavow.

Emphasizing the similarity among women is subversive because doing so highlights all women's dependence — although this is, of course, part of the point. In addition, the fact that the likeness Brontë stresses is not woman's selflessness but some internal difference, which is figured variously as madness and as sexuality, suggests that what women have in common would actually undermine the ideological ideal. That this "heterogeneity" is what Rochester has always admired in Jane, moreover, implies that the trait is the embodiment of womanliness. Jane's own descriptions of herself repeatedly foreground this heterogeneity, and she portrays her maturation as a growth from the "desperation" of childhood rebellion to the "restlessness" of unspecified desire (9, 95; chs. 2, 12).

Positioning Jane within a series of women and characterizing her as "restless" and passionate transform the difference that contemporaries thought ought to exist among women into a difference within all women — the difference of sexual desire. This similarity thus subverts the putative difference between the governess and the lunatic or mistress, just as it obliterates the difference between the governess and the wife. Having Jane marry Rochester — transforming the governess into a wife — extends the series of aberrant women to include the figure who ought to be the norm. As the boundary between these two groups of women, the governess belongs to both sides of the opposition: in her, the very possibility of an opposition disintegrates.

Teaching *Jane Eyre* in relation to this complex of cultural assumptions and anxieties helps students see that inconsistencies in the novel are signs of the literary text's participation in and attempts to resolve the ideological instabilities that characterized a particular historical moment. The meaning of the inconsistencies must therefore be sought not in the closed system of the text but in the interaction between the literary treatment of a problem and other, contemporary treatments. The fact that Brontë represents her heroine as a governess only to diminish, ostentatiously, the importance of this role makes sense when we understand that the dangers associated with the governess threatened to undermine the integrity of the role with which Brontë crowns Jane's development — that of wife and mother. To reduce these threats, Brontë specifically dismisses the class and sexual anxieties aroused by the governess. Having introduced them, however, she cannot fully dispense with their destabilizing effect, for the ideology that distinguished between the governess and the wife was also based on the likeness that it repressed. Brontë's depiction of the governess, then, simultaneously reproduces the contradiction in this ideological configuration and renders it available for twentieth-century readers to grasp.

TEACHING THE LITERARY
AND PHILOSOPHICAL TRADITIONS

Jane Eyre, Bertha, and the Female Gothic

Tamar Heller

I teach *Jane Eyre* in a course, Literature by Women, that tackles the challenging, and even daunting, task of selecting works that represent the broad range of women's contributions to English and American literature. The popularity of the subject attracts a diverse group of students: some are English majors, while others have taken only freshman English. I have found that *Jane Eyre* works particularly well in this class, both because it appeals to most of the students, whatever their background, and because they find it a useful introduction to feminist theories of narrative and genre, or what Nancy K. Miller calls "plots and plausibilities" in women's fiction. The first novel we read, *Jane Eyre* provides a paradigmatic example of how a woman writer responds to and revises traditional plots for women. In my discussions of the novel, I identify two traditional plot lines that undergird it: the tale of the woman alone — a female bildungsroman whose independent heroine is a significant innovation in a nineteenth-century context — and the tale of the woman and man, represented by the romance between Jane and Rochester. It is the intersection, indeed the collision, of these two plots that complicates each and creates the aesthetic and ideological complexity of the novel.

The character of Bertha Rochester, the "madwoman in the attic," may be seen as a signifier for the tensions between the bildungsroman and the courtship plots in *Jane Eyre*. She is linked to the bildungsroman plot by being, as Sandra M. Gilbert and Susan Gubar have argued, the monstrous version of Jane that indicates Brontë's ambivalence about the anger and rebellion her female characters express either openly or covertly. Bertha, of course, also suggests the sinister side of the courtship plot; through her presence, Brontë juxtaposes the romance between Jane and Rochester with a female Gothic narrative about women's domination by men. Here I draw on feminist analyses of the "female Gothic," a term coined by Ellen Moers to define a tradition of Gothic writing by women, popularized by Ann Radcliffe, that represents the female experience within domesticity as one of imprisonment, claustrophobia, and terror (Moers 90–110; see Modleski 59–84; DeLamotte 149–92, and, on *Jane Eyre*, 193–228). Confined by her husband in the family manor, Bertha is Brontë's figure for this plot and its negative portrayal of women's position within marriage and the family.

In my classes on *Jane Eyre*, I have used the female Gothic as the focal point of our exploration of the novel's multiple and intersecting plots. By helping to organize a discussion of the bildungsroman and courtship plots, an emphasis on the female Gothic allows students to examine the tension between female individuality and domesticity that is a central theme in the novel. The Gothic also provides an accessible avenue for students to encounter the text, although initially they may not think so. One problem in teaching a class on women's literature that covers a great deal of ground and enrolls students at differing levels of expertise is that many may be unfamiliar with a literary-historical category like the Gothic. In my experience, however, students know much more about Gothic, bildungsroman, and courtship plots than they might themselves realize, since these narratives are staples of the stories contemporary culture tells about gender. Discussions of the Gothic elements in *Jane Eyre* — and the implications of this genre for women — are enriched by appealing to the cultural knowledge that students already possess.

In the first class on *Jane Eyre*, when students have read through the account of Helen Burns's death, in chapter 9, I underscore Gothic themes in the novel, although I try not to use the word *Gothic* at this point. My strategy, again, is to get the students themselves to work toward a definition of what the Gothic means without, just yet, imposing my own. Sometimes students use the term *Gothic* as a synonym for *eerie* or *oppressive* as they describe the atmosphere of the novel. Although I note the significance of the word and tell them we will define it more fully in the next class, I ask students to concentrate for now on identifying what kind of world women inhabit in these first chapters. The images we focus on are those of confinement and imprisonment. In his discussion of the influence of the female Gothic on Wilkie Collins's *The Woman in White*, D. A. Miller has aptly defined the genre as the "feminine carceral" (120), and, with this description in mind, I underscore *Jane Eyre*'s images of domestic space as prison: Gateshead as nightmarish home and Lowood as coercive institution for feminine socialization anticipate Thornfield, which for Bertha of course is the home *as* institution.

One of the scenes we look at in depth in this first class, and to which I will refer in subsequent classes on the Gothic, is that of Jane's imprisonment in the Red Room. The Red Room is a complex Gothic site that suggests both Brontë's indebtedness to the Radcliffean tradition and her innovative development of it. Locked up because she dared to protest the domestic violence epitomized by John Reed's attack on her, Jane is not just the victimized heroine but a miniature version of the monster of passion Bertha will later embody; the moment in the Red Room in which Jane looks into the mirror and seems not to recognize herself (11; ch. 2) is echoed in the later scene in which Bertha invades Jane's room before her marriage to Rochester and, looking in the glass, tries on her wedding veil (249; ch. 25). In the Red Room scene it is already apparent how Brontë transforms imprisoning domestic space into the abode of "passion" (with its double meaning of anger and sexuality) and of Jane's experimentation with different types of feminine identity.

Before the second class, when students will have read through chapter 27 — in which Jane leaves Thornfield after finding out that Rochester is already married — I give them a handout so they can think about the relation between Bertha's story and Jane's. In the handout, containing a passage from *A Room of One's Own*, Virginia Woolf objects that Bertha's laugh, which Jane hears as she laments women's restricted sphere of action (96; ch. 12), is an "awkward break" that expresses the "jerk" of Brontë's anger — a quality Woolf claims makes her books "deformed and twisted" (72–73). In my opinion, Woolf's comment reveals more about her own attitude toward anger than it does about Brontë's art, and students often express their discomfort with Woolf's vocabulary when I ask them, at the beginning of the second class, what they thought about her criticism of the novel. Although setting up a straw man — or woman — is not always a good way to initiate a discussion, Woolf's ambivalent response to anger in women's literature is a useful introduction to Brontë's similar ambivalence as expressed through the figure of Bertha. In particular, Woolf's passage allows us to start exploring the connection between Bertha's manifestations at Thornfield — her maniacal laughter and nighttime attempts to murder men — and Jane's bildungsroman of personal and psychological development. I tell students that the main questions to consider are how the female Gothic plot mirrors the story of Jane's feminist discontent and what the significance is, in both these stories, of women's anger as well as of their oppression.

I turn, next, to a discussion of the term *Gothic*, noting that we had used it to describe the eerie and claustrophobic domestic spaces at the beginning of the novel. I ask students whether they have read any Gothics. Several confess to a knowledge of drugstore Gothics; few have read (or even heard of) Radcliffe's *The Mysteries of Udolpho* (1794), a novel I describe briefly, to provide a sense of the tradition of female Gothic. More, however, have read Daphne du Maurier's *Rebecca* (or seen the movie) and are quick to explain its striking resemblance to *Jane Eyre*. I then ask a question that provokes some (delighted) embarrassment: whether anyone has read Harlequin romances. After eliciting a few confessions, I ask students if Harlequins remind them of *Jane Eyre*, too, and point out that critics have identified Brontë's novel as an important influence on popular culture narratives for women, including Harlequins and modern Gothics (e.g., Russ 31; Modleski 15, 46–47). Here I identify the Harlequin as a pure example of the courtship plot, which traces the relationship between a man and a woman and ends in their marriage, giving as a more canonical parallel *Pride and Prejudice* and other Austen novels. To focus the discussion, I draw two columns on the board, labeling one "Female Gothic Plot" and the other "Harlequin (Courtship) Plot" (obviously, not all courtship narratives have Harlequin plots, but, for the purpose of isolating important themes, we stick to the romance novel as our model for this type of story). Then, once again drawing on their own cultural knowledge, students supply the archetypal ingredients of each narrative. Here are the kinds of lists we usually end up with:

Female Gothic Plot

Gothic "paraphernalia" — castles, convents

Historical or archaic setting

Supernatural, or apparently supernatural, events

Heroine — pure, good, imprisoned

Male tyrant — father, guardian, husband

Evil other woman

Good lover (different from tyrant figure, *or* tyrant becomes good lover by end of story)

Harlequin (Courtship) Plot

Exotic settings (European or tropical)

Shy virgin (who is poor)

Harsh Byronic man (who is rich)

Vampy woman who has been lover of Byronic male

Wimpy lover of heroine, eventually rejected in favor of newly sensitized Byronic man

As we compile these lists, it becomes clear not only that the female Gothic and courtship narratives closely resemble *Jane Eyre* but that the two are essentially the same plot, albeit with different emphases. To the extent that the plots differ, the female Gothic is a dark mirror of the courtship (Harlequin) plot; the former accentuates the anxiety about male domination already present in the romance narrative. In both the Gothic and courtship stories, tyrannical men terrorize repressed, virginal women, although in the Radcliffean Gothic the authoritarian male is not the woman's lover but, like Montoni in *The Mysteries of Udolpho*, the obstacle preventing the woman from marrying her sensitive male lover (again, examples are *Udolpho*'s Emily and Valancourt). In more recent transformations of the genre, however, the tyrannical male often *is* the woman's husband — a point succinctly conveyed by the title of Joanna Russ's essay on the modern Gothic, "Somebody's Trying to Kill Me and I Think It's My Husband." As Russ describes modern Gothics, the typical "latter-day Jane Eyre," attracted to a "dark, magnetic, powerful, brooding, sardonic *Super-Male*," is unsure whether he "1) loves her; 2) hates her; 3) is using her; or 4) is trying to kill her" (32).

At this point it's easy to turn back to Brontë's novel and to the feminine paranoia of the Gothic Bertha plot. We discuss whether Jane, too, has reason to be paranoid. Does Jane and Rochester's turbulent and interrupted courtship conform more to the model of the Gothic or the Harlequin? Precisely how dangerous is Rochester to Jane's autonomy? I remind students of Jane's comment about tales that "run on the same theme — courtship; and promise to end in the same catastrophe — marriage" (174; ch. 19). Dwelling on the pun implicit in a word that means not just conclusion but disaster, we examine to what extent the projected marriage with Rochester is *catastrophic* to Jane's cherished independence.

In pursuing this discussion, we return to the symbolism of domestic space that we had explored in our first class. At Thornfield, as at Gateshead and Lowood, domestic spaces are linked both literally and figuratively to sites of incarceration and terror, with the cozy and handsome inhabited wing of the house adjoining the Gothic region of decaying and crumbling domesticity that contains Bertha's prison. In this context, the imagery of the charades Jane witnesses at Thornfield is significant, since a sketch of a wedding is followed by one of "Bridewell," the debtor's prison (162; ch. 18). Jane's own financial indebtedness to Rochester during their engagement causes her not only to feel constrained by the increasingly unequal terms of their relationship but to anticipate losing her identity within marriage: "one Jane Rochester, a person whom as yet I knew not" (242; ch. 25).

Indeed, Jane's self-alienation as she puts on her wedding gown — "I saw a robed and veiled figure, so unlike my usual self that it seemed almost the image of a stranger" (252; ch. 26) — is mirrored by the Gothic image of Bertha haunting her room the night before the marriage, clad in white clothes that resemble a "shroud" (249; ch. 25). We explore the connections between Jane's feelings of repressed anger toward Rochester during her courtship and engagement — her reluctance, for instance, to let Rochester buy her an expensive wedding veil — and Bertha's destruction of this veil.

Throughout this discussion of Bertha, I am influenced by Gilbert and Gubar's argument that Bertha is Jane's double. I try, however, to pursue some of the ideological implications of this doubling by referring to the female Gothic tradition and its pessimistic commentary on the traditional courtship plot. In the Radcliffean narrative, the imprisoned woman, like Emily in *The Mysteries of Udolpho*, is also the pure and good heroine, while the story's evil other woman — in *Udolpho*, the adulterous murderer Signora Laurentini — is less the victim of men than of her own passion. With the figure of Bertha, Brontë recalls this Gothic convention of isolating the heroine's covert rebellion and sexuality in a female avatar who is then scapegoated and punished. Yet by having the incarcerated Bertha echo the imprisoned heroine as well as the wicked other woman, Brontë makes the connection between the female doubles at once more explicit and more complex than in earlier versions of the female Gothic. Nonetheless, Brontë's efforts to delineate the difference between Rochester's two wives, such as the writer's use of a language of racial otherness to describe the West Indian heiress, underscore her ambivalence about the qualities in Jane — passion, anger, and sexuality — that Bertha supposedly embodies. Brontë's most creative innovation of the Radcliffean tradition, indeed, may well be the way that this ambivalence develops the theme of feminine self-suppression in the female Gothic narrative.

We spend a great deal of our last class on *Jane Eyre* discussing the extent to which Brontë resolves the issues of female rebellion, individuation, and domesticity raised by her revision of the female Gothic. What do students think of the fact that Bertha's death is the precondition for Jane and Rochester's marriage? I read to them a passage from *The Madwoman in the Attic* in which Gilbert and Gubar, having identified Bertha as Jane's "truest and darkest double" (360), claim that the aspect of Jane that Bertha represents will not be "exorcised until the literal and symbolic death of Bertha frees her from the furies that torment her and makes possible a marriage of equality — makes possible, that is, wholeness within herself" (362). We consider whether Bertha's death — and her destruction of Thornfield, the site of the feminine carceral — signals a happy ending to the female Gothic narrative she embodies and whether her role is finished once Jane and Rochester have worked toward a more egalitarian relationship.

To complicate Gilbert and Gubar's rather rosy interpretation, however, I ask why Bertha's death is as violent as it is, pointing out the image of her "brains and blood" (377; ch. 36) scattered on the pavement. Similarly, Rochester's mutilation — his being both literally and figuratively cut down to size to equalize the distinctions between him and Jane — may suggest that the domestic relationship between men and women continues to be troubled. Moreover, could Bertha's death presage, for Jane, not "wholeness" but instead the further fragmentation of her personality, as Brontë casts out her "bad, mad, and embruted" side (257; ch. 26) to leave only the persona of the good wife, Rochester's "prop and guide" (395; ch. 37)? With these queries, I encourage students to examine whether they agree with Gilbert and Gubar's positive reading of the ending or whether they think that Bertha's "exorcism" is a way of taming and containing the feminine rebellion that she represents. In this debate — and I have found that students tend to be fairly evenly divided in reading the ending as positive or problematic — I stress the ideological and aesthetic complexity of the tension between bildungsroman and courtship plots that Brontë conveys through her use of the female Gothic. In this sense, Bertha, even though she is finally exiled from the text, continues most creatively to haunt it.

"Beauty and the Beast": Growing Up with Jane Eyre

Phyllis C. Ralph

What better way to approach a novel of growing up than to examine the way it exemplifies the stages involved? Viewing adolescence through the distancing lens of literature may be helpful for students in coming to terms with the maturation process. That lens can be focused by presenting the literature first in the familiar form of the fairy tale. Although some feminist critics see fairy tales as socializing agents that teach women their "proper" — that is, passive — role in society, another interpretation is possible. In animal groom tales such as "Beauty and the Beast," the protagonists are active participants in their own transformations and, as such, provide appropriate models for novels of a woman's development. Like Jane Eyre, Beauty makes choices and takes actions that effect change in herself and in others — unlike the reactive characters in such tales as "Cinderella" and "Sleeping Beauty." For example, in the most widely known "Cinderella," based on the version by Charles Perrault and popularized in this country by Walt Disney, the central character initiates no action, passively waiting to be rescued and transformed.

The class in which I have taught *Jane Eyre* is a sophomore-level literature and composition course titled Growing Up Female. The course examines the psychological interpretations of some popular fairy tales and considers what underlying meanings are suggested by the use of these fairy-tale themes in the novels read. We begin with a study of selected fairy tales, using as resources such works as *The Classic Fairy Tales*, by Iona Opie and Peter Opie, and *The Uses of Enchantment*, by Bruno Bettelheim. Although there are other background sources, including Julius E. Heuscher's *A Psychiatric Study of Fairy Tales* and Peter Blos's *On Adolescence: A Psychoanalytic Interpretation*, Bettelheim's volume is the most accessible and readable, and it works well as a supplemental resource. Next we look at a casebook containing versions and interpretations of the "Cinderella" motif, which takes the heroine only to the threshold of love, and then move on to the animal groom pattern, which shows that personal growth is required for union in an adult relationship. This motif encompasses such tales as "Snow White and Rose Red" and "The Frog Prince," but we focus on its best-known example, "Beauty and the Beast." Derived from the myth of Cupid and Psyche, the tale provides the structural paradigm for *Jane Eyre* and the other novels we study.

The animal groom tales can be especially useful in analyzing developmental novels featuring adolescent women. Symbolically representing the development and acceptance of mature sexual identity, most versions of this kind of tale include the same basic elements. In repayment for a favor done either for herself or for her father, the heroine goes to live with an animal or a monstrously ugly man. Although their union may be a forced one, she comes to love the monster but, in most variants, recognizes her feelings only after a separation proves almost fatal to one of them. Her love transforms the beast into his true state as a handsome prince, or at least alters her perception of him. According to Bettelheim, these tales teach "that for love, a radical change in previously held attitudes about sex is absolutely necessary" (282). Thus the tale depicts a crucial step in female adolescent development.

Young women are discouraged both by cultural standards of behavior and by fear of the implications of sexuality from accepting their physical natures. Bettelheim explains how their hesitancy is represented in the tales: "The animal groom stories convey that it is mainly the female who needs to change her attitude about sex from rejecting to embracing it, because as long as sex appears to her as ugly and animal-like, it remains animalistic in the male; i.e., he is not disenchanted" (286). Since the development of a mature sexual identity is necessary for effective functioning in the adult world, these tales also explore the nature of love and the formation of a relationship. All the stories suggest that real love includes the acceptance of the beloved as he or she really is, not as the lover perceives him or her to be. Mature love, then, requires the ability to see beyond the appearance to the reality, and the acceptance of that reality in all its aspects. While in the tales themselves the animal groom seems magically transformed by the heroine's devotion and acceptance, the implication is clearly that it is not the man who has been changed but the young woman's perception of him. This concept is important in understanding the growth of Jane Eyre and her evolving relationship with Edward Rochester. As Jane moves toward emotional and psychological maturity, she sees beyond Rochester's bestial appearance and behavior to the human strengths and weaknesses beneath.

Two aspects of animal groom tales that parallel important stages in the developmental process involve the role played by the father and the heroine's initiative in effecting the transformation of the beast. In "Beauty and the Beast," Beauty is the youngest daughter of a rich merchant who loses his fortune. She turns down many marriage proposals because she will not abandon her father in his distress. Coming home in a storm from a business trip, the merchant finds shelter in a house in which all his needs are magically fulfilled. As he leaves, he gathers a branch of roses for Beauty and is berated by a frightful beast for stealing the flowers after he has been so well treated. The Beast threatens the man's life but releases him on the condition that he send one of his daughters to suffer in his place. Thus it is the father who is responsible for the relationship between his daughter and the Beast, through his financial improvidence and his theft of the roses.

Accepting the conditions of her father's bargain, Beauty goes to the Beast's palace. Having ascertained that she came of her own free will, the Beast makes her welcome and provides a chest of gold for her family. Every evening he visits her, and gradually she grows fond of him. She agrees never to leave him if she can first visit her father, who has grown ill as a result of their separation. Promising to return in one week, Beauty goes home. Tricked by her envious sisters into extending her visit until a dream reveals the Beast close to death, she returns to find her dream a reality. When she thinks she is losing Beast, Beauty realizes that she loves him: "[T]he grief I now feel convinces me, that I cannot live without you" (Opie and Opie 149). Her agreement to marry Beast transforms him into a handsome prince, who tells her of his enchantment by a wicked fairy. The spell may be interpreted as the prohibitions against sexual expression for young women by their mothers or other female guardians, making them perceive men as threatening.

The deep love between Beauty and her father may represent her oedipal attachment, which is broken only when she acknowledges her devotion to the Beast. Faced with a conflict between her love for her father and the Beast's needs, she deserts Beast to go to her father, only to recognize how much the Beast means to her. In Bettelheim's view, no other well-known fairy tale makes it as obvious as "Beauty and the Beast" that a child's oedipal attachment to a parent is "natural, desirable, and has the most positive consequences for all, if during the process of maturation it is transferred and transformed as it becomes detached from the parent and concentrated on the lover" (307). He concludes that only after Beauty leaves her father's house to be reunited with the Beast, or has resolved the oedipal ties to her father, "does sex, which before was repugnant, become beautiful" (308). While such an outcome could be interpreted as a rationalization rather than a transformation, Bettelheim's reading is consistent with the stages of adolescent psychological growth.

Although the action of the narrative itself and Beauty's relationship with her father support the view that the tale is about the development and acceptance of sexuality, there is more to the narrative than this issue. Just as growing up entails more than physical maturity, so other changes must take place in Beauty to make her final choice understandable. At the beginning of her life with the Beast, Beauty's singular lack of curiosity about her surroundings embodies the latency stage that precedes the demonstration of initiative in pursuit of autonomy. In this next stage of development, Beauty makes the best of the threatening situation in which she finds herself, accepts the Beast for qualities that overcome his repulsive appearance, and chooses to return to him when she could have stayed with her family. Her independence is also symbolically represented by the chest of gold that provides for her family when Beauty first goes to live with the Beast. Bettelheim summarizes, "The story's essence is not just the growth of Beauty's love for the Beast, or even her transferring her love for her father to the Beast, but her own growth in the process" (308).

As we discuss the fairy tales and their interpretation, I provide background information on personal growth as determined by psychologists in the field, focusing especially on the stage of adolescence. The desired outcomes of adolescence are the formation of a relatively stable character and the achievement of a psychic structure that will allow the young adult to relate satisfactorily to the external world. Self-discovery, the quest for identity, is the crucial psychological task of adolescence, with the accompanying development of autonomy. Most authorities on adolescence see the establishment of a firm sexual identity as a main attribute of a cohesive self-representation. In addition to self-discovery, adolescents must acquire self-reliance; they do so by accomplishing a series of tasks, not unlike the tasks of primitive initiation rites. They must effect a separation from parental authority figures, test their own abilities by choosing and initiating action, assume responsibility for themselves, and define their own values.

Observing the growth of Jane Eyre, the heroine of this novel of development, we see her following the path described here in her movement toward maturity: taking risks, questioning conventional beliefs, determining her values and acting on them, assuming responsibility for herself, and, ultimately, deciding how and with whom to spend her life.

There are many surface references to fairies and other supernatural beings in *Jane Eyre*, but more significant is the underlying psychological meaning conveyed by the themes and patterns from the tales, especially that of the animal groom. As in Beauty's family, it is the poverty of Jane's father that creates the situation of the narrative; and like Beauty's choosing to live with the Beast to fulfill her father's promise, Jane decides to go to school and leave her cruel foster family, the Reeds. Also like Beauty, Jane makes the best of the threatening situation in her new environment. Having survived eight years at Lowood Institution, she separates herself from this "family" too, when she seeks a wider range of experiences. The enclosed atmosphere of the school and the lack of contact with the outside world represent the latency period preceding the transformation to adulthood. As with the maturing adolescent, Jane's completion of one stage signals the movement to the next developmental level.

The similarities between *Jane Eyre* and the animal groom tale continue. Brontë departs from the pattern in making clear that, unlike Beauty in the tale, Jane is emphatically plain, but Rochester is consistently described in terms suggesting a bestial appearance and a brutish personality. Since the issue is essentially one of perception, Jane becomes beautiful to Rochester as he grows to love her, even as her view of him is altered. Following their initial interview, Rochester often summons Jane in the evening, even as the Beast usually joins Beauty at night for conversation. Jane's refusal to call Rochester handsome echoes Beauty's agreement that the Beast is "very ugly" (Opie and Opie 145), and, like the Beast, Rochester seems pleased with such frankness. As the two become better acquainted, in both the tale and the novel, appearance no longer seems to matter. Just as seeing the Beast so often has accustomed Beauty to his deformity, making her look forward to his visits rather than dread them (Opie and Opie 147), so Jane concludes: "And was Mr. Rochester now ugly in my eyes? No, reader. Gratitude, and many associations, all pleasurable and genial, made his face the object I best liked to see" (129; ch. 15). Although his actual appearance has not changed, her feelings toward him have made her perceive him differently.

In the tale little information is provided about the sorceress who has turned the prince into a beast until a beautiful virgin will consent to marry him. The sorceress may represent the mother who has tabooed sex until marriage makes it permissible. Since such a restriction is a part of most children's education, the sorceress is not punished at the end of the tale. Sexuality is the issue in *Jane Eyre* as well, but Rochester suggests that it is fate or destiny that has played the role of sorceress. Telling Jane about his past, he says, "When fate wronged me, I had not the wisdom to remain cool: I turned desperate; then I degenerated" (119; ch. 14). He vows to be a better man, but, like the Beast, he must wed a young virgin to be transformed; marriage is impossible, however, because of his wife, Bertha. Seen from this perspective, perhaps Bertha fulfills the role of the sorceress who has caused Rochester's imprisonment in his present unhappy state.

Like Beauty, Jane leaves Rochester to care for an ill relative when she is summoned to the bedside of her dying aunt Reed. Since Jane's father is dead, her aunt represents her only known family tie and perhaps, by extension, the same kind of attachment. Rochester, unsuccessful in dissuading her from going, says, "Promise me only to stay a week," the same vow that Beast requires of Beauty. Jane refuses to commit herself to a time limit but pledges to return (196; ch. 21). A month elapses before she goes back to Thornfield; and although Rochester is not dying, as the Beast is at Beauty's return, this event culminates in their engagement. However, after the revelation of his previous marriage, Jane refuses to allow him to touch her, and their final separation, the one that brings Rochester near death, begins.

While living with her Rivers cousins, Jane completes the last of her testing tasks in her quest for adulthood. Here she establishes her economic independence by teaching school and struggles with the decision of whether to marry St. John Rivers. Her inheritance, coming as it does from an unknown relative, parallels the magical chest of gold that Beast provides for Beauty's family. Although St. John is everything that Rochester is not—handsome, learned, religious, and single—Jane overcomes the force of his personality and acknowledges to herself and to St. John that a marriage between them would be harmful for both. He urges her to reconsider, and, as she hesitates, a voice cries out, "Jane! Jane! Jane!" On the verge of weakening in the face of St. John's persistence, Jane hears Rochester's despairing cry across the miles and answers from her heart: "'I am coming!' I cried. 'Wait for me! Oh, I will come!'" (369; ch. 35). Jane seems called to Rochester's side, as Beauty was to the dying Beast, by a supernatural summons. Leaving the Riverses so that she can find Rochester, Jane rejects St. John, her last male familial authority figure.

Throughout the novel there are indications that Jane's influence is civilizing Rochester's bestial nature. When Jane responds to the supernatural summons and sees Rochester for the first time since their separation, however, he seems to have regressed: "But in his countenance, I saw a change: that looked desperate and brooding—that reminded me of some wronged and fettered wild beast or bird, dangerous to approach in his sullen woe" (379; ch. 37). Jane assumes the task of turning this "beast" back into a human; "It is time some one undertook to rehumanise you, . . . for I see you are being metamorphosed into a lion, or something of that sort" (384; ch. 37). Rochester, like the Beast, questions, "Am I hideous, Jane?" And she replies, "Very, sir: you always were, you know" (385; ch. 37). Because she is able to see beyond his bestial appearance to the reality beneath, her return restores Rochester to some semblance of humanity, and their marriage completes the transformation.

Since in the animal groom tales the curse can be undone by the heroine's love of and marriage to the Beast, this ending of the novel is necessary at a deep structural level. Actually, in the tale it is not the marriage itself but the promise of marriage that transforms the Beast, and this is equally true in the novel. Rochester's transformation really begins when Jane shows her affection for him and then agrees to marriage. The ending may be seen as the representation of the heroine's reintegration into society after completion of her testing tasks, culminating in the symbolic death of the child in her experience on the moors and her rebirth as an autonomous adult at Marsh End.

Essentially, the issue on which the transformation to adulthood depends is the acceptance of sexuality in a mature love relationship. Once the heroine has established a secure sense of her own identity, she is ready to share that self with another. This possibility is revealed to her by her altered perception of the suitor who had once seemed beastly but is now seen in his true human state. Like the fairy tales that provide this pattern, the novel—without ever directly mentioning anything sexual—conveys the message that sex, which at first may seem repugnant, in due time proves beautiful.

Jane Eyre, one of several novels in this course, is among the most effective because Jane can be seen either as a Cinderella or as a heroine comparable to Beauty. A comparison of the tales—in most versions of the former, the heroine makes little effort to achieve her goals, while in the latter, she assumes an active role—reveals for students the satisfactions of taking a shaping role in the events of their lives. They gain insights into themselves and see an application of literature to life as it provides perspective on the process of growing up.

Jane Eyre and Christianity

Susan VanZanten Gallagher

One of the important historical and cultural contexts informing the appearance of *Jane Eyre* in 1847 is the pervasive influence of Christianity. Charlotte Brontë's own life includes a number of encounters with the different forms of Christianity practiced in Victorian society, and *Jane Eyre* not only specifically addresses several issues associated with Christianity but also has been accused, both in its own time and more recently, of being anti-Christian and irreligious. Reading *Jane Eyre* in the light of its Christian context and content, then, can significantly affect our interpretation of the work. The novel's concern with contemporary religious issues forms as important a part in Jane's growth and development as her discovery of society's oppression of women. In fact, the two issues — Jane's spiritual growth and her social-psychological growth — are intertwined.

Such a contextual approach to *Jane Eyre* begins with a general understanding of religious issues in the early nineteenth century. At that time, Christianity was, paradoxically, both existing under siege and conducting forays into new territory. Doubts and questions concerning the premises of the Christian faith were prevalent. What J. Hillis Miller has termed "the disappearance of God" haunted many early Victorian writers, who struggled with the implications of Darwinian science and the new German higher criticism of the Bible. The efficacy of Christianity is a subject of primary interest to many nineteenth-century writers, as Tennyson's impassioned "In Memoriam" (1850) suggests.

Even as many writers' faith eroded, however, a widespread religious renewal was occurring. A transformation of British Christianity had begun in the eighteenth century with the Methodist revivals led by George Whitefield and John and Charles Wesley, and in the following century the numbers of dissenters continued to grow. But after the chaotic French Revolution, many British Christians associated Methodism with a threatening anti-authoritarian, leveling philosophy. They turned instead to Evangelicalism, a reform movement distinct from Methodism located within the established Church of England and calling for a new practical piety. By midcentury, Evangelicals had gained general acceptance and respect throughout British society, and their diligent work on behalf of the oppressed had resulted in significant social reforms in prisons, orphanages, hospitals, factories, and the slave trade (Hylson-Smith 66–69). Elisabeth Jay points out that historians cite "Evangelicalism as one of the two most important influences in Victorian society" (6). Both Methodism and Evangelicalism contained opposing factions of Arminianists, emphasizing free will, and Calvinists, stressing election and reprobation. In fact, the complicated web of British religious groups — including the traditional Church of England, the Evangelicals, and the

Methodists — was woven of various opposing threads such as personal salvation and social reformation, salvation by faith and salvation by works, God's grace and God's judgment, heaven and hell.

Patrick Brontë, Charlotte's father, was an Arminian Evangelical. A member of the clergy of the Church of England who was sponsored in his training by an Evangelical society, Brontë "belonged to a closely-knit group of Yorkshire Evangelicals" and wrote several essays and one novel extolling Evangelical perspectives (Jay 31). As the daughter of a cleric, Charlotte Brontë grew up fully cognizant of the contours and demands of Christian faith, as well as of the images and ideas contained in the Bible. Besides the broadminded philosophy of her father, Brontë was exposed to the Wesleyan Methodism of her aunt Branwell, who raised the Brontë children after their mother died. Winifred Gérin argues that the aunt's faith emphasized a Calvinistic "haunting sense of sin and dread of judgement" that thoroughly frightened the Brontë children (*Evolution* 34). However, Tom Winnifrith, carefully distinguishing a belief in sin and hell from a belief in predetermined damnation, has questioned Gérin's denomination of aunt Branwell as a Calvinist. Indicating that Patrick Brontë, along with many other non-Calvinistic Evangelicals, affirmed the ideas of sin and hell, Winnifrith suggests that Brontë probably found the more severe Calvinistic doctrine of reprobation in her reading (*Background* 29–42).

Whatever the exact origins of Brontë's exposure to these various beliefs, her biographers and critics have differed over her final reaction to Christianity, some arguing that she completely rejected the basic doctrines of the Christian faith and others asserting that she eventually embraced a more liberal but still Christian belief in a providential God. These biographical conundrums are reflected in questions that continually arise concerning *Jane Eyre* and Christianity. Students often first encounter the issue of the relation between the novel and Christianity when they read (in either the Penguin edition or the Norton Critical Edition) Brontë's comments in the author's preface to the second edition. Speaking to those who have criticized her novel, "whose ears detect in each protest against bigotry . . . an insult to piety," Brontë offers a tart rebuttal: "Conventionality is not morality. Self-righteousness is not religion. To attack the first is not to assail the last. To pluck the mask from the face of the Pharisee, is not to lift an impious hand to the Crown of Thorns" (Dunn [1971, 1987 eds.] 1). From this defense, students quickly infer the kinds of attacks the novel received. I also tell them about the novel's initial success, with a third edition being necessary only five months after publication of the second. One of the reasons for that success, I suggest, may be the controversy over the novel's treatment of Christianity. The Norton edition's collection of contemporary reviews, "Charlotte Brontë and Her Readers," provides readily accessible illustrations of the kind of debate the novel continued to provoke even after the third edition appeared.

Because of the religious disagreements of the time, the attacks on the novel, and Brontë's defense, we enter our reading wondering about the novel's relation to the Christian tradition. At the outset, I encourage students to look for and identify three elements: Jane's encounters with professed Christians and their beliefs, Jane's experiences with the supernatural, and Jane's prayers. Since I teach at a private religious college, most of my students have the background knowledge to note such characterizations and references. Other teachers may have to point out these aspects of the novel. The class then uses this basic textual analysis to discuss what Brontë is saying about Christianity. As we trace the references and attitudes toward Christianity, we uncover the progress of Jane's spiritual growth and development and thus read *Jane Eyre* as a bildungsroman, a novel of growth during which the protagonist eventually comes to find both her social and spiritual identity. Our discussion focuses on some of the following scenes and references to Christianity.

Jane's understanding of Christianity is first influenced by the cold and uncaring attitudes of the Reeds, those professed Christians who raise her. When Jane is locked in the Red Room, she is assured that "God will punish her." Miss Abbot advises, "Say your prayers, Miss Eyre, when you are by yourself; for if you don't repent, something bad might be permitted to come down the chimney, and fetch you away" (10; ch. 2). From this emphasis on sin and punishment, we are not surprised that, as a child, Jane is afraid of the spiritual world and unable to recognize God's loving care for her. In the Red Room, the scene of her banishment, she reflects "that if Mr. Reed had been alive he would have treated me kindly" (13; ch. 2). But when she wonders whether this father figure's ghost might return to the tabernacle-like room in which he died to protest her ill treatment, she becomes terrified. A sudden streak of light heralds "some coming vision from another world" (14; ch. 2), and Jane responds with a hysterical seizure. Rather than welcome supernatural intervention in her oppression, she fears it. Although the ballad that Bessie sings in the nursery afterward testifies to another view of God as a father and friend "to the poor orphan child," Jane experiences only an "indescribable sadness" as she listens (18; ch. 3).

In her dealings with Brocklehurst, Jane meets another professed Christian whose primary concern is the sin and punishment of those who disagree with him. Repeatedly described as "a black pillar," Brocklehurst quotes Revelations to Jane and gives her a didactic religious pamphlet containing "an account of the awfully sudden death of Martha G——, a naughty child addicted to falsehood and deceit" (30; ch. 4). The reverend's public condemnation of her at Lowood as a liar irrevocably labels her "a little castaway: not a member of the true flock" (57; ch. 7). Brocklehurst's hypocrisy is further revealed as he lectures the pupils on the vanity of fancy dress and hairstyles while his family parades in the latest fashions. On her first day at Lowood, Jane puzzles over the connection between the name "Lowood Institution" and the biblical text from Matthew inscribed on a stone tablet over the door (42; ch. 5). After considering these passages, I note that the phallic imagery, Brocklehurst's fear of "nature" in his reaction to naturally curling hair (55; ch. 7), and his strict rules governing the girls' appearance all connect sexual repression with a masculine and judgmental form of Christianity. However, I also ask the class to discuss whether Brontë's condemnation of Brocklehurst's hypocrisy necessarily implies her complete rejection of traditional Christianity. At this point, we may refer to the comments in the preface to the second edition. Biographical information about Brontë's own traumatic experience at the Cowan Bridge School for Clergymen's Daughters may shed further light on her rendition of Brocklehurst. A consideration of nineteenth-century Evangelicalism, moreover, shows that in Brocklehurst's obsession with sin rather than grace and his neglect of the students' physical well-being, he lacks true Christian compassion. Although he was ostensibly an Evangelical social activist, Brocklehurst's extreme Calvinism and hypocrisy result in his failure to carry out one of the major goals of the Evangelical movement.

An entirely different kind of Christianity is embodied in Helen Burns, whose beliefs are much closer to the primary Evangelical concern with compassion. Instead of concentrating on sin and judgment, Helen testifies to the existence of a beneficent supernatural world: "[T]here is an invisible world and a kingdom of spirits: that world is round us, for it is everywhere; and those spirits watch us, for they are commissioned to guard us" (60; ch. 8). When Jane asks Helen, "What is God?" the dying girl echoes Bessie's song: "I believe God is good; I can resign my immortal part to Him without any misgiving. God is my father; God is my friend" (71; ch. 9). Whether or not Helen succeeds in taming Jane's passions and turning her from too great a love of human beings, she provides a way of viewing God that is radically at variance with any that Jane had previously experienced. At Lowood, Jane utters her first recorded prayer, as she asks first for liberty, then for change, and finally for "a new servitude!" (74; ch. 10).

Jane finds, at Thornfield, a professed profligate, one who argues that people can legislate their own morality, make their own laws. As she gradually falls in love with Rochester, Jane steadfastly argues against his free-thinking position but nonetheless undergoes a significant change in her spiritual life. In the wisdom gained in narrative retrospect, she admits, "My future husband was becoming to me my whole world; and more than the world: almost my hope of heaven. He stood between me and every thought of religion, as an eclipse intervenes between man and the broad sun. I could not, in those days, see God for his creature: of whom I had made an idol" (241; ch. 15). After their marriage is halted, Jane once again prays: "God help me!" (268; ch. 27) and is rescued by a supernatural vision of a white maternal form advising, "My daughter, flee temptation" (281; ch. 27). As she hastily departs from Thornfield, she prays again for providential direction (290; ch. 28).

The Rivers family provides Jane with her final encounters with Christianity. In our discussion of this part of the novel, we compare the forms of Christianity presented here with the previous forms we have identified. Diana and Mary are warm and loving; St. John, another member of the clergy, resembles Brocklehurst in his cold demeanor, doctrinal emphasis, and resemblance to a pillar. Like Brocklehurst, he seems to fear sexuality and is content to marry Jane even though she does not love him. However, St. John is no hypocrite. He is a "cold cumbrous column" (346; ch. 34), but he is consistent. Placing the same demands on his own life as he sets out for others, he renounces his love for Rosamond and is willing to sacrifice himself on the mission field. He also seems to hold before Jane the possibility of spiritual change. His Evangelicalism is thus much more complex than the extreme represented by Brocklehurst.

We also compare and contrast St. John and Rochester, since the two men are rivals. While Rochester tempts Jane to give up God for love, St. John asks her to give up love and follow God. The cleric's emotional manipulation and loveless proposal are just as much a perversion of the institution of marriage as Rochester's previous domineering ways are. Again in the wisdom resulting from maturity, Jane sees St. John's desire to control her life as a spiritual temptation akin to that offered by the idol-like Rochester: "I was almost as hard beset by him now as I had been once before, in a different way, by another. I was a fool both times. To have yielded then would have been an error of principle; to have yielded now would have been an error of judgment" (368; ch. 35). Once again she entreats heaven to show her the path, and she then hears a voice crying, "Jane! Jane! Jane!" "Oh God! what is it?" she responds (369; ch. 35). Returning to Rochester as a result of this answered prayer, she discovers that he has repented and has begun to pray sincerely (393–94; ch. 37). He too was pleading with God for a change in his life, when he heard her voice carried on the wind. Faced with this evidence of supernatural intervention in response to prayer, Jane says, "I kept these things then, and pondered them in my heart" (394; ch. 37). Her words echo those of Mary in Luke 2.19 after she learns of the appearance of the angels to the shepherds.

By the time we reach the end of the novel, I have already incorporated some of the ideas of Sandra M. Gilbert and Susan Gubar into our discussion. The pattern of oppression and escape, the distinctive elements of the female bildungsroman that they identify, provide useful ways to examine many elements of Jane's progress. But during our final discussion, I introduce their interpretation of the novel as anti-Christian, noting the similarity of their charge to some of the comments of Brontë's contemporaries. Gilbert and Gubar's conclusion that *Jane Eyre* is, in essence, anti-Christian is based on their belief that Christianity is merely one more aspect of the oppressive patriarchal society that Jane must overcome. Christianity requires "a crucifying denial of the self" that the novel rejects. In their view, Brontë's often noted references to *Pilgrim's Progress* are the kind of misreading of a "master" text identified by Harold Bloom, "an 'irreligious' redefinition, almost a parody, of John Bunyan's vision" (Gilbert and Gubar 370). Other twentieth-century critics, such as Maggie Berg, have offered similar readings (112–16).

By identifying and analyzing some of the passages of the novel referring to Christianity, students can test the validity of the accusations made both in Brontë's time and their own. After they have read the novel and debated some of these issues, I point out other expectations that a nineteenth-century reader might have had since *Jane Eyre* closely follows the genre of the popular governess novel, which typically manifested a central religious concern with the governing hand of providence (Beaty 640). Readers who saw *Jane Eyre* as a governess novel would have no doubt that Jane's progress includes a steady growth in her awareness of providential guidance in her life. However, readers sympathetic to the extreme forms of Calvinism found in Brontë's time might readily take umbrage.

Similarly, our understanding of different kinds of Christianity might affect our reading of the novel today. Readers who believe Christianity to be inherently patriarchal and oppressive might well conclude that the novel is anti-Christian. Another understanding of Christianity might lead to a different interpretation. In considering these different options, I present my own reading of the novel as a Christian feminist bildungsroman, to give my students yet another perspective against which to develop their own reading. I suggest that although the Christianity professed by the powerful males in the novel is destructive to, and exploitative of, women, the novel might embody a Christian feminism that sees God as both masculine and feminine and advocates the values of love, sexuality, and a marriage of partnership. The feminism of the novel, Jane's progress from oppression to liberation, is actually supported by the kind of supernatural being that Brontë envisions. Throughout the novel, God's providential care encourages Jane's movement toward freedom and equality. In the two instances of supernatural intervention, God speaks first in a female voice — appearing as Jane's lost mother — and then in a male voice — that of Rochester. Similarly, the God who is the "mighty, universal Parent," according to Helen Burns (71; ch. 9), could be both the tender "Father" of Bessie's song and the loving mother of Jane's vision.

To counter the oppressive masculine images of God so prevalent in her own society, however, Brontë emphasizes feminine spirituality. The aptly named Miss Temple provides a positive model of spiritual and intellectual achievement, as do both Diana and Mary Rivers, whose respective names evoke Greek and Catholic spirituality. In my discussion of Jane's dream vision at Thornfield (281; ch. 27), I note its similarity to the mystical visions of the fourteenth-century Julian of Norwich, who sees the feminine side of God as manifested in the nurturance, guidance, and care of Jesus. Throughout the Christian tradition, minority voices have affirmed feminine qualities and women's gifts, and such recognition was growing stronger in the nineteenth century with the prominent role played by women as Methodist preachers, Quaker leaders, and Evangelical social reformers. Brontë thus may be participating in an alternative Christian tradition.

The God of Bessie's song, Helen's testimony, and Diana's and Mary's compassion is more concerned with nurturing than with judgment. Yet that (feminine) nurturing also includes (masculine) discipline and authority; Jane must learn both how to become Rochester's equal and how to put divine love before human love. In this reading, Jane's return to Rochester is not motivated by her acquiescence to her own passion; rather, it is a response to providential direction in her life in the tradition of the governess novel. Faced with the dilemma of how best to serve God, Jane is tempted to follow the influence of St. John, but the answer that she receives to her prayer is a call to an earthly vocation: the sacrament of marriage. *Jane Eyre* suggests that Christian vocations encompass more than the mission field and that domestic life is a valuable avenue of service. This emphasis is typical of nineteenth-century Evangelicalism, which saw "the family as a unit particularly favoured by God" (Jay 142). The accompanying view that celibacy was somewhat perverse (Jay 133–42) explains Brontë's negative depiction of St. John's rejection of Rosamond and of Eliza Reed's retirement to a convent. The complementary equality of Jane and Rochester in the social bond of marriage reflects not only the balance that should be achieved between passion and reason in an individual but also the balance that exists between the masculine and the feminine sides of God.

Brontë's affirmation of Christian compassion, authority, and marriage is congruent with much nineteenth-century Evangelical thought, but her characterization of God in feminine terms is unusual (although not unprecedented in women's writing). The novel's religious assertion of a woman's right to self-identity and its depiction of marriage as a relationship of equality rather than of dominance and submission anticipate twentieth-century Christian feminism. As a Christian feminist bildungsroman, *Jane Eyre* suggests that a strong, free, and self-determining woman who follows God's commands has achieved true maturity.

Jane Eyre: Charlotte Brontë's New Bible

Keith A. Jenkins

Writing about the use of the Bible in Victorian fiction, George Landow offers the following warning:

> Although it is a commonplace that we have lost the intimate knowledge of the Bible that characterized literate people of the last century, we have yet to perceive the full implications of our loss. . . . When we modern readers fail to recognize allusions . . . we deprive many Victorian works of a large part of their context. . . . [W]e under-read and misread many works, and the danger is that the greater the work, the more our ignorance will distort and inevitably reduce it.   (3)

Perhaps more than any other "great" Victorian novel, *Jane Eyre* exposes the extent to which biblical illiteracy hinders our ability to read insightfully. Charlotte Brontë is undoubtedly one of the most biblically allusive of the major Victorian novelists. The editors of the Clarendon editions index over four hundred biblical quotations or allusions in her four novels. While these citations offer a rich teaching opportunity, they present, at the same time, a serious methodological difficulty. Teachers who are unfamiliar with the Bible will probably feel unequal to the task. The footnotes in modern critical editions can be helpful, but they merely inform the reader of sources and parallels without offering any suggestions about how the use of biblical material establishes, augments, or complicates character, plot, or theme. Therefore, many teachers forgo any consideration of the relation between the Bible and the novel. It is possible, though, that students can move beyond seeing *Jane Eyre* simply as a rich collection of biblical allusions to be mined for isolated parallels.

Instruction that too closely resembles either an annotated list of allusions or a hermeneutical commentary with occasional references to the novel is misguided. While *Jane Eyre* does carry on an extensive dialogue with the Bible, the amount of shared language is finally less notable than the radically altered form in which the action and imagery of the sacred text find their place in the novel. It is this process of textual transmutation and the way it creates and enhances meaning that must be the focus of our teaching.

Many characters in *Jane Eyre* are linked to biblical figures by direct statement but with little textual elaboration or development of possible plot similarities. Such instances, while easy to spot, are often deceptively simple. In chapter 24, when Rochester offers Jane half his estate rather than satisfy her curiosity about his secretiveness, she calls him "king Ahasuerus" (230). Surely we would be guilty of underreading if we dismissed this allusion as an incidental bit of repartee. The Norton Critical Edition offers the following footnote: "The Persian king who, deceived by his usurious prime minister, nearly permitted a pogram [sic]. The story is told in the Book of Esther" (230). Although the note is accurate, it adds little to our appreciation of the allusion. It does, however, call our attention to parallels that can be expanded once their complexity has been recognized. Viewing Rochester and Jane against the backdrop of Esther's story deepens our understanding of how Rochester's tendency to lord it over Jane in the manner of an Eastern potentate, in spite of his protestations of love and desire for equality, makes her position at Thornfield so vulnerable. Ahasuerus's act of summoning Vashti "to show the peoples and the princes her beauty" (Esther 1.11) foreshadows Rochester's attempt to dress Jane in "rich silk of the most brilliant amethyst dye, and a superb pink satin," just as Jane's unwillingness "to wear his choice" (236; ch. 24) reminds us of Vashti's refusal "to come at the king's command" (Esther 1.12). Though quite different, both women resist imperious male attempts to compromise or define their status.

Nevertheless, the reference clearly points, if only indirectly and only through her association with Rochester, to Jane as a parallel to Esther more than to Vashti. When Vashti is banished for her unthinkable rebellion against patriarchal power, Esther becomes queen in her stead. Risking death to save her people, Esther rebels in her own right, violating custom by appearing unbidden before the king. But rather than react with anger, Ahasuerus somewhat casually offers her half of his kingdom because she has "found favor in his sight." However, the king's easy magnanimity—characteristic of his position of assured masculine power—pales before Esther's earnest willingness to sacrifice herself. In much the same way, Jane combines a restless chafing against male-defined roles for women with a willingness to live (and write) within that male-dominated sphere. The reference to this powerful story is brief, and Jane quickly moves on to another, quite different, biblical parallel. But the story's implications for reading the novel can transcend the actual dimensions of the passage. This two-word allusion to an ancient Persian king provides a point of entry into central issues in the novel.

Another common form of reference alludes to biblical events or places, again fairly directly, often by the use of simile or metaphor. In chapter 27, Jane speaks of the abrupt change in her situation produced by the "discovery" of Bertha Mason Rochester: "My hopes were all dead—struck with a subtle doom, such as in one night, fell on all the first-born in the land of Egypt" (260). Once again, a footnote identifies the source of the allusion (Exodus 12), but, without encouragement, few students will read the biblical account of the Passover. From the novel alone we can sense the devastating blow that Jane's "first-born" love has suffered. Without further explication, though, we might not detect subtle evocation of these important themes: the irony of Jane's linking herself—usually cast as the rebellious slave—with the archetypal biblical tyrant nation Egypt, the self-loathing of the rejected and displaced female orphan contained in the images of plague and death, or the connection of this figure with the novel's other references to exile and escape or sacrificial atonement. Any number of similar references, studied either separately or in patterns, can open new perspectives on familiar themes, often complicating or unsettling some that have become well established.

Much of the biblical material in *Jane Eyre* is far more intricate than these two examples. Clusters of narrative and imagery containing direct biblical references like those discussed above, woven together by more general use of biblical symbolism, resist simple classification. Though many such networks can be found in *Jane Eyre*, I focus on a progression of three in particular, as a model for teaching the novel in a manner supporting the thesis that Charlotte Brontë sought to subvert patriarchal authority — both societal and hermeneutical.

From the earliest reviews to the most recent essays, critics have recognized the rebellious spirit that pervades this novel. Jane Eyre, writing from the vantage point of ten years after her marriage to Rochester and her presumably happy settling at Ferndean, opens her autobiography at a moment of rebellion against masculine authority in the person of Master John Reed. As she dissects her biblical sources into units of imagery or narrative that she can then reassemble to serve her own purposes, Jane constructs nothing less than an alternative to that patriarchal view of the world, in revolt against which she begins, carries out, and ends her self-creation.

The major stories of the Bible depict that intersection of the declining spiral of the human drama with the constant upward pressure of God's redemptive energy, which critics call *Heilsgeschichte* 'saving history.' Creation and apocalypse mark the temporal extremes between which this divine-human interaction occurs, while the Passion and Resurrection of Christ form the central episode. These same three motifs dominate Jane's telling of her story. In Jane's world, however, the biblical orientation toward the *eschaton*, or end times, is reversed, and the redemptive movement of history resolves itself in an earthly re-creative act that returns to the primal state of innocence in the "paradise of union" (224; ch. 23) preceding the Fall. A consideration of the central narrative and imagery of the Eden myth suggests the extent of the novel's contact with the myth.

The novel's pivotal twenty-third chapter opens with an idyllic setting. At the "sweetest hour of the twenty-four" the dew is falling in the "Eden-like" orchard where Jane is walking (217), secluded by a high wall from the rest of the world. Suddenly aware of Rochester's presence, Jane tries unsuccessfully to hide. Alone with him, she grows uneasy, feeling guilt and shame. After questioning Jane, who conceals part of her feelings — only finally to betray herself by her answers — Rochester pronounces the dreadful sentence: she is expelled from the "Eden" of Thornfield. Class and gender expectations remain largely intact: Jane combines the roles of Adam and

Eve, the guilty and evasive creatures, while Rochester acts the part of God: owner of the garden, questioner, and judge. As in the Genesis story, expulsion from Thornfield-Eden will mean the loss of "paradise" and separation from Rochester-God, though in Jane's case through no fault of her own. Our initial impression, then, is of the irony of the parallels, for Jane is truly innocent, while Rochester practices deceit.

At this point, however, Jane's adaptation of the story becomes much more fluid. Discrete elements of the orthodox Christian version remain, but with altered significance. Freely trading roles without warning, Rochester and Jane take on aspects of every character in the Eden myth. Rochester's striking simile for his bond to Jane—"a string somewhere under my left ribs, tightly and inextricably knotted to a similar string situated in the corresponding quarter of your little frame" (221; ch. 23)—clearly recalls the creation of Eve from one of Adam's ribs (Genesis 2.21–22). Resisting Rochester's advances, as Eve resists the serpent's temptation, Jane raises legitimate objections to the "sin" he proposes. But not knowing the true extent of their legitimacy (i.e., the existence and imprisonment of Bertha Mason), Jane allows herself to be dissuaded. Seated under the horse-chestnut tree with Rochester, Jane suddenly becomes the forbidden fruit that Rochester-Eve plucks and tastes. Her eventual agreement to marry Rochester marks her Adam-like entry into complicity in the sin. For the moment, Rochester and Jane are both unaware of the consequences of their plans; their eyes have been opened only enough to see each other and their "paradise of union." Their short-lived joy is destroyed by a sudden weather change, a lightning strike transforming their "tree of knowledge," symbol of self-determination and freedom from restrictive social conventions, into the tree of life, from which Adam and Eve are cut off by the "flaming sword" (see Genesis 3.24).

Such a radical reshaping of the Eden myth suggests that no single, constant meaning can be attached to the novel's echoes of the biblical story. Indeed, this freedom in using a sacred source reveals a theological independence less interested in establishing a connection with orthodox religious thought than in using traditional materials in a new and decidedly untraditional way. When we hear these resonances of the Eden story in *Jane Eyre*, we see the radical quality of Jane's autobiographical rebellion. The symbols of the biblical Eden—the man, the woman, the tree, and the fruit—now stripped of their traditional associations with sin, can be shaped into Brontë's new Eden, in which the role of the divine is greatly reduced and male and female share equally the responsibility for the success or failure of their union.

Similarly complex allusions to the Passion and Resurrection of Christ appear in the novel. Once again in chapter 23, when Jane accepts Rochester's proposal of marriage, his response is troublesome and enigmatic: "It will atone—it will atone. . . . It will expiate at God's tribunal. . . . For the world's judgment—I wash my hands thereof" (225). This obvious reference to Christ's Passion exhibits the same fluid recombination of biblical imagery we noticed in the treatment of the Eden myth. Rochester combines the roles of the "Christ" who atones for sin — though by his devotion rather than his suffering — and Pontius Pilate, who sets the atoning death in motion without realizing or admitting his complicity in it. A definite association persists in the novel between sacrifice and the eventual restoration of union between Rochester and Jane (accomplished, ironically, as much by Bertha Mason's gruesome death as by any action of Rochester or Jane). The violent change of weather that immediately follows Rochester's cryptic statement, producing the lightning that splits the horse-chestnut tree, certainly resonates with the gospel account of Jesus's death (see Matthew 27.45–51 and Mark 15.33–38). While the language of this scene suggests an atoning passion of some kind, whether it will heal the broken community symbolized by the chestnut tree as a reminder of the sin of Eden remains to be seen.

An extended cluster of death and resurrection imagery begins in chapter 28. At Whitcross, Jane enters a deathlike period of wandering and deprivation lasting for three days, finally to be restored to life when taken in by the Rivers family. Jane's arrival at Marsh End marks a kind of resurrection, but in a partial sense at best, for she lies "motionless as a stone" for another three-day period, recovering her strength (298; ch. 29). Her initial interview with the Rivers family (which occurs between these two periods of three days each) resembles Jesus's trial before Pilate. Asked where she is from and what is to be done with her, Jane will give no full account of herself and passively accepts her fate. If this is the beginning of her "passion," then her "resurrection" must somehow lie beyond Whitcross, back at Thornfield with Rochester. Such tampering with biblical chronology frustrates any strict, linear interpretation. Jane's two alternative resurrection experiences lie in opposite and mutually exclusive directions. She can move forward into the world of St. John Rivers or return whence she came. Jane opts for the former until she discovers it leads to death rather than to new life. Only after following this path to its end does she conclude that, for her, rebirth lies in the healing embrace of this life.

The third motif in the pattern is apocalypse. Nonnarrative qualities make these references less susceptible to the kind of reconstruction we have observed in the other two types. Additionally, most of these references reflect an orientation toward the future that is basically inimical to Jane's recreative vision. They serve chiefly to indicate an extreme that initially attracts Jane but that she ultimately finds the strength to reject.

In chapter 35, St. John Rivers, while ostracizing Jane to express his disapproval of her refusal to accompany him to India as his wife, reads aloud the biblical description of a new heaven and a new earth (see Revelation 21). Transported by the power of his voice, Jane feels as if she were back at Lowood, listening to Helen Burns speak of her private vision of heaven as "a rest — a mighty home, not a terror and an abyss" (51; ch. 6). When

St. John's voice alters slightly, however, Jane senses that his next words are aimed directly at her: "[T]he fearful, the unbelieving, &c. shall have their part in the lake which burneth with fire and brimstone, which is the second death" (367; ch. 35; see Revelation 21.8). Suddenly St. John sounds more like Brocklehurst. Though Jane begins to feel ill at ease, she remains under the dominance of her cousin's will. At the point of surrender, she is saved by an intervention no less dramatic than the abrupt change of weather that drove Rochester and her from the orchard at Thornfield a year earlier. The "known, loved, well-remembered voice" of Rochester calls to her: "Jane! Jane! Jane!" (369; ch. 35). Her gradual seduction by St. John's apocalyptic worldview suddenly and decisively ends. The only heaven she desires she will seek and find on this earth.

St. John Rivers is associated with the Book of Revelation once more when he writes from India, near the point of death, to share the hope of his vision with Jane. Though Jane seems to validate St. John's vision by giving it a privileged place at the close of the novel, she no longer desires to share it. If anything, her serenity in relating his words tends to diffuse the earlier intensity of the apocalyptic vision. Having found Eden, Jane has no desire for the heavenly city. By placing these words at the end of the story, Jane does not suddenly recant her radical vision. Rather, she sets it in glorious relief against the stony background of traditional religious fears and hopes to which her new view of life is totally alien.

Rochester also echoes the language of Revelation, but his words resonate with that fluid reversal and recombination typical of the novel's appropriation of scriptural material. In telling Jane his version of the experience that led to their reunion, Rochester calls Jane "the Alpha and Omega of my heart's wishes" (394; ch. 37). The Christ of the Revelation uses these same words to express his sovereignty over all that was, is, and shall be (Revelation 22.13). From a traditional Christian viewpoint, Rochester's words verge on blasphemy. He speaks of renewed faith in "the beneficent God" (393; ch. 37), and yet he freely admits that Jane — not God — is the center, if not the source, of his existence. Conscious of the debt he owes God, who "in the midst of judgment . . . has remembered mercy" (395; ch. 37), Rochester speaks of his gratitude numerous times and exhibits a changed attitude toward life as proof of it, but his experience of judgment and mercy produces a somewhat unconventional faith in him. As a thoroughly human "new Adam," Rochester must center his life on another creature — one who "corresponds" to him (see Genesis 2.18) — not on the ineffable and transcendent God.

Through the vehicle of autobiography, Jane not only creates her own Eden with Rochester, she consummates her rebellion against patriarchal religious traditions by redefining the will of God. The redemptive power of suffering no longer leads to a cosmic paradise attainable only through the crisis of apocalypse (either personal or historical) but rather restores the "paradise of union" that existed in Eden before the Fall. Redemption becomes re-creation and renovation of earthly possibilities, not a cataclysmic *eschaton* that destroys and then begins anew. Thornfield is destroyed, but Rochester and Jane are not. True, they are transformed, but they remain definitely *of* this world as well as *in* it. And while Ferndean may not strike us as particularly Edenic, perhaps collapsing traditional boundaries between paradise and the fallen world, it remains an earthly (even earthy) residence. Jane's rejection of the cosmic, apocalyptic visions of St. John Rivers (and of Helen Burns) is absolute. As we follow Jane from Thornfield to Marsh End to Ferndean, if we listen to the way in which she echoes familiar biblical sources, only to alter them once she has called them to our mind, perhaps we can catch a glimpse of her radical vision — of an ending that recaptures the lost innocence and shattered hope of its beginning.

Clearly, a plan for teaching *Jane Eyre* that takes into account its extensive borrowing of the Bible's language, imagery, and action, either by a brief, random consideration of individual passages or by a more extensive and organized effort to demonstrate a particular thesis, offers rich possibilities, regardless of the setting. Since our goal is to explore how these references enrich the novel rather than to exegete the biblical texts themselves, previous knowledge of the Bible and extensive training in biblical interpretation are not required. If we take Landow's warning seriously, by slighting or even ignoring *Jane Eyre*'s nearly unprecedented intertextuality, we risk misreading and, worse yet, misteaching this important and compelling novel.

TEACHING SPECIFIC CONTEXTS

Jane Eyre and Narrative Voice

John O. Jordan

Who is the narrator of *Jane Eyre*? When I teach Brontë's work to undergraduates in my survey course on the nineteenth-century English novel, I
regularly begin by asking this deceptively simple question. Before we attempt
to answer it, however, I warn students that the question is a tricky one and
that the obvious answer — Jane Eyre — though not incorrect, may prove insufficient for our needs. We agree to hold the question open as long as we
can and to return to it periodically as we discuss other aspects of the book.

My purpose in beginning with the narrator question is to complicate students' habits of reading by calling their attention from the outset to the
presence of a narrative voice in Brontë's text and by asking them to think
about the ways in which this voice, through its use of emphasis, selection,
sequencing, and other narrative devices, shapes and controls the story. In
this way, I hope to lay the groundwork for later discussion of such topics
as Jane's identity, the relation of form to ideology in the novel, and narrative
closure.

My thinking about narrative voice draws generally on the work of Gérard
Genette and in particular on the chapter entitled "Voice" in his book *Narrative Discourse*. For Genette, voice refers to those determinations "dealing
with the way in which the narrating itself is implicated in the narrative,
narrating in the sense in which I have defined it, that is, the narrative situation or its instance, and along with that its two protagonists: the narrator
and his audience, real or implied" (31). In focusing on the concept of voice,
I not only emphasize the constructedness of the narrative text but call into

question any easy assumptions students may have about the existence of a unified autobiographical subject. Implicit in my reluctance to foreclose the narrator question is at least a hint that the novel's fictional "I" may prove more elusive and dispersed than it at first seems to be.

As a second point of entry into the text, we turn to the facsimile title page of 1847 (reproduced in the Norton Critical Edition) in order briefly to consider the implications of the novel's full title, *Jane Eyre: An Autobiography*. We discuss the conventions of autobiography as a literary genre, including its customary use of first-person retrospective narration as well as its affinities, especially during the nineteenth century, with the tradition of the bildungsroman, or novel of development. My goal here is to stress the ways in which genre influences reader expectations. From the title alone, I argue, we are led to expect that *Jane Eyre* will be a story, told in the protagonist's own voice, of how her younger self grew to be the person that she is at the end of the book — in other words, that Jane's search for and achievement of identity will be the novel's central theme. I then propose, somewhat paradoxically, that the novel's use of the first-person pronoun tends to undermine the very notion of identity that the book presumably takes as its theme. Drawing on the ideas of Emile Benveniste (usefully summarized in Silverman), I point out that the pronoun *I* can never achieve identity, since it always designates two separate subject positions — positions that Benveniste calls the speaking subject (*le sujet de l'énonciation*) and the subject of speech (*le sujet de l'énoncé*). In Benveniste's terms, the mature Jane who narrates can thus never be identical to the narrated Jane who appears as a character in the text, although both appear to inhabit the signifier *I*. The narrative voice and its self-representations can be apprehended only in relation to each other; they can never be collapsed into a single unit.

Continuing with the title page of 1847, we consider the phrase "edited by Currer Bell," which authorizes Jane's fictional autobiography. In addition to the biographical questions and issues of female authorship raised by Brontë's sexually ambiguous pseudonym, I steer discussion toward the general question of names in the novel and their relation to subjectivity. Having noted the slippage between the names Currer Bell and Charlotte Brontë, I invite the class to play with the name Jane Eyre and to give me any puns, homonyms, anagrams, or other verbal associations (in French as well as in English) that this name calls to mind. In proposing this game — one that I sometimes assign as a homework exercise, with instructions to consult a good dictionary — I am of course drawing on the work of various critics (e.g., Adams, "Woman's Estate"; Gilbert and Gubar; Politi; Boumelha) who have found Jane's surname suggestive.

On the chalkboard, we make a list of these puns and associations, indicating parenthetically their potential thematic relevance for the book. The list generally includes the following: *air* (Jane as spirit, fairy); *err* (to make a mistake, to sin; also to wander, cognate with *eyre*, archaic English word meaning a journey in circuit); *ire* (anger, rage); *eyer* (sight, spying, vision and blindness; Jane as visionary); *"I"-er* (Jane as autobiographer; consider also the initials JE = "je"); *heir* (inheritance, genealogy); *aire* (French word for eagle's nest, cognate to English *aerie* or *eyrie*: birds, wildness, heights); *Eire* (Ireland, non-English identity); *eery* (anagram of Eyre: weird, uncanny). The list is not exhaustive, nor is it meant to be; but it is sufficiently diverse to suggest the multiple and potentially contradictory possibilities inherent in the surname and, by extension, in the character who bears that name. Unlike her surname, however, Jane's given name, we note, does not lend itself to such "errant" permutation. "Plain Jane," by its very English ordinariness, suggests the homely and familiar, in contrast to the more exotic *(unheimlich)* and unstable "Eyre." One result of this admittedly incomplete exercise is a series of formal and thematic oppositions that can be incorporated into our consideration of narration and narrative voice. Schematically, the oppositions look something like this:

Jane/Eyre :: familiar/exotic : stable/unstable : single/multiple

Sometime during the second or third class meeting, when I feel reasonably sure that most students have finished the novel, I mention another possible meaning for Jane's surname. "Eyre," I suggest, might also refer to the letter *R*, as pronounced in French. We then review the various characters and families in the book whose names begin with this letter — Reed, Rivers, and Rochester — considering the ways in which each of them offers (or denies) Jane the possibility of affiliation, vocation, and intimate relationship. Of the three male characters in this group — John Reed, St. John Rivers, and Edward Rochester — it is Rochester whose name holds the most interesting implications for the question of narrative voice. Since the novel's final chapter reveals that Jane and Rochester are married, it then becomes possible to identify the narrator of *Jane Eyre* as Jane R, or Jane Rochester.

What difference does it make, I then ask, for us to think of the novel's narrative voice as belonging not to the rebellious and oppressed younger Jane but to the mature wife and mother who asserts a "perfect concord" with her husband in the novel's closing chapter (397; ch. 38)? How might the values of this narrator (including her religion, race, nationality, marital and economic status, and newly secure class position) influence the account she gives of her past life? Indeed, what motivates Jane Rochester to tell her story in the first place? In posing such questions, I tell the students, I am in effect asking them to consider reading the novel "backward," starting at the moment of narrating and moving toward the beginning, rather than the customary way of reading stories "forward," from start to finish.

Foregrounding the question of the narrator in this way has important implications for teaching the novel. For one thing, it provides a basis on which to undertake an ideological critique of the narrative voice. Drawing on the work of Jina Politi and Gayatri Spivak, two excellent political readings of the novel, I ask my students to consider several passages in which the narrator's class, economic status, race, and nationality appear to influence her representation of people and events. Among the passages we examine from this perspective are the interview with Mr. Lloyd in chapter 3, in which young Jane states her wish "not . . . to belong to poor people" (20). To what extent, I then ask, is the narrator's handling of the story as a whole prompted by similar motives, or at least by a wish to justify her own rise in social position at the end of the book?

In this connection, we also look closely at the representation of Bertha, Adèle, and Grace Poole, in an effort to determine how much Jane as narrator may be collaborating with the marginalizations of these "foreign" women (Grace Poole is "foreign" by virtue of her class) in order to position herself at the center of her story. Of particular importance as well are chapters 28 and 29, in which, after a period of wandering outside the bounds of human society following her flight from Thornfield, Jane discovers what turns out to be her proper class identity with the Rivers family. In her dialogue with the Riverses' servant Hannah, we can hear a tone of social superiority that becomes increasingly evident in her narration as well — for example, in the condescending attitude she adopts toward her students at Morton school and in the general xenophobia that characterizes her judgment of most things Continental. Finally, we consider the "providential" plotting of the novel's last chapters, especially the supernatural summons of chapter 35, and ask not why Brontë uses this device but how it serves the narrator to do so.

Examining the relation of form to ideology by interrogating the motives of the narrative voice produces a reading of *Jane Eyre* that emphasizes its conservative social and political agenda. According to this view, "Mrs. Rochester" as narrator tells her story in a way that legitimizes her own privileged position and silences any discordant or oppositional voices in the text. Once the possibility of such a reading has been established, however, I dissuade students from accepting it completely. I remind them that *Jane Eyre* was condemned by at least one contemporary reviewer as "pre-eminently an anti-Christian composition," whose "tone of mind and thought" is the same that "has overthrown authority and violated every code human and divine abroad, and fostered Chartism and rebellion at home" (Rigby, rpt. in Dunn [1987 ed.] 442). Keeping this review in mind, I ask the class to locate passages in the novel that might have provoked such a negative response. Inevitably, the passage that we end up discussing is the famous feminist text in chapter 12 that begins: "It is in vain to say human beings ought to be satisfied with tranquillity: they must have action; and they will make it if they cannot find it" (96). Among the questions I press students to consider are, Who is speaking? and, What is the effect of the present-tense narration? After close examination of the passage and its context, we conclude that the voicing is ambiguous. The indignant protest against domestic confinement and the defiant claim for an equal sphere of action with men that animate the paragraph belong equally, I maintain, to the young governess of Thornfield and to the mature narrator, speaking from Ferndean. To the extent that this outburst can be understood as coming from Jane Rochester, it suggests a somewhat different view of the novel's ending from what either the narrator's claim of perfect mutuality in her marriage to Rochester or the ideological reading suggested above would lead us to believe. Jane's statement "Millions are condemned to a stiller doom than mine, and millions are in silent revolt against their lot" (96; ch. 12) reads very differently, for instance, if we take "mine" as a reference to Ferndean and "silent revolt" as an expression, however partial or oblique, of her feelings about marriage. Rather than attempt to resolve these contradictions, I encourage students to take them as further evidence of a lack of unity in the narrative voice, a lack that contributes to what Karen Chase, speaking of the narrator, calls "the elusiveness of this self that keeps receding from its own manifestations" (76).

Turning finally to the problem of narrative closure, I ask another deceptively simple question: Where does the novel end? Like the question of the narrator with which I begin, the matter of the ending is more complex than it first appears. Although in one sense the novel can be said to end on its final page, in another its conclusion is spread out over the entire text as narrative discourse. Jane's final action, after all, is not to marry Rochester but to tell the story of her life. For her, in effect, closure becomes disclosure — an act of telling that brings her into intimate relationship not with Rochester but with another figure marked by the letter *R*, namely, "Reader."

But even the act of telling must have an end, my students correctly point out. Why then, they ask, does the narrative voice conclude the book with two paragraphs devoted to St. John Rivers? I approach this puzzling question by way of two passages we have already considered: the mysterious summons of chapter 35 and the feminist outburst of chapter 12. Comparison of these two passages can help students understand more clearly certain equivocations that appear not only at the end of *Jane Eyre* but throughout the novel. In narratological terms, the voice that Jane hears calling "Jane! Jane! Jane!" (369; ch. 35) can be understood as the text's own summons to closure. It is the voice of Rochester, if you will, but it is also a voice that points the way toward the novel's happy ending — that is, toward Ferndean, the "perfect concord" of marriage, and the cessation of narrative desire. The fact that Jane can hear this voice indicates not so much her powers of telepathy as the extent to which she has internalized her master's voice and stands ready to obey it as a means of bringing her wanderings to a close. The voice that Jane hears in chapter 12, however, actively resists such closure, whether in the form of domestic confinement (Thornfield, Ferndean) or in that of narrative finality. Instead of closing off narrative possibilities, the words that speak to her in this instance insist on keeping them open. "Then my sole relief . . . ," she writes, was "to open my inward ear to a tale that was never ended — a tale my imagination created, and narrated continuously; quickened with all of incident, life, fire, feeling, that I desired and had not in my actual existence" (95–96; ch. 12). The contrast between the two passages is striking. In these two voices, I suggest, with their different attitudes and goals, we can recognize the opposing facets of Jane Eyre's character already signaled in the differential components of her name. If the former is the voice of "Jane," with her familiar, practical singleness of purpose, then the latter voice — restless, heterogeneous, desiring — belongs to "Eyre."

The paragraphs devoted to St. John at the end of the book represent the narrative's effort to mediate between the demands of these opposing narrative and characterological tendencies. On the one hand, the impulse toward closure seeks satisfaction by invoking the traditional consolations of religious life as embodied in the saintly dedication of the missionary. On the other hand, the impulse toward narrativity seeks its satisfaction in the shift of focus away from England and Ferndean's secure domestic routine toward India, with its promise for Jane of a larger, more heroic (and more dangerous) sphere of action, something that in various forms she has always desired.

If the closing passage remains puzzling, it is largely because the narrative voice remains undecided which of these alternatives to embrace — or, indeed, if either is wholly satisfactory. Jane's unattractive representation of St. John elsewhere in the narrative, moreover, makes his appearance as an emblem of finality even more deeply problematic. In any event, here, as throughout *Jane Eyre*, the indeterminacy of the narrative voice — its uncertainties and equivocations — provides a useful focus for teaching the novel.

Fire and Light in *Jane Eyre*

Mary Burgan

Even though most undergraduate students in my classes have not read widely in literary criticism or theory, they come to *Jane Eyre* with convictions about the mythic significance of its pervasive imagery of fire and light. They have been sufficiently in touch with the conventions of Gothic fiction to know that the burning of Thornfield, Bertha Mason's fiery death, and Rochester's blinding by a falling timber in the conflagration are central occasions of revelation in the narrative. Moreover, if they have encountered the compelling chapter on the text in *The Madwoman in the Attic*, they tend automatically to read Charlotte Brontë's novel as an allegory of gender rage that must break out in flaming apocalypse. In my own teaching of *Jane Eyre*, I defamiliarize the novel in order to expand my students' interpretive range. I believe that their critical assumptions bring premature closure to a fresh experience of the text and that their lack of historical context for nineteenth-century fiction deprives them of a sense of Brontë's power as a social critic.

To appreciate fully the achievement of *Jane Eyre*, for its own historical setting as for ours, students must see that its fire and light imagery is closely chronicled, precisely controlled, and thereby decisively implicated in the narrative. Some of the early reviews (included in Dunn's 1987 edition of the novel) provide a useful antidote to interpretive abstraction by showing that the surface of domestic materiality was the means by which *Jane Eyre* struck many of its first readers as an unimpeachable record of the daily lives of women. In his 1847 appraisal, G. H. Lewes pointed to the blend of detailed representation and psychological acuity as the main virtue of Brontë's novel: "We do not simply mean the power over the passions — the psychological intuition of the artist, but the power also of connecting external appearances with internal effects — of representing the psychological interpretation of material phenomena" (Dunn 437). Violent reactions against the novel, like that of Elizabeth Rigby, further indicate that Brontë's knowing invocation of the miseries of domestic dispossession in Victorian society was so vivid as to provoke conservative reaction (Dunn 440–43).

I usually begin my class sessions on the text itself — the exploration of various critical approaches comes later — by asking students to imagine as literally as they can Jane Eyre's opening declaration of pain: "dreadful to me was the coming home in the raw twilight, with nipped fingers and toes" (5; ch. 1). Teachers might turn out all the lights in the classroom to give some notion of the sensory impact of Jane's narrative; asking students to write two or three sentences describing how they experience cold can help to dramatize a world in which fire and light are luxuries rather than givens.

Once readers think about Jane's bodily condition — as the narrator insists they do by depicting her frequent physical discomforts — they can begin to perceive that the novel enacts a complicated dialectic between physical sensation and the imagination. Having thus suggested the difficulty involved in Jane's trying to read Thomas Bewick's *History of British Birds* in a cold window seat by the light of the waning day, I bring my students to the possibilities of research into the "facticity" of *Jane Eyre*. Here it is useful to turn to what we know about domestic lighting in the nineteenth century, to demonstrate how social and economic history enriches our reading of the novel.

There are several good sources of information on fire and light in the Victorian period. Richard D. Altick's discussion of the physical constraints impeding the evolution of the "English common reader" describes the main features of the development of literacy in England in the nineteenth century; Altick gives not only the cost of candles but the size of print for books; he examines the impact of the window tax on limiting natural light in poor homes and the incidence of eye strain among readers (90–94). Biographically inclined students may want to link this last point to Elizabeth Gaskell's observation that Charlotte Brontë's eyestrain as a young girl, "which prevented her doing anything for two years," caused her to be "short-sighted" thereafter (Dunn 447, 450). David Spring's study of the landed estate in the nineteenth century shows the class contexts of fire and light; he notes, for example, that the bill for candles was one of the most prominent items in the household accounts of the duke of Bedford, prompting the duke's steward to try to institute surveillance of servants to prevent wasting or stealing of light (30, 188). The paucity of candles in Jane Eyre's childhood, then, suggests not only their costliness but their designation as the property of the wealthy; the poor could do with smelly "dips" — wicks soaked in animal fat either floating in a vessel or attached to a stand.

There are two general histories of lighting that furnish fascinating detail (and useful illustrations, if one has access to a slide projector or overhead projector). *Flickering Flames: A History of Domestic Lighting through the Ages*, by Leroy Thwing, is a privately printed hobbyists' chronicle; *Disenchanted Night: The Industrialization of Light in the Nineteenth Century*, by Wolfgang Schivelbusch, is a more theoretically expansive and readily available survey. Thwing provides illustrations of every imaginable instrument of domestic lighting (from candle snuffers to "pickwicks") and helpful definitions of extinct essentials like the rushlight (a rush or reed dipped in animal fat and held at an angle by a pincer on a stand). The second book is a fount of information that also theorizes in the manner of Michel Foucault. For example, Schivelbusch emphasizes gaslight as an urban device for the policing of city streets — its earliest use signifying metropolitan extravagance, disorder, and vice. (Rochester may be alluding to such an association when, in narrating his discovery of Céline Varens's infidelity in Paris, he mentions that he could see her on the street because "it was moonlight and gas-light besides" (124; ch. 15).

Such social and economic facts may reinforce sensitivity to the accuracy of Brontë's narrative. And other excellent topics for research papers include money, servants, dress, disease, domestic space, and inheritance laws. Research assignments on such subjects can give students the relief of information to report rather than another critical argument to rehearse; moreover, through looking at the physical details, students come to see that although her imagination is fired by her yearning, Jane Eyre's desires are not the free-floating daydreams of conventional Gothic romances but reflections of the impulse for survival.

Although I would not attempt to explicate for undergraduates Elaine Scarry's complicated analysis of the connection between the body and imagining, I ask them to think about the ways in which the imagery of the pain of blindness and cold helps to construct psychic desire in *Jane Eyre*. The theorist I do introduce in some detail is Gaston Bachelard; his writing is accessible, and the implications he sees in embodied images involve a comprehension of the structuring of metaphor. His suggestion, for example, that the lamp "is the center of a dwelling, of every dwelling" (*Flame* 11) sheds light, for us, on the topography of the Reed household: the privileged children have access to the parlor fireplace, but the orphan is exiled to the perimeter. Extrapolating from this insight, students can see that Jane's position in the window seat and then in the lightless Red Room is a deeply engrained emblem of her utter homelessness. Once students become aware that the light-dark issue is central to the novel, they notice that Brontë rarely sets up a scene without establishing its sources of warmth and illumination.

At Lowood, Jane immediately discovers that life at school provides little comfort; her realization can be seen in small acts, like her initial adjustment to cold and dark in the anteroom of the school: "I stood and warmed my numbed fingers over the blaze, then I looked round; there was no candle" (36; ch. 5). In this phase of her story, the stress falls on environmental conditions, accommodating Jane's increasing freedom to castigate institutions like Mr. Brocklehurst's. When she is led into the common room, where all the girls are gathered, for example, she inventories the sparse illuminations that dimly reveal the setting: there are two pairs of candles, one set burning at each end of the hall; apparently no other lights shine for the eighty girls who work there, although mention of "the dim lights of the dips" suggests the possibility of additional rushlights (37; ch. 5). After dinner Jane peers through the gloom on the way to bed, noting that there is but a single light in the great dormitory that houses rows of the girls' beds, and at dawn only "a rush-light or two burnt in the room" (38; ch. 5). In her first full day at Lowood, Jane further observes that fires burn only at opposite ends of the schoolroom, and once again she is "nipped" by the cold when the girls are forced outside for exercise (42; ch. 5). Later she records the injustice of the "great girls" surrounding the hearths and thus blocking heat from "the younger children crouched in groups, wrapping their starved arms in their pinafores" (52; ch. 7).

Of course, *Jane Eyre* is not merely a catalog of social wrongs; it is one of the great symbolic articulations of feminine subjection and release. Indeed, an exploration of the metonymic images shows their participation in the metaphoric structure of the work in a variety of ways. One way, the comic, addresses an aspect of the novel frequently neglected; Brontë stages Jane's escape from Lowood through a wry attention to the status of her candle. Impatient to read the reply to her advertisement for a position, Jane must wait till after the day's labors to open her letter. When she is at last free, however, she is trapped in her room with a garrulous colleague and with only the short end of a candle, which—in exasperation—she watches burn down. To her relief, her roommate has eaten a heavy supper and falls asleep while there is yet "an inch of candle" to read by; Jane has just enough time to study the letter before "the socket of the candle dropped, and the wick went out" (77; ch. 10). This orchestration of a turning point in Jane Eyre's history is antithetical to the old Gothic device of the candle sputtering out at the crucial moment; rather, it portrays a self-sufficient and observant heroine—not the passive victim of Gothic romance—who can be satirical about incidental barriers like "the inevitable Miss Gryce" (76; ch. 10). Jane's venture into the larger world is thus launched through initiatives against trivial inconveniences as well as against the more profound deprivations of freedom and love.

Because criticism has canvassed the metaphorical possibilities of fire and light imagery at Thornfield, my approach to the resolution of the novel does not linger on the fires set by Bertha Mason to destroy Rochester and Jane, on the lightning that destroys the horse-chestnut tree, or on the Gothic chiaroscuro of Jane's moonlit meetings with her lover. Leaving these to student discussion, I focus on the extravagance of fire and light that Rochester marshals to magnify the great world at Thornfield. Jane, longing for the brightness and warmth of home, finds them in her early days with Mrs. Fairfax, whom she first encounters in "a room whose double illumination of fire and candle at first dazzled me . . . ; when I could see, however, a cozy and agreeable picture presented itself to my view" (83; ch. 11). Later, significantly, Jane's comfort is dispersed by the blazes kindled for the visit of Blanche Ingram. In this sequence, which a number of critics have identified as predominantly specular in orientation, even the costumes of the privileged women carry their own light: "each came out gaily and airily, with dress that gleamed lustrous through the dusk" (147; ch. 17). When Jane makes her command appearance in the drawing room, the emphasis is on the dazzle of the scene: "We found the apartment vacant, a large fire burning silently on the marble hearth, and wax candles shining in bright solitude." Then Jane peers into the dining room, "with its lit lustre pouring down light on the silver and glass"; as the ladies finally enter, they remind her of a "flock of white plumy birds." After Rochester's arrival with the men of the party, Jane is overcome by the light: "I sit in the shade — if any shade there be in this brilliantly-lit apartment" (149, 150, 152; ch. 17).

The network of fire and light imagery in *Jane Eyre* is clearly complicated: fire and light are good; too much fire and light are bad. Their absence in Jane's childhood figures her isolation, and the deprivation she felt will not be assuaged by the public display of icy glitter. I suggest that what Jane needs is the socialized light of familial home; in such a reading, the narrative's crucial turning point is not the dramatic flight from Thornfield. It is, rather, the "beacon" of candle that penetrates the darkness of her wanderings on a dim landscape after she leaves Rochester. Drawing close to the window that frames the taper, she observes a room in which the objects reflect "the redness and radiance of a glowing peat-fire" (292; ch. 28) and Diana and Mary Rivers bend over their books. Jane will regain home only when she is invited into the kitchen at Marsh End, where peat and candle combine to create a domestic site of reading among sisterly women. Eventually, when she has access to these necessities, she will share them, becoming Rochester's "light" as his reader at Ferndean.

Scrutinizing episodes of the novel, then, my students are ready to assent to the proposition that *Jane Eyre* portrays the history of a woman whose desires — variously interpreted as they have been — are imagined out of the pain of growing up without enough heat to warm herself or light to see by. But my intent in tracing such patterns is not to fabricate a simple gauge for assessing each instance; rather, it is to exhibit the spectrum of possibilities — the grammar of metaphor arising from the sense impressions of earliest childhood, reinforced by the conditions and the aspirations of daily experience, and finally worked into the fabric of a life story. I want students to see that when Jane's rebellion gives way to the fiery images of mental desolation frequently glossed by critics, there are many ways to interpret her actions. It is this spectrum that Bachelard has memorably evoked in his study of the imagination's fascination with fire: "metaphors are not simple idealizations which take off like rockets only to display their insignificance on bursting in the sky, but . . . on the contrary metaphors summon one another and are more coordinated than sensations, so much so that a poetic mind is purely and simply a syntax of metaphors" (*Psychoanalysis* 109).

Contrast and Liminality: Structure and Antistructure in *Jane Eyre*

Mark M. Hennelly, Jr.

When I teach *Jane Eyre* in a survey course on British fiction, I begin by citing Fielding's remark in *Tom Jones* that understanding the principle "of contrast, which runs through all works of creation" significantly "open[s] a new vein of knowledge" (5.1.161). When I teach the novel in a course on Victorian fiction, I note Dickens's comment in *The Old Curiosity Shop*: "Everything in our lives, whether of good or evil, affects us most by contrast" (493; ch. 53). Fielding is particularly concerned with character "foils," and Dickens with contrasting pure little Nell with her curiously grotesque environment. Students gradually recognize, however, that Charlotte Brontë uses contrast more comprehensively, to coordinate the levels and stages of her text, from the largest structural units and thematic motifs to the style and syntax in individual sentences.

Thus Brontë explores "the force of contrast" (362; ch. 35), and students point out that, like the difference Rochester assumes to exist between himself and St. John Rivers, it is often an "overwhelming contrast" (388; ch. 37). Jane, for example, characteristically uses the principle to evaluate her past and present milieus and Rochester's and Rivers's forms of love as she analogously begins to integrate the "strange contrasts" Rochester observes in her (276; ch. 27). At the same time, the attentive student learns to compare and contrast Jane's subsequent choices—whether based on bicameral judgment or feeling (208; ch. 21), conscience or passion (261; ch. 27) —with norms supplied by both dramatic and narrative irony. And as I have argued in "*Jane Eyre*'s Reading Lesson," the studious reader realizes that Jane's often unreliable narrative installments may not jibe with those of other, interpolated voices, so that the novel becomes a tale at least twice-told. In fact, I ask students to consider the possible pun in the repeated phrase "fateful third story" (183; ch. 20), which suggests the added difference, or, better, Jacques Derrida's *différance*, of Bertha's suppressed point of view. At any rate, students very easily pick up such glaring cues and clues. They feel, consequently, that they are beginning to comprehend and even practice the unfamiliar craft of literary criticism, especially since students readily understand, once the obvious is pointed out, that every conflict by definition involves a struggle between apparently opposing forces.

Leading students through an increasingly subtle series of juxtapositions, however, illustrates that what M. M. Bakhtin has dubbed the dialogic is by no means as simple or reductive as it first appears. For instance, St. John confronts the contrasting attractions of "the standard of the cross" and Rosamond Oliver, "the Rose of the World" (331; ch. 32), which clearly present a foil for Jane's divided loyalties between Rivers himself and Rochester. This conflict, simultaneously, introduces the more complicated motif of the cross, which itself implies opposing energies — perhaps most dramatically when Jane's flight from Thornfield takes her to Whit*cross*, where "four roads meet" (284; ch. 28). But the crossroads theme occurs whenever Jane "cross[es] the threshold" (297; ch. 28) of a dwelling, particularly the boundaries of the five major locations that serially subject her to liminal rites of passage. When St. John undergoes such an initiation, a liminal context is also implied — "What struggle there was in him between Nature and Grace in this interval" (363; ch. 35) — and this fairly obvious structural reading prepares students for the final class on the more difficult "antistructural" contrasts in Victor Turner's liminal theory (discussed later in this essay). The thematic conflict between the rose and the cross corresponds to the cosmogonic "war of earthly elements" (208; ch. 21) Jane speaks of and to what might even be called a Rosicrucian motif in the novel. (Apropos of Thornfield, Midsummer Eve, and St. John of the Cross, and following the insights of William M. Burgan in "Masonic Symbolism in *The Moonstone* and *The Mystery of Edwin Drood*," I ask students to consider the relevance, in *Jane Eyre*, of Rosicrucian and Masonic elements beside the more familiar legend that roses did not bear thorns until after the crucifixion.) Such questions, in fact, can suggest opposing readings of the end of the novel: that is, whether it reflects a resolution of all levels of binary contrasts or whether, as David Lodge contends in his study of the war of earthly elements, it leads to a paradoxical (or even indeterminate) irresolution. My experience has been that a basic understanding of "the force of contrast" prompts students to enter this debate in a more informed fashion. Explaining to students that, for Derrida, *différance* expresses both difference and deferral of judgment challenges them to consider an unresolvable dialectic between comparison and contrast as the pulse of *Jane Eyre* — a pulse that beats most uncertainly but most strongly during the concluding correspondence between Jane and St. John.

Teaching contrast also facilitates the class's appreciation of such image patterns as eyes. For example, Rochester demands, after the aborted wedding, that the institutions of religion and law, respectively vested in Wood and Briggs, judge between Jane and Bertha: "Compare these clear eyes with the red balls yonder" (258; ch. 26). Conversely, Jane herself notes ocular similarities: Dowager Lady Ingram's "fierce and hard eye . . . reminded [her] of Mrs. Reed's" (151; ch. 17). Students are no less quick to perceive that the Socratic, stichomythic exchanges in the novel, particularly between Jane and her two suitors, often become "cross-examinations" in which, as Rivers and Jane illustrate, both the "earthly elements" and the energetic personalities may project apparently contrasting impulses: "I am cold: no fervour infects me"; "Whereas I am hot, and fire dissolves ice" (338; ch. 33).

When students perform such dialogues in a classroom version of the Victorian reading circle, these contrasts become even clearer and provoke lively debate. Furthermore, reading aloud enables students to contrast not only their own different interpretations but also, as I suggest in "*Jane Eyre*'s Reading Lesson," their previous silent and isolated reading experiences with the participatory and communal performances of Victorian common readers. Thus, once introduced to "the force of contrast" in the novel, the class can use it as a heuristic tool. Moreover, Brontë's dialogic method informs the rhetorical balance and juxtapositions in even her smallest grammatical units: "The strong blast and the soft breeze; the rough and the halcyon day; the hours of sunrise and sunset; the moonlight and the clouded sky, developed for me, in these regions, the same attraction as for [Mary and Diana]— wound round my faculties the same spell that entranced theirs" (308; ch. 30).

I next discuss the way the text plays with (compares and contrasts itself with) familiar genres, like the confessional autobiography, or bildungsroman, that have developed self-defining conventions. As Jane writes, "[T]his is not to be a regular autobiography" (72; ch. 10). The genre topics that have proved most provocative in class include the Gothic and detective story; the romance; the fairy tale; the progress novel; social satire (introduced with Brontë's celebrated criticism of Jane Austen); the governess novel; the *Kunstlerroman*, or portrait of the artist; the *roman à thèse* (the "feminist" thesis); and even a kind of protonaturalistic novel (generally an examination of the nature-nurture arguments in the text). My objective here is for students to understand that this medley of genres reflects not only identifiable literary conventions but also contrasting philosophies of life. A remark like Blanche's "chapter of governesses" (155; ch. 17) shows that the characters themselves (as is even clearer with romance models in Brontë's *Shirley*) are often intimately aware of these conventions and of the debatable relation between art and life, though perhaps unconscious of their own ironic misreadings of the genre signals.

When we discuss the romance tradition, particularly its "emblems of love," I hold up a valentine representation of Cupid, and we explore the textual relevance of its contrasting iconography: flighty wings, blinding and role-playing mask, vulnerable nudity, innocent childishness, and painful arrows. Jane, for instance, laments the "barbed arrow-head in my breast" (283; ch. 27) when she flies from Rochester. The last time I taught *Jane Eyre*, I even made time to screen the fifth part of Joseph Campbell's *The Power of Myth* PBS video series, "Love and the Goddess" (transcribed and enlarged as chapters 6 and 7 of the Doubleday edition of *The Power of Myth*). It proved a huge success, and among many relevant motifs, the class especially noted the importance of eyes ("scouts of the heart") and the contrasting demands of *agape*, *eros*, and *amor* in the troubador tradition, as well as the unexpected "feminist" significance of Isis: "the Goddess who goes in quest of her lost spouse or lover and, through loyalty and a descent into the realm of death, becomes his redeemer" (Campbell 177). In this context, we also discussed Northrop Frye's notion of romance in terms of "the up-and-down movement" of the Persephone myth and its "contrast between two worlds"—the "idyllic" and the "demonic" (53).

When we compare romance conventions with fairy-tale motifs, students invariably bring up Cinderella. I try to move them beyond the predictable Disney version parallels to some of the variant motifs developed by Bruno Bettelheim in *The Uses of Enchantment* that suggest, for instance, a similarity between Jane's "dividing the ripe from the unripe" apples (243; ch. 25) and Cinderella's ability "to separate good from evil, as in the sorting of the lentils" motif (Bettelheim 273). Such insights make challenging paper topics, particularly in advanced classes. For the sake of contrast, I frequently pass out copies of Charles Perrault's version of "La belle au bois dormant" ("Sleeping Beauty"), which was available to Brontë in Cluer Dicey and Richard Marshall's 1764 chapbook translation, if not in the original, so that the class can explore the significant parallels between that fairy tale and Jane's awakening process (sometimes I use this theme, too, as a writing assignment).

At this point we discuss the dominant fairy-tale motif of the "transforming process" itself (73; ch. 10), which implies contrasting stages of selfhood and also suggests the way the novel may adapt this motif from tales like "Sleeping Beauty" and "Beauty and the Beast." Such a discussion inevitably leads to the feminist thesis and the famous passage in chapter 12 that seems symbolically to trigger Bertha's lugubrious laughter (96). I tell the class that when I first read Jane's story of her "sad childhood" (62; ch. 8) as an adolescent, I identified wholeheartedly with Brontë's heroine, with no thought whatsoever of our gender differences. In fact, only recently—as I became more aware of the importance of the *timing* of Bertha's appearances or awakenings—have I begun to appreciate feminist readings. I use the evolution of my own responses to stimulate a class debate on the values of male and female reactions to the novel. We try, at the same time, to link feminist and Gothic concerns, and I stress that it is not enough to say that Bertha is Jane's foil, her shadow, or even her "mirror" self. As Laurence Lerner has suggested, we must be more precise in trying to determine, for instance, whether Bertha represents Jane's latent sexuality and attraction to Rochester, her submerged hostility toward Rochester's masculine tyranny, or both. A discussion of the conclusion of chapter 25 and the beginning of chapter 26 is essential in order to compare and contrast Jane's reported vision of a "shape" that "had never *crossed* [her] eyes within the precincts of Thornfield Hall before" and now appeared as a "reflection . . . in the dark oblong glass" (249; ch. 25; emphasis added) with her own reflection in bridal attire the next morning: "a robed and veiled figure, so unlike [her] usual self that it seemed almost the image of a stranger" (252; ch. 26). Here my reminder to the class that this "spirit" self first significantly appears when Jane "had to *cross* before the looking-glass" in the Red Room as she labors in "the mood of the revolted slave" (11; ch. 2; emphasis added) usually provokes more comparisons of Jane and Bertha and allows me to note the relevant plot twists in Jean Rhys's *Wide Sargasso Sea* and Doris Lessing's *Four-Gated City*. In advanced classes, we take more time to consider Bertha as a personification of Derrida's *différance*, an "undecidable" like the unconscious itself.

Sometimes, before the class begins the novel, I introduce image patterns by asking different students to note the recurrence of a prevalent image and then to explain its thematic functions. This activity immediately demonstrates the force of comparison and contrast because the class "experts" are quick to discover, for instance, that Brocklehurst and Rivers are both compared to marble columns, while eyes, as we have seen, often reflect the internal differences between characters. As Rochester points out, "The soul, fortunately, has an interpreter — often an unconscious, but still a truthful interpreter — in the eye" (279; ch. 27). Other images that work well in this exercise are hair, children, food, disease, each of the four elements, boundaries (windows, doors, gates — prefiguring discussion of the liminal), colors (especially red, green, white, black, and gray), books, clothes, the moon, writing, birds, money, school, vegetation, houses, physiognomy (and phrenology), hands (or "the science of palmistry" [170; ch. 18]), doubles and halves, twilight, and mothers — especially Jane's and Bertha's "absent" mothers. Students at all levels are amazed at the frequency with which their particular motif occurs and delight in demonstrating to their classmates the variety of forms the image assumes. Significantly, most students experience difficulty in isolating their image from others, since Brontë usually compares and contrasts overlapping motifs in given episodes, as we have seen in Jane and St. John's personification of fire and ice. Students can also be asked to consider the relevance of specific books that appear in *Jane Eyre* — that is, to compare and contrast the novel with John Bunyan's *Pilgrim's Progress*, Samuel Johnson's *Rasselas*, Walter Scott's *Marmion*, and Friedrich von Schiller's *The Robbers* (see "*Jane Eyre*'s Reading Lesson" 698–99), among others, and, if they are not already familiar with the texts, to consult a source outlining the plots of major works. During this exercise, the class experts invariably detect intriguing parallels between, say, Schiller's Amalia-Franz-Karl love triangle and that involving Jane, Rochester, and Rivers, or they discover illuminating Gothic-romance contrasts between Constance, Lady Clare, and Marmion, on the one hand, and Jane, Blanche, and Rochester, on the other.

A more integrative classroom approach to the contrasting motifs is, again, to create a Victorian reading circle for a favorite passage (students can even act out such episodes with appropriate costumes and props). I have had most success with the Red Room experience (ch. 2), Jane's first twilight meeting with Rochester (ch. 12), the "Bridewell" charade (160–62; ch. 18), Bertha's appearance two nights before the planned wedding (ch. 25), and Jane's mysterious summons (369–70; ch. 35). Each of these is interesting and provocative for different reasons. For example, with some help from Susan D. Bernstein's "Madam Mope: The Bereaved Child in Brontë's *Jane Eyre*," we highlight issues like childhood depression, separation anxiety, and even anorexia in connection with the Red Room trauma. Students have a great deal of fun with Bridewell as a "metacommentary" on the text: first in seeing that the simple governess, typically excluded from the gathering, proves a more astute critic or reader than the sophisticated guests in solving the charades, and then in discovering the ironic relevance of comparable states like marriage (or passion, if *bride's well* is a sexual pun, as Cowart argues [35]) and prison. But I have found that the mysterious summons passage is the most productive in suggesting the relative validity of contrasting world-views, as well as the value of contrasting readings of Jane's ultimate belief system. Personified (in one sense) in St. John, religion "calls" to Jane, but obviously so does something else. Is this Other "calling" the already implied mental telepathy between loving soul mates, Jane's exclusive intuitive powers if not her awakening self, base "superstition," or a mysterious "Mighty Spirit" who may be God, Mother Nature, or even the ghost of Jane's natural mother (370; ch. 35)? After we debate these contrasting readings, I ask the class to compare them with Rochester's own account of the moment (393–94; ch. 37) and (recalling Gothic contrasts between scientific, spectral, psychological, and skeptical solutions) to consider whether his "empirical" validation sustains one or another reading and whether it elevates or reduces the mysterious effect of the summons.

I conclude this account of using the "force of contrast" as a focus for teaching *Jane Eyre* by sketching the relevant cross-cultural comparisons of the anthropologist Victor Turner, who elaborates the "threshold," or liminal, antistructures in rites of passage. Turner's seminal essay appears as chapter 4, "Betwixt and Between: The Liminal Period in *Rites de Passage*," in *The Forest of Symbols: Aspects of Ndembu Ritual*. In preparation for the last class on the novel, I require my advanced students to read this essay, and one student then compares its pertinent insights with Sarah Gilead's helpful but quite general liminal reading of *Jane Eyre*. Besides serving as a road map to crucial thematic intersections in the novel, Turner's theory allows students to experience the rewards of a comparative, interdisciplinary approach. In a course on Victorian fiction, the "transitional" nature of liminal phenomenology also provides students with a firmer grasp of the transitional context of Victorian culture. And obviously the liminal approach is essentially a dialogic or contrasting one itself, since it compares the everyday values of the neophyte's familiarly structured world with the unfamiliar antistructures of liminal versions of the *mundus inversus*, or what Brontë, in her remarkably clear use of liminal vocabulary, terms a "house turned topsy-turvy" (344; ch. 34) or "a state between" (251; ch. 25).

Turner derives his theory from Arnold van Gennep's classic *Rites of Passage* (1909) and its development of the three stages of the ritual process: separation, threshold (*limen*), and aggregation (see Hennelly, "In a State Between"). Within this framework, I ask the class to consider Jane as a model of "arrested" or "prolonged" liminality as she tries to transform and then reintegrate herself into society without sacrificing or even compromising her antistructural ideals. *Jane Eyre* repeatedly emphasizes the liminal "fascination of the locality" (308; ch. 30) with gates, doorways, windows, stairs, and crossroads (see, for instance, 188–90; ch. 20), and the novel also stresses liminal time frames, particularly twilight, midnight, and "season[s] of general holiday" (342; ch. 34) like solstice intervals. Again, these spatial and temporal zones are often thresholds to transitions and transformations as they forcefully contrast here with there and then with now. In fact, I ask my class to note the repetition of the word *threshold* (and *interval*) in the novel, and students quickly discover that it appears almost as frequently as the word *contrast*. For instance, after Jane's initial adventure with Rochester on Hay Lane at twilight, she ironically reflects, "I did not like re-entering Thornfield. To pass its threshold was to return to stagnation" (102; ch. 12).

For Turner, every threshold entrance *entrances* the initiate, or "passenger," just as Rosamond's "entrance" prompts St. John to admit "my senses are entranced" (323, 328; ch. 32). I ask students to consider Jane's entranced state during the betrothal scene on Midsummer Eve (ch. 23; a liminal reading of this chapter can also provide a valuable paper topic) as a crucial and sustained example of liminal motifs, since her transformation provocatively illustrates Turner's account of the "first fruits or harvest festival" (95). At the outset, we note that the interlude begins at twilight and concludes at midnight. During the interval, "sunset is thus at meeting with moonrise" (219; ch. 23) as both planets preside over the garden's ripening fruit; students can consider this natural process in the light of Turner's contention that female rituals involve "growing a girl" ("Betwixt" 101) and that "lunar symbolism" often reinforces this feminine growth. Throughout the novel, "moonlight at intervals" (243; ch. 25) punctuates Jane's development, and even its conspicuous absence suggests Jane's liminal dormancy. For example, "the moon shut herself wholly within her chamber" (244; ch. 25) after ominously forecasting Jane's symbolic link to the apparently arrested development of "the cloven halves" (243; ch. 25) of the chestnut tree. Or "the moon appeared momentarily in that part of the sky which filled their fissure; her disk was blood-red and half overcast; she seemed to throw on me one bewildered, dreary glance, and buried herself again instantly in the deep drift of cloud" (243; ch. 25). The stages of this celestial, social, interpersonal, and psychological transforming process significantly end, students should again note, at "the stroke of twelve" as Jane is about to "pass the threshold" at what appears to be the same time that lightning strikes the tree so that "half of it split away" (225; ch. 23). The narrator herself even interprets this critical experience as contrasting a "paradise of union" with a "nightmare of parting" (224; ch. 23). And students easily see that its "crisis" is what Turner calls the "life-crisis" or "critical moment of transition" and "transformation" during which "change is bound up with biological and meteorological rhythms" ("Betwixt" 93–94). In *Jane Eyre* the repeated "ceremony of parting" (198; ch. 21) illustrated here is a transforming process that invariably "opened the doors of the soul's cell" (371; ch. 36). Once we grow familiar with Turner's leads, I ask my class to chart Jane's characteristic reflections before each contrasting stage of transformation, such as, "A phase of my life was closing to-night, a new one opening to-morrow: impossible to slumber in the interval; I must watch feverishly while the change was being accomplished" (78; ch. 10). After tracing this process, which, again, is most evident during Jane's Midsummer Night's dream trance (ch. 23), my class reconsiders whether Jane ultimately returns to structured society or whether she and Rochester remain in the state of what Turner's later work calls *liminoid* antistructurality, the socially subversive condition characterizing individuals in deritualized, industrial cultures (see "Liminal to Liminoid").

Next the class reviews Turner's remarks on the dependent status of the neophyte. For Turner, masters and guardians are significant threshold custodians whose power contrasts with the neophyte's powerless position at the "seclusion site" ("Betwixt" 98), just as Rochester's powerful experience contrasts with Jane's status as a "neophyte" who has "not passed the porch of life, and [is] absolutely unacquainted with its mysteries" (120; ch. 14). Students should compare such remarks with Rivers's demanding from Jane "a neophyte's respect and submission to [her] hierophant" (359; ch. 34). In liminal fashion, though, Jane typically wavers "between absolute submission and determined revolt" (352; ch. 34) during her initiation into the mysterious paradoxes of selfhood that her different suitors personify. Turner's discussion of the paradoxical statuslessness of the neophyte recalls Jane the governess who governs almost nothing. His discovery of contrasting "symbolism both of androgyny and sexlessness" ("Betwixt" 98) in the neophyte, as student response is usually quick to demonstrate, reflects both plain Jane's apparent disdain for "feminine" displays and her "man's vigorous brain"and "woman's heart" (359; ch. 34). Even the "tombs and wombs" ("Betwixt" 98–99) that Turner links with neophytes appear in the contrasting images of birth and death or dreams of dead children as "baby-phantom[s]" (194; ch. 21). In sum, I want my class to understand that when Jane feels as if she "did not exist" (242; ch. 25), she precisely articulates Turner's definition of the neophyte's condition.

Moreover, what Turner calls the therapy of "comradeship," or the antistructural bond of *communitas*, is relevant to the novel because its relationships allow initiates, like Jane and Helen or (as students are ready to argue) even Jane and Rochester, to be themselves—Jane insists, "I will be myself" (228; ch. 24)—without performing structured roles. In the repeated idiom of the text, they develop "sympathetic communion" (174; ch. 19) and a "community of vitality" (243; ch. 25). During liminality, all antistructural roles are further played out in the subjunctive mood, so that the neophyte has the freedom to invert and even subvert the structured value system, as

Jane suggests when she contemplates her possible destinies with "thoughts of what might, could, would, and should be, and that ere long" (339; ch. 33). Consequently, I ask students to find and discuss other such significant subjunctive passages (see, for instance, 314; ch. 30). The liminal (at least as it again evolves into the *liminoid*) also invokes a carnivalization of contrasting genres, which we have already noted in the novel. In addition, it extensively employs performative displays, like the charades, and less dramatic, reflexive "metacommentaries," like Jane's beguiling watercolors, which from a liminal perspective usually stimulate innovative student response, and like "the tapestried room" with its "pictorial cabinet" (257; ch. 26) or "mystic cells" (184; ch. 20). The cabinet, a portentous threshold to Bertha's den, situated directly above Jane's own bedroom, particularly challenges student ingenuity with the encoded mysteries of its illustrated panels implying a comparison between St. John and Judas.

Finally, the "heart of liminal matter" is "the communication of the *sacra*" (Turner, "Betwixt" 102), or sacred symbols such as mirrors, pictures, and masks or veils, which students can easily locate in *Jane Eyre*. With her "bloated features," Bertha graphically expresses Turner's notion of the *sacra*, which are (a)typically disproportionate, monstrous, mysterious, dreamlike, and often theriomorphic. Besides her "corpulent" form, this "big woman" or "clothed hyena" boasts a "purple face" and "the gambols of a demon" (258; ch. 26), and a provocative paper topic is a discussion of Bertha as a living *sacra*, or personification of the different antistructural elements in Jane's rite of initiation. For Turner, *sacra* profoundly reveal "the arcane knowledge or '*gnosis*' obtained in the liminal period" ("Betwixt" 102). Like the "antipodes of the Creole" (274; ch. 27), this gnosis ultimately involves the "Other" — the mystery of the *coincidentia oppositorum*, or some paradoxical integration of contrasting values, which students should try to identify in Bertha.

When my class explores the liminal content of the novel's "lurid hieroglyphics" (125; ch. 15), especially as these *sacra* relate to Bertha and the repeated Gothic and gnostic term *mystery*, student insights appreciably deepen. For example, after discussing Turner's invocation of the Eleusinian Mysteries of the Great Mother, class members wonder whether Brontë's "mystic lore" (349; ch. 34) invokes comparable folkloric, "Hindustani," and, again, even Rosicrucian mysteries as it ushers Jane into the gnostic paradoxes of her own selfhood. Armed with the insights of Turner's essay on liminality, my students invariably find this mystic lore, or gnosis, "incarnate" in Bertha Mason, that apparent contrast to Jane but actual "living enigma, that mystery of mysteries" (178; ch. 19), exactly like Jane herself. Paraphrasing one student's delight in the novel's puns, we might say that Bertha's death mysteriously conceives Jane's birth; Bertha is the midnight mason who deconstructs and reconstructs Jane's selfhood. Pursuing the pun further with the comparative leads of Turner, we could add that Bertha personifies the Masonic Mysteries

— not just of brotherhood or even of comparable sisterhood but of a sympathetically shared selfhood. As Brontë conversely writes of Mr. Yorke in *Shirley*, "he was without the organ of Comparison — a deficiency which strips a man of sympathy" (76 [Penguin ed.]). In this sense, sympathetic students ultimately discover that "the force of contrast" and of antistructure in *Jane Eyre* often yields remarkable comparisons — even with oneself.

Jane Eyre and Pictorial Representation
Margaret Goscilo

Charlotte Brontë's interest in pictorial representation is more pronounced in *Jane Eyre* than in her other novels because its main character is an artist manqué: Jane not only paints and draws throughout the book but also frequently couches her aesthetic or moral judgments in visual terms. Although this artistic inclination is an aspect of Jane's characterization that students often overlook, it provides a fruitful line of inquiry into the novel's cultural contexts. With the narrative-pictorial connection as my springboard, I take an interdisciplinary approach to the novel through the iconography of Romantic and Victorian pictures, selected according to my triple goal of illustrating zeitgeist, introducing biographical factors, and considering Brontë's creative processes. I present these images to the class soon after we have started the novel, in a slide show that emphasizes lecture but invites discussion too. (Since slides dominate class attention, they are the most effective way of working with visual parallels, but students are also responsive to reproductions in books passed around the room. Commentary becomes more difficult in such a dispersed encounter with smaller images, however. Sources for the images I use appear within the text and refer to the list at the end of the essay.)

I have used this pedagogical approach in The English Novel: Victorian and Modern, a sophomore nonmajors course, in which *Jane Eyre* is our first text, followed by *Great Expectations, Tess of the D'Urbervilles, Women in Love,* and *To the Lighthouse* or *Mrs. Dalloway.* Thus my slide presentation of *Jane Eyre* lays the groundwork for other Victorian texts, while also preparing for further correspondence, in the modern novels we examine, between fiction and the visual arts. Generally students respond enthusiastically to this interdisciplinary tactic, welcoming the visuals as a fresh stimulus — and gaining from them a sensitivity both to the figurative nature imagery that pervades Jane's language and to the pictorial emphasis of her descriptions. Often, too, they focus a paper on visual-art influences or intertexts in the subsequent novels.

Usually I spend a minimum of two weeks on *Jane Eyre*, assigning and discussing it in installments. By the time I turn to the slide show, in the third class period (chs. 12–18), Jane is settled at Thornfield and we have had formalist sessions on characterization, point of view, and imagery. My starting point for considering visual representation within and in relation to the novel is the scene in chapter 13 in which Rochester peruses three of Jane's paintings, described in painstaking detail (110–11). By asking the class to characterize the contents and mood of the paintings, I elicit such replies as "gloomy," "unreal," "imaginary." I next remind students that we have seen such images earlier — in the very first chapter, in fact, as Jane pores over

Thomas Bewick's *History of British Birds*. Turning to the beginning of Jane's life story to examine what her art has to do with Bewick's illustrations, students will remark that they are likewise gloomy, watery, and cold landscapes. From here it is a smooth step to Romanticism's rediscovery of nature and scenery and its emphasis on human responses to the beauty, power, and moods of the natural world. First I observe that Bewick (1753–1828) spanned the years subsequently labeled the pre-Romantic and the Romantic periods. Then as we look at the Bewick engravings (Cirker) best matching Jane's specifications, I note other Romantic codes and constructs in the images, in Jane's verbal evocation, or in both: the allure of exotic, far-off lands; pensive solitariness; mysterious, irrational forces; the yearning for infinity; intense sensibility and passionate response; the powers of the imagination; the importance of childhood; the ruins of time. Moreover, the progressive gloominess of the images Jane cites ("the cold and ghastly moon glancing through bars of cloud at a wreck just sinking," "the quite solitary churchyard," "marine phantoms" [6; ch. 1])[1] invites a brief mention of Romanticism's morbid or graveyard strain, on which I subsequently elaborate when I show Henry Fuseli's Gothic representations (in Antal and in Tomory). Intrigued by the idea of seeing exactly what Jane looks at, students discovering Bewick are often surprised to find such small, black-and-white images corresponding to her enthusiastic remark "Each picture told a story . . . as interesting as the tales Bessie sometimes narrated on winter evenings" (6; ch. 1) — and to learn that woodcuts were the typical form of book illustration until the advent of photoengraving, in 1880.

Through Jane's pronounced preference for Bewick and her simultaneous fascination with narrative and illustration, I introduce biographical background to the novel. If Bewick's engravings capture Jane's imagination and his many versions of sinking ships provide telling analogues to her first watercolor — the cormorant over a shipwreck — it is because Charlotte Brontë herself and her siblings had fallen under Bewick's spell in their earliest years: hence I provide a brief outline of the Brontës' childhood, motherless and isolated both geographically and socially in the Haworth parsonage, and their collaborative immersion in fantasy as an escape from the harshness of their life. Attracted, like Jane, to pictures and tales equally, they copied and recopied Bewick woodcuts even as they wove their stories about Glass Town — later about Angria and Gondal — under the influence of Shakespeare, Scott, the legendary Celtic bard Ossian, and, especially, Byron. And before bequeathing to her fictional alter ego her admiration for the engraver, Charlotte at seventeen wrote "Lines on Bewick," to commemorate the "rapture" his work had afforded the siblings (Fraser 51). Among her extant illustrations, such animal studies as a drawing of her sister Anne's spaniel Flossie and a watercolor of a pine marten (Wilks) reflect a Bewickian naturalistic detail; however, little of his brooding atmosphere touches her landscapes, which include pencil sketches of Bolton Abbey, Yorkshire, and Miss Wooler's school at Roe Head (Fraser), both prosaic enough to recall Jane's finely executed "landscape in water colours" (80; ch. 10) hanging on her superintendent's wall rather than the mysterious, fantastic vision of the three pictures Rochester examines. Perhaps Charlotte's and Branwell's continual copying of engravings for manual skill, detail by minute detail, precluded the sweep and energy found in Jane's fictional pictures. Or perhaps Jane's frustrated recognition ("I was tormented by the contrast between my idea and my handiwork: in each case I had imagined something which I was quite powerless to realise") and Rochester's blunt appraisal ("You had not enough of the artist's skill and science to give [your thought] full being" [111; ch. 13]) echo a self-critical awareness that had kept Brontë herself from attempting grand subjects on a grand scale.

But if Jane's visions have little in common with Brontë's own art work, they evoke another Romantic artist with great influence on the Brontës' imaginations — John Martin, whom Jane does not name yet whose imagery is particularly suggestive alongside hers, with which it shares a grand scale, intense colors and textures, and sublime intimations. Of Brontë's familiarity with Martin there is no doubt: not only did his engravings, including *The Fall of Babylon* and *Belshazzar's Feast*, decorate the parsonage walls in her childhood but a letter from 1850 explicitly testifies to her adult admiration for his *Last Man*. Indeed, Rebecca Fraser's recent biography devotes two paragraphs to the likely effect of Martin's visions on the young Brontës, whose imaginative response to the world, she suggests, "achieved its most impressive plastic expression in the imagery of John Martin" (48). The best segue to Martin is his *The Assuaging of the Waters*, with its Bewickian combination of sea, rock, and birds, while other paintings like *Sadak in Search of the Waters of Oblivion*, *The Deluge*, *Manfred on the Jungfrau*, *The Bard* (all in Johnstone), and *Manfred and the Witch of the Alps* (Twitchell) make concrete such terms as "visionary," "transcendental," and "sublime." Of course Martin's *Manfred* series further links art and literature in its visualization of poetry by Byron, that crucial influence on the Brontës' adolescent and mature characterizations of male protagonists — among them Rochester — as demonic hero-villains. Finally, I note another visual-verbal correspondence in Martin's illustration of Milton, whose imagery Brontë invokes by having Jane refer to her third watercolor as representing "the shape which shape had none" (111; ch. 13; Death in *Paradise Lost* 2.660).

From the painters with no direct influence on Brontë's imagination but whose art yet crystallizes the Romantic vision consonant with Jane's watercolors and the novel as a whole, I choose J. M. W. Turner and Caspar David Friedrich. In their representations of infinity, of natural elements dissolving into each other, Turner's sublime and apocalyptic visions have much in common with Jane's epiphanic images of the evening star and death. His *Fire at Sea*, *Snowstorm: Hannibal and His Army Crossing the Alps*, *Snowstorm: Avalanche and Inundation*, *Sunrise with Sea Monsters*, *Death on a Pale Horse*, and *Angel Standing in the Sun* (all in Buttlin and Joll) certainly convey the mystic grandeur of nature that Jane's pictures intimate. And Friedrich's landscapes have a quality, which Peter Quennell sums up as an "indefinable atmosphere of calm, mystery and breathless silence" (250), even more in harmony with her representations. Friedrich's images that best complement Jane's visions, not only in subject matter but also in spiritual mood, include *Cemetery Entrance*; *Landscape with Grave, Coffin and Owl* (Traeger); and *The Arctic Shipwreck* (Borsch-Supan) — all three reminiscent of Bewick — *Ravine*; *Two Men by the Sea at Moonrise*; *The Monk by the Sea*; *The Northern Lights*; *Abbey in the Oakwood*; *Winter*; *Monastery Cemetery in the Snow*; *Man and Woman Gazing at the Moon*; and *Mountain Landscape with Rainbow* (all in Borsch-Supan).

Finally, to illustrate the Gothic imagination — and, particularly, the undercurrents of madness, monstrousness, and sexual repression — at work in the novel, I draw on the macabre iconography of Fuseli. First I pick up on Friedrich's numinous quality by noting the eerie, fantastical mood of Jane's first meeting with Rochester — which is preceded by her crayonist's analogy ("as, in a picture, the solid mass of a crag, or the rough boles of a great oak, drawn in dark and strong on the foreground, efface the aërial distance of azure hill, sunny horizon, and blended clouds, where tint melts into tint" [98; ch. 12]) and which Sandra M. Gilbert and Susan Gubar have specifically characterized as "something out of Coleridge or Fuseli" (*Madwoman* 351). Then we look at Fuseli's *Young Woman Imprisoned with a Skeleton*, *Solitude in Twilight* (Antal), *Fear*, *The Three Witches*, *Lady Macbeth Grasping the Daggers*, *Self-Portrait*, *Mad Kate*, *Lord Byron's Vision*, and, finally, *The Nightmare*, one of the most popular and influential — even notorious — Gothic images (all in Tomory). Besides recalling "the fiend" and the "black, horned thing" of Jane's Bewick reading (6; ch. 1) and the atmosphere of her enclosure in the Red Room, this supernatural, nocturnal representation, complete with feverish eroticism, embodies some of the psychosexual energies of the night mysteries and visitations Jane experiences at Thornfield. Its depiction of suffering and passive femininity is a crucial motif that will recur in certain Victorian paintings, while, more immediately, the horse as dynamic or libidinal drive provides an interesting parallel to Rochester's first appearance in the novel.

From the novel's Romantic ideology, I move to its reflection of the mid-nineteenth-century society in which Brontë lived as an adult and wrote her novels. None of Jane's art speaks for the Victorian ethos in the way that her landscapes espouse Romanticism; yet, after learning of Rochester's attentions to Blanche Ingram, she undertakes her task of portraiture in a "course of wholesome discipline" (141; ch. 16) suggestive of the contemporary period's moral emphases. Here Jane essentially turns her talent to a sermon against affection for Rochester, and her prefatory remark about "endeavor[ing] to bring back with a strict hand such [thoughts and feelings] as had been straying through imagination's boundless and trackless waste, into the safe fold of common sense" (140; ch. 16) encapsulates in metaphor the domestication of Romantic energies by the subsequent era. Taking the sober tone of this passage as a cue, I begin my pictorial documentation of the period with similarly didactic pictures that either exhort to virtue (for example, Ford Madox Brown's *Work*, George Goodwin Kilburne's *Poor Relations*, Thomas Peel's *A Prayer for Health*, Alfred Rankley's *Old Schoolfellows*) or sermonize against the consequences of vice (Robert Braithwaite Martineau's *The Last Day in the Old Home*, William Powell Frith's series *The Road to Ruin*). (All these images are to be found in Wood's *Panorama; Work* and *Old Schoolfellows* in color also appear in Wood's *The Pre-Raphaelites* and Reynolds, respectively.) These few images serve to suggest some of the ideological hallmarks of bourgeois Victorian culture: domesticity, respectability, piety, industriousness, sentimentality, and social conscience. Nor are students slow to recognize elements in these paintings as visual analogues to the novel's voices of social repression thus far: Mrs. Reed and Mr. Brocklehurst.[2]

Of course, in this particular passage Jane herself enacts a Victorian moral lesson by juxtaposing her two pictures almost emblematically: "Portrait of a Governess, disconnected, poor, and plain" and "Blanche, an accomplished lady of rank" (141; ch. 16) become exemplars of womanhood reminiscent of the period's conventional paradigms for female identity. Moreover, Jane's injunction against illicit love before she starts the portraits conjures up the specter of the fallen woman, as prominent a figure in Victorian thought and art as her counterpart the Angel in the House. These two icons become my focus in the next few paintings, which I discuss with some debt to Nina Auerbach's interdisciplinary work *Woman and the Demon: The Life of a Victorian Myth* (and more recently also to Bram Dijkstra's *Idols of Perversity: Fantasies of Feminine Evil in Fin-de-Siècle Culture*). I start out with George Elgar Hicks's *Woman's Mission*, as a visual summa of the narrow prescriptions for female identity against which Jane protests in the famous feminist passage early in chapter 12 (96); the images in this triptych consist of *Guide of Childhood, Companion of Manhood*, and *Comfort of Old Age*, all variations on woman's selflessness and subservience (Nead). Other paragons of womanhood appear in such pictures as Charles Alston Collins's *Convent Thoughts* (Dijkstra), Albert Graefle's *Queen Victoria as a Widow*, Jane Maria Bowkett's *Preparing Tea* (Wood, *Panorama*), Brown's *The Last of England* (Wood, *Pre-Raphaelites*) — in the last of which Auerbach finds an ambiguous female dominance that proves relevant to our eventual discussions of Jane's demonic other, Bertha, and of Jane's equivocal ministering role at book's end.

Next, to represent the fallen woman, I show perhaps the two best-known Victorian homilies on her fate: Augustus Egg's three-piece *Past and Present* (Auerbach) and William Holman Hunt's *The Awakening Conscience* (Wood, *Pre-Raphaelites*; Ironside), inspired by Little Emily's fate in *David*

Copperfield. Both artists convey the heavy cost that awaits the mistress and the adulteress, thus anticipating Jane's difficult choice before leaving Thornfield and the horror of "excessive" female sexuality that the novel embodies in Bertha. By contrast, Brown's *Take Your Son, Sir!* (Ironside), which challenges the social ignominy accorded the unwed mother, was, significantly, never exhibited at the Royal Academy. Also less preachy is Richard Redgrave's *The Outcast* (Wood, *Panorama*), whose lower-class unwed mother, forbidden to enter her father's home, perhaps represents the exploitative seduction of poor women, especially servants, to which Jane herself alludes before drawing her two portraits and which was a commonplace in Victorian life and fiction. Indeed, Redgrave's depictions of working women constitute a social criticism much like Brontë's own, and two of his canvases in particular match her vision: *Fashion's Slaves*, which came out the same year as *Jane Eyre*, counterpoints a proud, rich woman and the humble milliner's girl receiving her commands; *The Poor Teacher*, which Redgrave painted in several versions and eventually retitled *The Governess* in 1845, captures the melancholy solitude of a position like Jane's (all in Wood, *Panorama*).

A final function of studying the Victorian images is to prime the class to understand more fully the impress of contemporary culture on Brontë's adult years, of which I offer a brief account to conclude the presentation. Moving to Branwell Brontë's 1834 portrait of Charlotte, Emily, and Anne (Wilks), which marked his decision to pursue an art career in London, I explain the contrast between the only son's options and those of his sisters, all destined to train as governesses. I outline primarily the years leading up to *Jane Eyre* — the father's hopes vested in Branwell's success, Southey's letter discouraging Charlotte's writing (Fraser 109–10), the Brussels teacher-pupil identity, the unrequited attachment to the married Héger, the sororial subterfuge with male pseudonyms — but touch also on Brontë's later life: the lonely spinsterhood spent caring for her elderly father, the eventual acceptance of a most un-Byronic husband, the death caused by pregnancy. Essentially, the images by Branwell and these other artists become pictorial glosses on Brontë's life as well as on Jane's — and especially on the two women's relation to Victorian patriarchy. I conclude with an eye to our final class discussion on the novel's reception, asking students to speculate, as they continue reading, about which elements in *Jane Eyre* might have provoked Victorian society's censure.

Exploiting the TV-screen orientation of today's students, I use this interdisciplinary session as an outline of nineteenth-century currents of thought, as a reminder that no artist — even one secluded in the Yorkshire hills — works in a vacuum, as a fixative for key themes and images of the novel, and as a tribute to the importance of the visual imagination in Brontë's work. My emphasis also seems to work in encouraging students to see more connections between their various courses than they are wont to do.

NOTES

[1]Some of the woodcuts that best fit Jane's descriptions are plate 192: 4, 5; plate 164: 9; plate 100: 1, 3, 4, 5; plate 217: 1.

[2]Wilks includes a pencil drawing that might be Brontë's own study for a portrait of Brocklehurst.

SOURCES FOR REPRODUCTIONS

Antal, Frederick. *Fuseli Studies*. London: Routledge, 1956.

Auerbach, Nina. *Woman and the Demon: The Life of a Victorian Myth*. Cambridge: Harvard UP, 1982.

Borsch-Supan, Helmut. *Caspar David Friedrich*. Trans. Sarah Twohig. New York: Braziller, 1974.

Buttlin, Martin, and Evelyn Joll. *The Paintings of J. M. W. Turner*. Vol. 1: *Plates*. New Haven: Yale UP, 1977.

Cirker, Blanche, ed. *1800 Woodcuts by Thomas Bewick and His School*. Introd. Robert Hutchinson. New York: Dover, 1962.

Dijkstra, Bram. *Idols of Perversity: Fantasies of Feminine Evil in Fin-de-Siècle Culture*. New York: Oxford UP, 1986.

Fraser, Rebecca. *The Brontës: Charlotte Brontë and Her Family*. New York: Crown, 1988.

Ironside, Robin. *Pre-Raphaelite Painters*. London: Phaidon, 1948.

Johnstone, Christopher. *John Martin*. New York: St. Martin's, 1974.

Nead, Lynda. *Myths of Sexuality: Representations of Women in Victorian Britain*. Oxford: Blackwell, 1990.

Reynolds, Graham. *Victorian Painting*. New York: Macmillan, 1966.

Tomory, Peter. *The Life and Art of Henry Fuseli*. New York: Praeger, 1972.

Traeger, Jorg, ed. *Caspar David Friedrich*. New York: Rizzoli, n.d.

Twitchell, James B. *Romantic Horizons: Aspects of the Sublime in English Poetry and Painting, 1770–1850*. Columbia: U of Missouri P, 1983.

Wilks, Brian. *The Brontës*. New York: Viking, 1976.

Wood, Christopher. *Panorama: Paintings of Victorian Life*. London: Faber, 1976.

———. *The Pre-Raphaelites*. New York: Viking, 1981.

Jane Eyre and Imperialism

John Kucich

Students respond so strongly to *Jane Eyre*'s psychological and feminist dynamics that the work's relation to imperialism may seem to many of them a peripheral topic — as it has seemed to most of the novel's critics. But *Jane Eyre* represents British colonialist issues more strikingly than most other nineteenth-century domestic novels. Saturated with the language and the concerns of empire, the novel lends itself readily to discussions of imperialist exploitation, racial otherness, and orientalism. In courses organized around these topics, Brontë's work can be illuminating; it provides, as well, opportunities to discuss such issues within the traditional nineteenth-century novel course. Nevertheless, in my experience the question of imperialism is not likely to rise spontaneously to the surface, even though, once the subject is brought up, students are often quick to observe its relevance to *Jane Eyre*. Classroom discussions about imperialism thus may require special guidance, but they can prove fruitful.

Beyond whatever immediate interest imperialism may provoke, there is a context in which the topic can be especially useful. Its prominence in the novel points, in a general way, to the often neglected public dimension of domestic novels like *Jane Eyre*. Students today often complain, in particular, about the compromising inwardness of the novel's feminism: Jane's marriage signals to many of them a distressing retreat from the public conflicts she has struggled with fiercely in the early sections of the novel, and a fundamental concession to the Victorian belief that love and marriage are the only means of female self-realization. One way to challenge this understandable tendency to see Brontë as a romantic, prefeminist writer (or, conversely, to prod students who are content with Jane's marital achievement) is to note the existence of an explicitly public, even nationalistic language with which Jane negotiates the major conflicts in her life. Such an approach can show how deeply issues like imperialism, race, and orientalism condition a writer's thinking about sexuality and private life and how preoccupations with sexual oppression led Victorian women novelists to reflect on other social issues.

The most obvious — but by no means the only — starting point for a discussion of imperialism in *Jane Eyre* is the simple fact that the central characters' sense of their own identity and independence depends on the fruits of empire. Students are often struck by the centrality of colonial sources for identity, both economic and psychological: Jane's inheritance, Rochester's first marriage and fortune, St. John's spiritual mission. A useful goal for discussion might be to answer the question, Does the novel as a whole endorse British imperialism through the protagonists' dependence on the resources of empire, or does such reliance lead to a critique of British exploitation? Further, does Brontë in any way link the oppression of women to the subjugation of colonized peoples? The connection between domestic and colonial spheres in the novel does not have to be approached this baldly, however, or with this kind of ideological emphasis. Discussions may flow more freely with more neutral questions: Why is Brontë calling our attention to the colonial foundations of her characters' lives in the first place? What symbolic role do the colonies play? How, exactly, do the colonies shape the identities of Brontë's characters?

Many students are likely to feel that Brontë thinks of the colonies simply as a distant source of profit and danger and that she is relatively indifferent to them for their own sake. My students have not always been impressed with the argument that such obliviousness in itself betrays an acceptance of colonialist expropriation. They usually agree that, as Jane's Madeiran inheritance illustrates, the autonomy of the middle-class British woman depends on financial independence. But they are often unmoved by the idea that the middle-class woman's financial autonomy must be purchased, within British capitalism, at the price of someone else's labor. Although some students will grant that Brontë links female liberation approvingly to the luxuries of a colonial economy, readers of any age or class are ordinarily not disturbed by such inequities unless there is a clear victim — certainly, the novel itself invites this moderate response. Similarly, it may be insufficient to note that Jane's divided love life, which splits her loyalty between the symbol of conquest, Rochester, and the figure of spiritual aid, St. John, seems to lend female support to the double logic of male imperialist roles — missionary zeal serving as an apology for economic exploitation, and exploitation serving as the reward for spiritual responsibility. These configurations of romance, money, and imperialism, however, can at least dispel any doubts about Brontë's frankly avowed, Toryish support for British national policy in general, which has been documented by Cora Kaplan, among others.

What seems to move students more uniformly is the narrative's active degradation of Bertha Mason — the most visible victim of colonialism in *Jane Eyre*. A white Jamaican Creole, Bertha, as the embodiment of the non-English world, is portrayed in terms that rely heavily on colonialist stereotypes. Groveling and crawling, Bertha blurs the line between human and animal. In her madness, her alcoholism, and her amorphous propensity for "vice," she is clearly a projection of racism and prejudice. *Jane Eyre* is a generally xenophobic novel — as, for example, the treatment of the unscrupulous Frenchwoman Céline Varens suggests. But as the "mixed" product of European and non-European cultures, Bertha presents unmistakably the fears of contamination that afflict the imperialist imagination. Such apprehensions have geographical inflections in the novel as well: it is useful to point out that conventional Victorian attitudes about the vulnerability of the white middle-class woman to tropical climates — an assumption made by all in the novel who hear about Jane's possible voyage to India — map out a kind of racist terrain that insinuates the purity and delicacy of white women. What is even more crucial about the stereotyping of Bertha, however, is the way in which Jane's identity depends on the complex relationship of doubling between herself and Rochester's first wife. It is at this point that issues of imperialism can be easily introduced into more familiar discussions of Jane's psychology. Students are quick to see that Jane's desires for power and rebellion cannot be removed from the context of European domination, as figured in her juxtaposition to Bertha.

Jean Rhys has shown in *Wide Sargasso Sea*, for instance, how Jane's rags-to-riches story excludes the parallel plight of the Creole woman. Many students will have heard of or read Rhys's novel, but for those who have not, a basic summary indicates that Brontë sacrifices the potential correspondences between the victimization of the two women. Both women are viewed by Rochester as his property, for example, both are literal or figurative prisoners, and both have an unequal share in basic legal and economic rights. Rhys once claimed that she was motivated to write *Wide Sargasso Sea* because *Jane Eyre* had not done justice to Brontë's West Indian character (Thorpe 99). The suggestion that Bertha's victimization is effaced from the novel, and that Rhys has rewritten *Jane Eyre* from the point of view of Bertha as victim, is a striking point of departure from which students can perceive the hierarchy created between Jane and the non-middle-class women in the novel: her condescension toward servants like Bessie, Grace Poole, and Hannah, for instance, or her sense that the working-class children in St. John's school are degraded and vulgar.

More important, however, is the way in which Bertha seems to express Jane's own darkest impulses: her rage against Rochester, her sexual passion, her fierce independence, and her appeals to the authority of nature over culture. Students are often intrigued by the parallels and contrasts between the two women, especially in the light of Jane's reflections about the relative merits of reason and passion. For the most part, students see the Jane-Bertha linkage as a scapegoating of the non-European woman, a way to define the moral superiority of the white middle-class woman by portraying the Creole woman as debased by passion.

I have found it useful and not at all intrusive to summarize, in this context, the recent debate that has broken out within feminist circles over the iconic opposition of European and non-European women in *Jane Eyre*. Many students (at least in advanced English classes) have heard of Sandra M. Gilbert and Susan Gubar's *The Madwoman in the Attic* and observe that one of the foundational works of feminist literary criticism takes Bertha — the figure of suffocated rage — as the archetypal image of the female self that both fascinated and appalled Victorian women. If, in this reading, Jane and Bertha are presented as two embodiments of one character, it is because Bertha shows where Jane's own rebellious desires might take her. Bertha's role in the text is thus seen entirely as a projection of Jane's potentially criminal self, a useful foil against which she can define her own choices, her own emotional balance, her own selfhood. More recent feminist writers have complained, students often point out, that this interpretation erases Bertha's identity by incorporating her negatively into the white middle-class woman's psyche. As Gayatri Spivak has argued, it is disturbing to find, in the very writers in which one would expect sympathy for oppressed women, the complete effacement of the racially "other" woman. Students sometimes respond to this sketching of feminist debates by confessing and repudiating their own tendency to obliterate Bertha as a character with textual significance of her own, to read her only as a symbol for Jane's psychic condition or as an obstacle to Jane's happiness. Others make the connection to what they see as the radical exclusiveness of some versions of Western feminism. A fruitful topic for discussion is whether this exclusiveness is simply a property of some kinds of feminist interpretations of *Jane Eyre*, whether it is a tendency of Jane as autobiographer, or whether it signals the Eurocentrism of Brontë herself as a novelist.

Once this problem of racial exclusiveness has been established, it is easier to discuss another form of appropriation of otherness in the novel: the language, evocative of the East, with which Jane frequently adorns herself. While the narrative appears to be either indifferent to or threatened by figures of cultural otherness like Bertha, it seems remarkably free to employ an orientalist vocabulary, like that described by Edward Said, to hint at Jane's psychological and sexual mysteriousness. On the very first page of the novel, Jane hides in the window seat and sits "cross-legged like a Turk" (5; ch. 1). Oriental references are not a negligible part of Rochester's depiction of Jane as an enigmatic and enchanting being; she often seems flattered by his praise of her in such terms as "good genii" (133; ch. 15).

In the most extreme terms, *Jane Eyre* can be described as a kind of Ur-text of British imperialism, a novel that confirms important axioms of empire. Nancy Armstrong and Gayatri Spivak have argued this point forcefully, Armstrong claiming that, through Bertha, Brontë "brings alien cultural materials within a domestic framework and destroys their cultural otherness" (210). The evidence in the novel, while striking enough, is also ambivalent — so much so that students never fail to see this point as a controversy worth arguing about.

The other side of this debate — that Brontë did, in fact, recognize her solidarity with the nonwhite woman and did, therefore, seek to oppose the violence of imperialism — can begin with the same issue of language. Students will probably notice that Jane consistently describes herself as a "slave" and that she often characterizes her own oppression in terms of racial exclusion. When John Reed abuses her in the novel's opening scene, for example, Jane tells him, "[Y]ou are like a slave-driver — you are like the Roman emperors!" (8; ch. 1). She is dragged off to the Red Room "like any other rebel slave" (9; ch. 2); she later apologizes for Mrs. Reed by citing her own "racial" otherness: "[H]ow could she really like an interloper not of her race, and unconnected with her . . ." (13; ch. 2), Jane wonders. Even as governess, Jane refers to herself as part of the "anathematised race" (155; ch. 17) as she listens to Blanche Ingram speak of the way such women tend to produce "mutiny and general blow-up" (156; ch. 17). St. John refers to her, in anger, as one who is "worse than infidels" (360; ch. 34). Significantly, too, Helen Burns admonishes Jane that rebellion is the path taken by heathens and savages, not by good Christians — a connection that only underscores Jane's righteous identification with the slave. The language of racial otherness that Jane constantly invokes to describe her own condition suggests a solidarity with the outcasts of imperialist England. Victorian readers were not unresponsive to this alignment. In a famous condemnation of the novel, Elizabeth Rigby pointed out explicitly that what she took to be the novel's anti-Christian attacks on cultural authority resembled the insurrectionary potential of the colonial subject (see Dunn [1987 ed.] 440–43).

Background information on the slavery debate in Victorian England can help reinforce the self-consciousness of Brontë's strategy. As Cora Kaplan has observed, Brontë wrote the novel at a time when British women were heavily involved in antislavery agitation. One of the first forms of acceptable, collective female activism, in fact, was the abolitionist movement, which was held in predominantly good favor by the majority of the British population. Through agitation against slavery, British women were able to take public positions on political issues, in a way that symbolically aligned their own sense of oppression with that of a commonly recognized just cause. Though slavery was abolished in the British colonies in 1833, in the 1840s British women allied themselves with worldwide antislavery movements, including abolitionism in the United States. The analogy Jane makes between her own oppression and the oppression of the victims of colonialism, therefore, can be seen as Brontë's justification of her own protofeminism, as well as an accurate reflection of her support for abolition, which, in 1848, she called a "glorious deed" (Wise and Symington, *Brontës* 2: 198).

Further, Jane uses the language of slavery explicitly to resist Rochester's domination. She rejects his smile "such as a sultan might . . . bestow on a slave" and his talk of "seraglio" (236; ch. 24). In an extended fantasy, she imagines herself stirring up a "mutiny" against the slave-owning Rochester, if she were to encounter him as an oriental despot: she would "preach liberty to them that are enslaved . . . till you have signed a charter, the most liberal that despot ever yet conferred" (237; ch. 24). Jane's application to Rochester of the language of slavery suggests another dimension of Brontë's reference to the public controversy. A common feature of anti-slavery debates in the 1840s was the argument that servitude corrupts not only the slave but also the slave-holding class. While the Masons are the most obvious illustration of this assertion — the genetic madness of Bertha and the effeminacy of Richard Mason echoing British stereotypes of decadent eighteenth-century aristocrats — the potential for such degradation is linked to Rochester and to his class as well. It shapes Rochester's consciousness of his own class privileges in ways that Jane must reject, as when he argues, "[Y]our station is in my heart, and on the necks of those who would insult you" (231; ch. 24).

In this light, it is possible to read Bertha's suicide—which Spivak has bitterly compared with suttee—as a deliberate gesture of defiance and resistance. Laura E. Donaldson has argued against Spivak that Bertha's suicide is Brontë's attempt not just to symbolically enact Jane's aggression against Rochester but to give voice to the silence of the colonized woman—an interpretation that is certainly sustained in *Wide Sargasso Sea*. Bertha's self-immolation can be seen as a parallel to Jane's self-effacing flight from Thornfield and can be read as a ritualistic, if tragic, act of resistance. Jane and Bertha are to some degree linked, not opposed, in their need to overthrow Rochester's authority. While this interpretation risks condemning Bertha to yet another kind of marginalization and may even further demonize her rage, it at least seems to absolve Brontë of obliviousness to the parallels between Jane's and Bertha's oppression. In discussion, one might ask students to compare the expressive use of suicide here with similar strategies in feminist writers like Virginia Woolf, Sylvia Plath, and Anne Sexton.

The novel as a whole thus leaves considerable room for debate about its attitudes toward empire. It is fair to say that, as a commentary on imperialism, Brontë's work is provocatively unresolved, but students will undoubtedly resolve the issue for themselves in various ways. Whatever students feel about the direction of the novel's concern with imperialism, however, the strong political current demonstrates that, rather than retreat from social issues into a conventional romance plot, *Jane Eyre* actively makes use of a political subtext. Such a discussion can open up the issue of Jane's desire for independence to the connections between personal and national power. It can also lead to an examination of women's historical struggle for autonomy, in which their self-assertion suggests symbolic associations, both disturbing and empowering, between middle-class women and other victims of power. Finally, the debate can make it clear that feminism in midcentury England was a fledgling movement and that Brontë's compromises must be seen in the context of ambiguities about the relation between women's situation and the nation of which they were an indeterminate part.

Jane Eyre and the Politics of Style

Dennis W. Allen

Captivated by the plot of Charlotte Brontë's novel, students often ignore the language of the work. Yet a close look at Brontë's descriptions of objects and interiors demonstrates that the novel's language is "political" in the broadest sense, that it reflects the ideological assumptions of industrial capitalism. By emphasizing the ways in which domestic objects function as signs of social status, and in which the words of the novel themselves are seen as objects to be used and exchanged, the instructor can show students how Brontë's style is intimately related to the economic assumptions of her culture and to the class perspectives of the Victorian bourgeoisie.

One juncture at which the style of *Jane Eyre* becomes visible is in Jane's description of her arrival at Moor House. Having fled Thornfield, Jane is penniless and on the verge of starvation. As night falls and she wanders out on the moor, she sees a light emanating from "a clump of trees — firs, apparently, from what I could distinguish of the character of their forms and foliage through the gloom." Encountering a stone wall, Jane finds a gate bordered on each side by "a sable bush — holly or yew" (291; ch. 28). She then approaches the house, looking in a window to see a room "with a sanded floor, clean scoured; a dresser of walnut, with pewter plates ranged in rows, reflecting the redness and radiance of a glowing peat-fire. I could see a clock, a white deal table, some chairs." Jane observes these objects "cursorily only," since there is "nothing extraordinary" in them (292; ch. 28). A moment's reflection on the passage, however, suggests otherwise.

To begin with, if these objects are unimportant, Jane's description of them is nonetheless remarkably detailed; she notes what kind of wood the dresser is made of and that the plates are pewter rather than silver. But the passage is even more curious if one considers the situation. According to her account, Jane is, at this point, on the verge of collapse from inanition. She even sinks on the doorstep to await death when Hannah refuses her admission to the cottage. It is strange, then, that Jane should be so precise in her descriptions, even to the extent of attempting to ascertain the type of trees lining the path. (Such detail cannot be justified by the fact that Jane is recording these events some ten years later, well after she has learned that the trees are firs. Jane's expression of uncertainty re-creates the perceptions of the moment of the action.) Why, even at the occasional expense of probability, is *Jane Eyre* filled with specific characterizations of objects?

The traditional explanation given for the extended descriptions that abound in novels is that the works reflect the growth of empiricism at the end of the seventeenth century, the epistemological shift from a stress on universals to an attention to particulars. Associated with the rise of capitalism and of the middle class, empiricism emphasizes individual experience and the sensuous apprehension and practical manipulation of the world (Watt 9–34). The result in literature, Ian Watt has argued, is the development of "formal realism," which includes the sort of exact depiction of physical surroundings found in novels, the emergent genre of the middle class. Yet Watt's analysis seems finally inadequate, for, in it, "realism" becomes an end in itself. Although the minute portrayal of objects and interiors lends a sense of reality to the characters and events by surrounding them with the physical detail that we observe as the background to our lives, this notion of "realism" is itself entirely conventional. The question, then, is why the conventions of realism take this particular form.

The answer lies in the various values the object can have under capitalism. Let us take another look at that walnut dresser. Writing at roughly the same time as Brontë, Karl Marx pointed out that objects of human manufacture, like the dresser, have two related sorts of value—a use value and an exchange value. The use value is what we need an object for, the functions it can have: in the case of the dresser, to store things. Exchange value is more abstract, a way of determining the relative value of objects that have various uses and that take differing amounts of labor to create. Exchange value is what the object can be traded for—in short, its price. Jean Baudrillard has extended Marx's analysis by noting that, in addition to use and exchange values, the object has a sign value ("Sign Function" 33). Homes, clothing, and furniture are themselves signs, indicating social rank and wealth. Thus, just as contemporary Americans often draw conclusions about someone based on the kind of car he or she drives—the vehicle signifies a specific class affiliation and social status—a Victorian reader would have been able to draw multiple, subliminal conclusions from a novel's material descriptions.

Baudrillard goes on to argue that the sign value, the significance, of objects cannot be restricted to a simple correspondence between the object and a particular social class. Because of the social mobility created by a capitalist economic system, a person's possessions, taken together, reflect a complicated portrait of his or her actual social status, desired social status, and the tension between the two ("Sign Function" 40). Thus, even before the reader has encountered the Riverses and learned their story, the furnishings Jane sees through the window summarize the family's social position. The walnut dresser and the deal (pine or fir) table both have places in a symbolic hierarchy of woods, walnut suggesting middle-class affluence and deal indicating more humble social connections. The presence of the two types of wood in the same room encapsulates perfectly the Riverses' ambiguous social status: the antiquity and gentility of the family and their current precarious economic situation. The pewter plates convey the same message. Displayed as ornament, the plates are intended not for use at meals but as a sign of a certain level of affluence in which one can afford objects whose function is precisely that they are useless. However, the plates are pewter rather than silver, an indication that St. John, Diana, and Mary Rivers are not as affluent as, say, Mrs. Reed (whose furniture, by the way, is "old mahogany").

But the point is not simply that the description of material possessions allows the reader to determine, in a relatively complicated way, the social status of the characters. This attention to objects itself reflects the insecurities of the nineteenth-century bourgeoisie, a tension that animates the novel on a variety of levels. The rise of industrial capitalism in Victorian England provided an unprecedented level of social mobility; no longer were individuals automatically relegated to the social rank of their parents (Gay 65). Yet because status based on possessions is more precarious than an inherited social position, Baudrillard argues, the bourgeoisie is always apprehensive about the legitimacy of its social standing. Its insecurity was reflected in the decor of the Victorian home, in which the objects that asserted the owner's social position were organized according to two principles designed to reinforce middle-class values: saturation and redundancy. Crowded with furniture and knickknacks, the home represented sheer accumulation as a sign of status, and a multiplication of coverings and ornamentation framed the items to underline and duplicate the fact of possession ("Sign Function" 41). The principle is illustrated in Mrs. Reed's Red Room, in which the profusion of objects — beds, chairs, and tables — is accentuated by fabric: the curtains and counterpane of the bed, the "festoons and falls" of damask at the windows, and the "crimson cloth" covering the table (10; ch. 2). Crowded with massive furniture, the pieces themselves covered and draped with fabric, the Red Room reminds Jane of a tabernacle, and one thing it enshrines is the social status of the Reeds.

The social anxieties implied by Mrs. Reed's decor are not incidental to Brontë's novel, which is, on one level, a narrative of the insecurities of social position. Jane is, of course, the heroine as social outsider, a role reflected both by her status as an orphan and by her occupation as governess, that liminal figure in the social hierarchy (Gilbert and Gubar 349). Jane's tenuous standing is confirmed by her placement within the novel's domestic interiors. As the novel opens, Jane is hidden in the window seat, a position she will frequently occupy at Thornfield, situated in a space between the inside and the outside, both physically and socially. The novel as a whole, in fact, illustrates Victorian anxiety about social mobility, the desire both to advance socially and to pretend that the position one has achieved is one's "natural" position. Thus Jane not only takes her place in society by marrying Rochester but discovers that this place is indeed *hers* through her accession to (inherited) wealth and her kinship with the Rivers family.

The social tensions of the novel are encapsulated in Jane's reaction to objects and interiors. Quitting her job as schoolmistress when she learns that she is wealthy, Jane establishes as her first goal the refurbishing of Moor House. Although she leaves the bedrooms and sitting room untouched so that they retain "old associations," the rest of the house is carpeted and covered.

A spare bedroom is done up in "old mahogany and crimson upholstery," and the sitting room is graced with "an arrangement of some carefully selected antique ornaments in porcelain and bronze" (345; ch. 34). Such labor is the physical equivalent of the novel's plot. The old mahogany and antique ornaments are intended not simply to represent social status but to insist on it as a time-honored, secure fact, just as the novel's fantasy of social mobility insists finally that Jane's social status is hereditary. Thus the material descriptions that fill the novel do not merely reflect the conventions of novelistic realism. The conventions themselves reveal the importance of objects for the Victorian bourgeoisie in its struggle to define and ensure its social status, a struggle that provides the narrative of the work — Jane's search for a place in society.

Yet the sign value of objects does not explain Jane's portrayal of nature: her attention to the trees lining the path at Moor House or the fields and woods surrounding Lowood and Thornfield. The novel's descriptions must therefore be placed in another context. Ultimately, we are dealing here not with real objects but with verbal ones, with signs; and just as objects can function as signs, so signs are themselves objects. Moreover, Baudrillard has demonstrated that, like other objects in a capitalist economic system, signs have a use value and an exchange value ("For a Critique" 59). The use value of signs can be variously defined, but in its simplest form it is the basis for our everyday view of language: the function of words is to present meanings. If the use value of the sign stresses content, the exchange value of the sign emphasizes the act of communication itself, in which the exchange of words between individuals is more important than what is actually said. Both the use value and the exchange value of the sign are crucial to an understanding of the role of language in *Jane Eyre*.

The use value of the sign is the principle underlying traditional New Critical readings of texts, and students have little difficulty providing examples of the function of the novel's material descriptions. Such passages, as we have seen, are intended to create a mimetic illusion, and, as students quickly point out, some descriptions serve an additional symbolic purpose. The splitting of the horse-chestnut tree, for example, symbolizes divine displeasure at the projected marriage of Jane and Rochester, their eventual separation, and Rochester's physical debilitation. Moreover, Brontë's implicit belief in the use value of signs helps explain the overall assumptions of the traditional novel. Unlike contemporary fiction, which often asserts that reality does not exist except as a linguistic construct, Victorian literature assumes that signs refer ultimately to a reality that exists before language. And if the use of the sign is to have a meaning, then the use of a collection of signs, of a novel, is to convey the truth about that reality. This is the justification for fictions like *Jane Eyre*; even if the story is not literally true, it nonetheless tells us something about the nature of life or the ways of the world. Thus Brontë's novel is read, traditionally, for its "moral," whatever one takes this to be: that, for example, true love depends on a similarity between the lovers or that one must establish a balance between passion and reason. The belief in the use of signs to reveal the truth is even reflected in the structure of the novel (and, indeed, of most of Victorian fiction). Much of the interest of the narrative comes from a series of mysteries (the identity of "Grace Poole," the nature of Rochester's feelings for Jane) that are clarified both for the characters and for the readers in the course of the story. The novel's structure of mystery and revelation duplicates the suppositions of the use value of the sign; if you read long enough, everything will become clear. Words will uncover reality.

Taken as objects, then, the signs of the novel have various uses, conveying meaning on a number of levels. But use alone cannot explain the length of *Jane Eyre* or of Victorian novels in general. In reply to Rochester's complaint that her goodbye to him when she goes to visit the Reeds is too brief — "stingy" in fact — Jane says that "as much good will may be conveyed in one hearty word as in many" (198; ch. 21). Yet the novel itself, swollen by descriptions, seems to belie this sentiment. If one thinks of the work, however, as a collection of signs with both use value ("meanings") and exchange value, the novel, like most Victorian fiction, can be seen as an accumulation of verbal capital. In fact, the principles of saturation and redundancy would seem to apply not only to Victorian decor but also to the style of the novel. Thus the piling up of descriptions and the development of plot complications to extend the narrative represent the author's labor to produce a sort of verbal wealth, stockpiled in the text. For Victorian authors, who were often paid by the word, this linguistic capital could literally be exchanged for money, but *Jane Eyre* suggests that there is another, more subtle exchange value of the sign.

The novel opens with Jane reflecting on her alienation from the Reeds, and the theme of isolation continues throughout the narrative. Refused admittance to Moor House by Hannah, Jane laments her segregation from other people: "Alas, this isolation — this banishment from my kind!" (295; ch. 28). St. John's revelation that Jane is an heiress leaves her somewhat cold. She is pleased by the independence that wealth will bring, but the money comes, as she notes, "not to me and a rejoicing family, but to my isolated self" (336; ch. 33). It is the additional revelation that the Riverses are her cousins that thrills Jane: "Glorious discovery to a lonely wretch! This was wealth indeed! — wealth to the heart! — a mine of pure, genial affections" (339; ch. 33). If affection is a form of wealth, it can be, as here, inherited; but, the novel makes clear, it can also be gotten through exchange, through the exchange of words. The point is implicit when Jane first approaches Moor House and wonders how she can touch its inmates with concern on her behalf, inducing them to give her shelter. Language is the only thing she can exchange for a night's rest. It is not surprising, then, that Jane later says that, for her, the value of communication with "refined minds" is to cross the "threshold of confidence, and [win] a place by their heart's very hearthstone" (330; ch. 32). Communication is the exchange of the speaker's language for the sympathy of the listener, a principle that Jane's arrival at Moor House enacts. And the novel, Jane's accumulation of words in the text, is intended to re-create this process with the reader. The wealth of signs that is the novel is given to the reader in exchange for the "mine" of the reader's interest and affection. Thus the novel is long because, following the accumulative logic of capitalism, the more signs there are to be exchanged, the better. The more words Jane gives us, the more love she will receive.

The descriptions that fill *Jane Eyre* show students how the novel reflects the implicit assumptions of Victorian capitalism evident in the signifying function of material objects and in the belief that words are objects to be used and exchanged. And if the novel seems to reject capitalism by stressing Jane's yearning for family rather than for money, her preference is less a denial of bourgeois values than a solution to the social anxieties such values generate. If social status based on material objects is always insecure, the social integration produced by affection, the novel suggests, is not. Thus the value of the text is, finally, less what it means (its use value) than the social place it assures both for Jane and for Brontë (its exchange value). As Brontë states in the preface to the second edition, she has presented the public, the press, and her publishers with a "plain tale," and she thanks them for their kindness to an "obscure aspirant," an "unknown and unrecommended Author." Just like Jane at the door of Moor House, she has come before her readers as "a struggling stranger" (Dunn [1987 ed.] 1), exchanging language, the signs she has created and accumulated, for a place by their hearts' hearthstones.

Jane Eyre through the Body:
Food, Sex, Discipline

Diane Long Hoeveler

In introducing upper-level students to gender and class issues, as well as to the sexual and bodily dimensions that emerge from a reading of *Jane Eyre*, I focus on three central issues: the patterns of eating and starvation in the text, the relation of this pattern to Jane's body and her somewhat convoluted sexuality, and the connection of both issues to the text's depiction of "disciplinary practices" (the machinery of power that operates in capitalist societies to control the physical body). Taking Michel Foucault's writings as my primary theoretical background, I teach *Jane Eyre* as a paradigmatic work that presents the ideological construction of the "feminine" bourgeois body and depicts Jane's immersion in alternating loci of disciplinary power: clinics and doctors, schools and asylums, families and prisons. As Foucault argues, the bourgeoisie distinguished itself from both the aristocracy and the working class by making its sexuality and its health a primary source of its hegemony. Whereas "blood" was the source of the aristocracy's power, "sex" and its control became the predominant characteristic of the middle class, both male and female. In her fictional presentation of various bodies, Brontë suggests that gender and class issues alone do not determine one's ultimate social status. Only by cultivating the perfectly disciplined body, reified in an idealized companionate marriage, can one achieve bourgeois "salvation"—that is, social and economic hegemony.

My first class on *Jane Eyre* focuses on chapters 1 through 10, which recount Jane's childhood memories of life in the Reed encampment and her incarceration at Lowood. I instruct students before they begin their reading to note references to bodies and eating habits in this section of the text. If they are alert readers, they detect the clear pattern of self-starvation and self-abuse Jane has learned: if status is based on material possessions and inheritance, then Jane is worthless. She has no right, that is, to eat, to consume when she produces nothing ("you have no money; your father left you none; you ought to beg, and not live here with gentlemen's children like us, and eat the same meals we do" [8; ch. 1]). In such a situation Jane is forced to abuse her body in self-hatred.

The first paragraph of the novel situates Jane in relation to the dinner hour; this child is perpetually gnawed by hunger. As an orphan, unconnected to any nurturing familial structure, Jane can be aware only of her "physical inferiority to Eliza, John, and Georgiana Reed" (5; ch. 1). The novel, of course, reverses the physical advantages of these three pseudoaristocrats, so that they either implode (as does the anal-retentive Eliza) or explode (as do the orally greedy John and Georgiana), while Jane, through her sufferings and trials, earns the perfect "feminine" hegemonic bourgeois body, as symbolized by both her inheritance and the marriage that "rehumanises" Rochester (384; ch. 37). Both the money and the man allow Jane to overcome the class indeterminacy that has plagued her throughout the novel. The final bodies of Jane, the newly emerged and firmly established bourgeoise, and Rochester, the chastened aristocrat, complement each other in a fantasied image of perfection, a sort of erotic apocalypse symbolized by their son and their Miltonically ideal companionate marriage (see L. Stone and Hagstrum for background on this notion).

After an introductory discussion of the Reed family dynamics, we focus closely on the Red Room episode. Here my concern is to demonstrate Jane's learned strategy of passive aggression (her resigned comment that her "care was how to endure the blow which would certainly follow the insult" succeeded quickly by her rebellious and class-conscious outburst at John: "You are like a murderer" [8; ch. 1]). But, as Jane discovers, such a psychic configuration can result only in self-induced paranoia and hysteria ("I had a species of fit" [15; ch. 2]). The dissociation of Jane's mind from her body is reiterated in the mirror episode, as it is in her "Resolve" to kill herself by "never eating or drinking more" (12; ch. 2). I point out that the anorexic desire to stave off menstruation is not very subtly presented here (see Caskey). Significantly, after her emergence from the Red Room, Jane is unable to eat a favorite tart served to her on "a certain brightly painted china plate" decorated with a "bird of paradise" (17; ch. 3). Bird imagery reinforces Jane's fluctuating psychic state throughout the novel, and the rejection here of appetizing food and lovely plate forcefully illustrates Jane's self-hatred, her inability to consider herself worthy of any nourishment at all; she even projects herself onto the "little hungry robin" on the sill (25; ch. 4).

Short of dying, however, Jane desires to become a "stone" (13; ch. 2), a metaphor for her attempt to deaden her emotions and the needs of her body in compliance with bourgeois norms. Her desire is hypocritically repudiated later by Brocklehurst, who prays to God "to take away [her] heart of stone and give [her] a heart of flesh" (28; ch. 4). Jane knows, however, that she is living in a world inhabited by bourgeois automatons, not loving Christians with fleshly hearts. Self-preservation demands conformity to disciplinary practices, those learned behaviors that enable Jane and other lower- and middle-class women to function in a society that is structured as a panopticon — that is, as a prison presided over by the omniscient eye of power (see Foucault, *Discipline and Punish*). Indeed, the charge continually made against Jane, that she "always looked as if she were watching everybody, and scheming plots underhand" (21; ch. 3), serves as a projection of the family onto Jane. In an atmosphere in which Jane's every word and thought is observed by the matriarch and her brood, they accuse her of what they themselves have done. To survive in such a world, Jane knows she must go to school: "Bessie sometimes spoke of [school] as a place where young ladies sat in the stocks, wore backboards, and were expected to be exceed-ingly genteel and precise" (20; ch. 3). The female body (and mind) here is shaped to conform to conservative values thought appropriate for middle-class children. The young class-indeterminate Jane exists for the family as the very emblem of "passion" — anger and sexuality — and is associated explicitly with lower-class revolutionaries (an "infantine Guy Fawkes" [21; ch. 3]). The discipline in the ways of repression that Jane needs she finds at Lowood. As Jane "matures," she becomes more securely middle class and less "passionate," at least in the rebellious sense.

If life at Gatehead was at least sweetened occasionally by "a bun or a cheese-cake" brought by Bessie (24; ch. 4), life at Lowood is experienced as institutionalized starvation; "a thin oaten cake, shared into fragments" and "burnt porridge" are all the students receive (38–39; ch. 5). But the pur-pose of the routines at Lowood is not to feed the body; it is to subdue it in order to create appropriately submissive middle-class females who will serve the emerging industrialized culture — the body as machine ("pampering the body obviat[es] the aim of this institution" [54; ch. 7]). Thus I ask stu-dents to notice the emphasis on time management, the references to clocks (41; ch. 5), the continual demands for "Silence!" and "discipline" (40; ch. 5), forms of punishment (44–45, 58; chs. 5, 7), and the rejection of "nature" in favor of culture. In such an institution, Brocklehurst achieves his stated aims by claiming, in a sadistic piece of illogic, that to feed the body is to starve the soul (55; ch. 7). In addition to disciplining the girls through en-forced starvation, Brocklehurst cuts off their hair, a sort of distorted castration of female sexuality, a blatant example of how the machinery of power operates in conformity with sexual repression. And just to be sure we recog-nize the school as totalitarian "institution," Brocklehurst sends his wife and daughters up to the dormitory rooms to search the dresser drawers and to interrogate the help. The school functions as little more than a prison, a juridical system of power that actually produces — brings into being — the subjects that it later claims to represent.

At this point I introduce my students to a series of excerpts from Foucault's *Discipline and Punish.* I cite here only two brief passages:

> There are two images, then, of discipline. At one extreme, the disci-pline-blockade, the enclosed institution, established on the edges of society, turned inwards toward negative functions: arresting evil, breaking communications, suspending time. At the other extreme, with panopticonism, is the discipline-mechanism.   (209)

The panopticon, that is, reversed the dungeon as the site of punishment for eighteenth-century society. The new machinery of the *gaze* was institu-tionalized by a hidden supervisor observing from a central tower — like some sort of omniscient God — every action of the inmates. According to Foucault, "our society is one not of spectacle, but of surveillance. . . . We are neither in the amphitheatre, nor on the stage, but in the panoptic machine" (217). For a woman, to accept "discipline" means to accept her fate silently, whether that destiny calls for her to be a governess or a corpse. And a woman who rejects life's gruel and complains draws the attentions of the panopticon. In such a situation her behavior is closely marked and properly punished (see the works by Armstrong and by Kucich on this pattern in *Jane Eyre*). We approach here one of the meanings of the figure of Bertha.

I point out to my students that in addition to using the prisonlike school to codify ideological conservatism, late-eighteenth-century society invented "madness" and contained it in asylums (or attics). Construction by the "Enlightenment" of the madhouse stands, then, as a revealing parallel to the school as prison (see Foucault, *Madness*). If the heroine is under constant surveillance in society as panopticon, then Rochester's "Gothic castle" represents the reverse. Within the walls of Rochester's manor, Jane thinks (wrongly) that she wanders as if in dark and endless tunnels, with no one to see her movements, let alone acknowledge her thoughts. The radical disparity here in images — the exteriority, exposure, transparency of the panopticon and the interiority, enclosure, opacity of the asylum-attic — represents for Brontë the two poles of being female in a male-dominated, capitalist society. Women in both instances are contained, hidden or hiding, either as objects or as absences. In the school as prison, Jane learns the language of repression; she learns that silence can be her only protection from the tyranny and false accusations of power (as signified by Brocklehurst). Becoming as invisible as possible, she represses emotion, desire, hunger. In the Red Room episode or the Gothic castle as asylum, however, the dominant discourse system is hysteria, the language of Bertha. The malady that plagues Jane during her fits and Bertha throughout the text is desperation, terror at their complete objectification by others.

Speaking of objectification, I discuss Helen Burns at length, as the exact opposite of Bertha. In the depiction of these two women, Brontë practices what Roland Barthes has called, in *Mythologies*, "neither-norism" (81–83): the novelist rejects the sexuality and anarchy of Bertha while also repudiating the Christianity of Helen and St. John (female and male versions of the disembodied Christian). I read Helen as the woman who accepts her status as a completely self-erased signifier. She represents bourgeois values of self-denial, passivity, Christian forbearance, and masochism wrought to a dangerous degree. Society would not exist long if all women internalized the disciplinary code as well as Helen does. And yet she is strangely attractive to Jane, as she is later brought under the spell of St. John Rivers (a man who upholds the same values and hyperasceticism to a deadly degree). In this section of the novel, Jane does, of course, recognize the ideal female body: Miss Temple (the body as temple of the Holy Spirit). But the humanely disciplined Miss Temple, complete with lovely gold watch and secreted sweet cakes, is hopelessly out of Jane's reach — or, rather, the existence of Helen Burns, and Jane's tendency to masochism and self-hatred, are still too strong. The death, by metaphoric starvation, of Helen (and later, by implication, of St. John) stands as one route that Jane could have taken. She chooses another path, however, a journey into accepting her body and its needs. She meets Rochester.

In the heterosexual romance that forms the next long section of the text, chapters 11–27, we see a decrease in the number of blatant references to food, eating, and starvation and a concomitant increase in the number of references to visual and oracular imagery. The body, that is, no longer remains fixated at the infantile level of concern for nourishment; it has progressed to what we would recognize as the object-relations stage, to reaching out to others as either "same" or "different." The last section of the text, chapters 28–38, presents the final series of bodies that Jane deciphers and finally rejects or accepts. To Jane, Rochester and Bertha seem "different" from her, while she initially perceives St. John and his sisters as the "same." In these last two sections, Jane attempts to mediate the attraction that both "bodies" — ways of experiencing life and gaining power — have for her.

To explain the invention of the modern body, I provide the following schema for my students, a sort of abbreviated history of the body in the nineteenth century. I introduce here, as supplements to Foucault, the theories of Norbert Elias and M. M. Bakhtin. Elias's work traces the creation, during the nineteenth century, of what he calls *homo clausus*, an individual who makes biological self-control a private matter. Such an individual experiences the culturally imposed "rising threshold of shame and embarrassment" about bodily functions as an endorsement of increasing personal restraint, as the institution of "a wall, of something 'inside' man separating him from the outside world" (258, 259). And it was, according to Elias, the newly created and controlled "public body" (249) that society validated. This "public body" distinguished itself from the lower classes by its aping of the courtly value of self-control, along with its acceptance of shame as the secret sin at its bourgeois heart. It was through the imposition of such behaviors, Elias believed, that the modern state could come into existence. Bakhtin, in contrast, privileges the "carnivalesque" body of the early modern period: it enacts its essentially feminine values through intense release of emotion, it destroys authoritarian strictures, and it challenges and inverts imposed political and religious systems. Jane's attraction to these two bodies — *homo clausus* (St. John Rivers, Helen Burns, the Rivers sisters) and the "carnivalesque" (Rochester, Bertha) — can be seen as one locus of meaning in *Jane Eyre*. Jane is tempted, on the one hand, to conform, to conceal, to privatize, to repress; on the other hand, she is presented with the bacchanalian possibilities of Rochester and Bertha, the dream of becoming either an adulteress and a sexually illicit woman or an anti-bourgeois maenad.

Jane becomes the heroine of the text and deserves to inherit Rochester's considerably reduced estate when she rejects the body in the attic (with its "giant propensities" [269; ch. 27]) and indirectly precipitates Bertha's destruction (see works by Cohn and by Monahan). I read Bertha's last mad rampage as motivated by her desire to rid herself of Jane as a rival. Although we know that Jane has been gone from Thornfield for some time, Bertha lives in a decidedly different psychic world. Jane rather than Rochester is the target of the fire. The female bodies turn on each other here, the *homo clausus* body of Jane rejecting and abjecting the carnivalesque, hysterical female body of Bertha and surviving as a chastened shadow of itself, troped as in projection by Rochester's maiming. Rochester's "castration," or what we can recognize as a sort of ritual taming of his body, actually mirrors Jane's physical diminution, her renunciation of the carnivalesque. That is, before Jane and Rochester can be united in an ideal Miltonic companionate marriage, there has to be a good deal of ritual maiming of the flesh of both the male and the female. Female sexuality, potentially anarchic and threatening to the social order, must be excised (and so Bertha dies); male sexuality, so disabling to women's autonomy, has to be tamed (so Rochester is punished for his sexual indiscretions and disabled).

I ask my students to note other oppositions that reflect the conflicts between the *homo clausus* and the carnivalesque throughout the text: the body as stone (Brocklehurst, St. John Rivers, Eliza) and as diffuse, amorphous, transformational (Rochester as the Gypsy "woman," Jane as "elf," "sprite" and "changeling" [241; ch. 25]). Brontë seems to be suggesting through such imagery that conformity to bourgeois definitions of health requires the ability to adjust not simply one's mental and psychological makeup but one's physical appearance as well. We also discuss the significance of the bodies (real and dreamed) of children, juxtaposed as they are to the bodies of "big, brown, and buxom" aristocratic women (193; ch. 20). Adèle, of course, embodies Jane's suppressed fear of all things French and blatantly sexual ("there was something ludicrous as well as painful in the little [Parisienne]" (150; ch. 17). Jane obviously identifies with children, but not with the adult, aristocratic women who populate the text. One might claim that Jane's (and, by extension, Brontë's) xenophobia and sexual and class anxiety manifest themselves in the continual references to large, "robust," "dark" aristocratic women (Mrs. Reed, Blanche, Bertha, and Rochester's foreign mistresses), in contrast to Jane's repeated description of herself as "pale" and "little" (30, 86; chs. 4, 11). Her fondness for silent and defenseless children may indicate that her sexual needs are appropriately bourgeois — small, harmless, easily accommodated by Rochester (as Bertha's were not, as Blanche's might not be).

In chapters 28–38, we again note the connection between starvation and sexual abstinence as Jane flees Rochester, progressively starving as she journeys away from him. The scenes in which Jane tries to barter her worn gloves for a cake, eats pig slop, and begs bread from a suspicious farmer are poignant. Jane learns that she cannot deny her body; her efforts to suppress her sexual desires for Rochester are unavailing. Her models, as she seeks her final identity, are the bourgeois Rivers sisters, Diana ("Physically, she far excelled me: she was handsome; she was vigorous. In her animal spirits there was an affluence of life and certainty of flow" [308; ch. 30]) and Mary, women whose names suggest the two most powerful virgins in the pagan and the Christian traditions. Jane reenacts a triangular courtship, attracting another man — this one handsome indeed — away from a beautiful and rich ("aristocratic") woman, Rosamond Oliver. In St. John's repudiation of the cash-sex nexus, we know ourselves to be, of course, in the realm either of wish fulfillment, fantasy, and fairy tale or of abnormal psychology. Pointing out both options to my students, I generally get an interesting discussion going by asking, "How many of you think an extremely handsome man, highly educated and desirable, would prefer to marry a poor, homely woman who does not love him rather than a rich and beautiful woman who adores him?" The question is guaranteed to bring out the worst in everyone.

On a more substantial note, I mention the not very submerged incestuous theme (Jane and St. John Rivers as cousins) and demonstrate its exemplification of what Foucault labeled the shift, in the eighteenth century, from a "machinery of alliance" to a "machinery of sexuality" (*History* 105–06; see Sheridan 187–90). The primacy of kinship, or the incestuous associations of extended family members, was supplanted during this period by the institutionalization of the modern family, characterized primarily by its rigid denunciation of incestuous desires. But Jane does not reject St. John Rivers because she experiences his body as the "same" as hers; she rejects his denial of her body (not to mention his own). Jane needs a body that can be "different" from hers at the same time it can be "bone of [her] bone, flesh of [her] flesh" (397; ch. 38), and this she finds — somewhat paradoxically — in the blind and maimed (read exogamous) Rochester (see Monahan; Wyatt; Tayler for contrasting readings on this issue). She "rehumanise[s]" him, eats with him ("I am hungry: so are you, I daresay" [384; ch. 37]), and thereby claims her bodily inheritance: a son.

No one talks much about Jane's maternity (although an important discussion of a related topic can be found in the appendix to John Maynard's study of Brontë), but I stress the fact that she speaks only about bearing a male child (397; ch. 38). If Jane is the "apple" of Rochester's blind eyes, the son and heir is the apple of Jane's eyes. The psychic and socioeconomic dynamics have come full circle: the body of the starved and frozen (read poor and class-indeterminate) Jane has acquired what she lacked; because her ideal companionate marriage has produced an "aristocratic" son who will sire more bodies, death holds no sting for her. The final words of St. John actually bespeak Jane's own confidence, her rewriting of Helen

Burns's message of salvation through that ultimate disciplinary practice —
Christianity. Immortality for Jane has been achieved not through spiritual
apocalypse or physical extinction but through an erotic and bodily reclama-
tion of the perfectly tamed flesh. Jane as representative of the newly tri-
umphant bourgeoisie has survived the disciplinary practices that had the
potential to either "castrate" or kill her. Having seized the ultimate machinery of power for herself, she claims the life force, eats, reproduces, and
thereby consumes death. *Resurgam.*

Jane Eyre as a Novel of Vindication

Bernard J. Paris

I often teach *Jane Eyre* as part of a course in Victorian fiction in which I show how psychological analysis of realistically drawn characters reveals them to be, in E. M. Forster's words, "creations inside a creation" who are "often engaged in treason against the main scheme of the book" (64). I explore the tendency of such characters to subvert two schemes in particular: the education pattern that we find in such novels as *Emma*, *Great Expectations*, and *The Mill on the Floss* and the vindication pattern that we find in such novels as *Mansfield Park*, *Henry Esmond*, and *Jane Eyre*.

In the education pattern, character flaws lead the protagonists to make mistakes that bring suffering to themselves and others, and the novel's plot and rhetoric strongly suggest that out of this suffering comes moral and emotional growth. In the vindication pattern, deserving protagonists are discriminated against or devalued by parental figures or the surrounding community, are given opportunities to prove their worth, and are the recipients, by the end, of widespread approval and an appropriate social position. Both patterns have tragic and comic forms, and some novels contain both education and vindication plots. In *Middlemarch*, for instance, Lydgate is educated while Dorothea is vindicated; in *The Mayor of Casterbridge*, Henchard is educated while Elizabeth-Jane is vindicated. Though *Jane Eyre* is predominantly a novel of vindication, it also presents Jane as undergoing a process of growth.

In all the novels I have mentioned, psychological analysis of the protagonists shows the supposedly educated characters to be less mature at the end and the vindicated characters less admirable all along than we are meant to believe. In novels of vindication, the protagonists are often mimetically portrayed as having deprived childhoods that force them to develop compulsive strategies of defense; but instead of being presented as destructive, these strategies are glorified by the novel's rhetoric and, in the comic version of the pattern, are validated by the plot. The world of the novel is manipulated to satisfy the protagonist's rigid and often conflicting psychological needs. In teaching *Jane Eyre*, I begin by considering the horrors of her childhood and the defenses they generate, and I then examine the glorification of her defenses by the rhetoric and their validation by the plot. Jane's psychological problems are portrayed in vivid detail, but the implied author collaborates with Jane so completely that her inner conflicts are obscured and her glorification seems justified.

A case can be made, I think, that of all the terrible childhoods in Victorian fiction, Jane's is one of the worst. Jane is as despised and rejected as Heathcliff, but she is even more isolated, since Heathcliff has Cathy, whereas Jane has no ally at all. Like Pip's sister in *Great Expectations*,

Mrs. Reed feels burdened by having to care for an orphan, takes out her resentment on the child, and then excuses herself by blaming her victim, whom she sees as irredeemably bad. Tormented by the Reed children as well as by their mother, Jane leads "a life of ceaseless reprimand and thankless fagging" (16–17; ch. 3). Like Pip, she is made to feel unsafe, unloved, and unworthy by a foster mother who wishes her dead; but her case is worse than Pip's, for she must live "without one bit of love or kindness" (31; ch. 4) for the first ten years of her life, whereas Pip has Joe for emotional support.

Jane tries to defend herself in two ways, by striving "to fulfill every duty" (12; ch. 2) and to "please" Mrs. Reed (28; ch. 4) and by escaping through her reading into imaginary worlds. The opening episode shows that neither of these strategies works. Mrs. Reed excludes Jane from the family partly because she does not have a "franker, more natural" manner (5; ch. 1), and John Reed flushes her out of the window seat, where she is happy with Thomas Bewick's volume on her knee, in order to harass her (8; ch. 1). No matter what she does, Jane can neither win acceptance nor escape abuse.

It is part of the vindication pattern for Jane to be surrounded by detractors who treat her unfairly and who will later be shown to have been wrong in their estimate of her; but when we study the mimetic portrait of Jane, we can see that her mistreatment at the hands of the Reeds has damaged her emotionally and that Mrs. Reed's description of her "as a compound of virulent passions, mean spirit, and dangerous duplicity" (14; ch. 2) is, in fact, accurate. Though Mrs. Reed fails to understand her own responsibility for Jane's traits, Jane *is* "a compound of virulent passions," as the opening chapters show, for she is full of rage and resentment. She has a "mean spirit" in the sense that she is too fearful to express her outrage directly and she passively accepts abuse. "What a miserable little poltroon had fear, engendered of unjust punishment, made of me in those days!" (26; ch. 4), the narrator exclaims. The charge of duplicity is also understandable. Despite Jane's attempt to be "useful and pleasant" (10; ch. 2) in order to avoid being sent away, she is too full of hostility to play this role successfully, and her pretense is transparent. She is a sullen, brooding, silently accusing child (John Reed calls her "Madame Mope" [7; ch. 1]) whose demeanor arouses defensiveness and anxiety (see Bernstein).

Mrs. Reed cannot comprehend "how for nine years [Jane] could be patient and quiescent under any treatment, and in the tenth break out all fire and violence" (210; ch. 21). The novel begins with a series of scenes in which Jane is subjected to more than she can bear, becomes beside herself with rage, and turns violently on her oppressors. Though compliance has never worked, she has clung to it out of a fear of total rejection, but when John Reed denies her access to books and causes her to fall and cut her head, Jane's pent-up fury erupts. Feeling that "a moment's mutiny" has already rendered her "liable to strange penalties," she resolves "like any other rebel slave," "to go all lengths" (9; ch. 2). Jane switches from compliance and detachment to aggression as her primary defense (see Horney, *Conflicts*, *Neurosis*, and Paris, *Psychological Approach*, *Third Force* for discussions of compliance, detachment, and aggression as defenses).

Despite the trauma of her experience in the Red Room, Jane finds that the consequences of her rebellion are predominantly positive. Her hysterical behavior brings about the intervention of Mr. Lloyd, the apothecary, and arouses Bessie's sympathy for the first time. She is sent away from Gateshead, as she had feared, but to school, where she has a chance to prove herself, rather than to the poorhouse, as threatened. She rids herself of John Reed by fighting back as soon as he attacks, and she experiences an enormous sense of triumph when she puts Mrs. Reed on the defensive with her verbal assaults. Whereas Jane's compliance has failed, her aggressiveness works; the lesson she has learned is reinforced when Bessie praises her newfound boldness and warns her that if she dreads people, they will dislike her (34; ch. 4).

Jane's experience at Gateshead establishes the agenda for her vindication, not only in terms of plot and rhetoric but also psychologically (see Butery, "Flight," for a complementary analysis of Jane's psychology). Jane needs to prove that she is not mean-spirited and duplicitous; hence her boldness, her bluntness, and her repeated declarations that she is not afraid. She must show, too, that she is not bad, worthless, inferior to people like the Reeds; hence her need to be good at all costs, her boasts about all the recognition she receives, and her satisfaction in her social and economic advancement. Jane is extremely sensitive about her plainness (Abbot says that "one really cannot care for such a little toad" [21; ch. 3]); hence her critical or condescending attitude toward beauties like Blanche Ingram and Rosamond Oliver and her sense of triumph that Rochester and St. John prefer her to them because of her moral and intellectual superiority. The world of the novel is so arranged that after Jane leaves Gateshead, her feelings of personal, social, and economic inferiority, of friendlessness, isolation, and undesirability, and of weakness, vulnerability, and cowardliness are all reversed. Her value is attested by her intellectual and artistic accomplishments; the friendship of admirable people like Helen Burns, Miss Temple, and the Rivers sisters; the fondness of her pupils; the venerating love of Rochester, who can find no other woman to suit him; and St. John's appreciation of her sterling qualities. She proves herself fearless, truthful, and good in every situation, and her poverty, low status, lack of family, and frustration in love are all removed by manipulations of the plot.

I have taught *Jane Eyre* as a novel of vindication for many years, but in teaching it once more before writing this essay, I have come to see that there is also an education pattern in Jane's story. Jane gets her due not just because, according to the rhetoric, she is good, though unappreciated, from the beginning but also because she triumphs over her own passionate character, resists powerful temptations, and succeeds in living up to a lofty moral ideal.

The explosions of rage with which the novel begins give Jane an exhilarat-ing "sense of freedom, of triumph" (31; ch. 4), but they also fill her with anxiety and self-hate. After Jane tells Mrs. Reed that her mother, father, and uncle know "how you wish me dead," Bessie says that she is "the most wicked and abandoned child ever reared under a roof," and Jane half-believes her, for she has "only bad feelings surging in [her] breast" (23; ch. 4). When Jane attacks her aunt again after Brocklehurst's visit, the taste of ven-geance is at first like "aromatic wine," but the "after-flavour" gives her the "sensation" of having been "poisoned." Feeling her "indignation" to be "fiendish" (32; ch. 4), she leaves Gateshead with "a sense of outlawry and almost of reprobation" (200; ch. 21). Jane cannot behave aggressively with-out being tormented by self-condemnation.

At Lowood, Jane is indignant on behalf of Helen Burns, another aban-doned, abused child. Helen, however, rejects the lesson Jane has learned at Gateshead — that we should be good to decent people but "strike back again very hard" at the bad ones — calling this doctrine heathen and un-civilized. She advocates, instead, the imitation of Christ: "Love your enemies; bless them that curse you; do good to them that hate you and despitefully use you" (50; ch. 6). Jane cannot immediately adopt Helen's extreme com-pliance; but when she fully and freely forgives Mrs. Reed, who is unrelenting even on her deathbed, she proves to herself that she has spiritually matured (210–11; ch. 21). As narrator, she assumes a Christlike attitude: "Yes, Mrs. Reed, to you I owe some fearful pangs of mental suffering. But I ought to forgive you, for you knew not what you did" (16; ch. 3). Helen shows Jane how she *ought* to deal with her resentment, and Jane incorporates Helen's dictates into her idealized conception of herself, to which she forces herself to conform.

The author collaborates with Jane not only in bringing about her vindi-cation but also in making it possible for her to meet the seemingly impossible demands that she places on herself. If Jane were to continue to experience her anger, she would fail to live up to the teachings of Christ and would feel like a heathen, uncivilized outlaw. But what is she to do with her aggres-sion? Part of it is channeled into the feistiness that Bessie has encouraged and that so charms Rochester, but most of it is acted out for her by others, enabling her to satisfy her vindictive and rebellious impulses without losing her nobility. Jane's enemies are all brought down by the author, some rather horribly, making it easier for her to forgive them; and an alter ego is pro-vided in Rochester, "a bold, vindictive, and haughty gentleman" (136; ch. 16), whose fierceness, mysterious sufferings, and volcanic passions reflect the side of Jane that she cannot express and that the rhetoric denies.

Like Jane, Rochester is a victim of family and fate; but being an upper-class male, he can act out his resentment, and Jane can experience her own forbidden feelings through him. Rochester, a rebel against God and society, is troubled by conscience, while Jane is a conscientious woman with deeply repressed rebellious impulses. Jane and Rochester seem to complement each other perfectly, since the repressed side of each is dominant in the other. He looks to her for reformation, while she satisfies through him the bold, vindictive, and haughty side of her nature.

The match is not really perfect, of course, since Jane and Rochester have contradictory needs that reflect their own inner conflicts. Rochester wants a wild, free thing who is absolutely virtuous, while Jane wants a worldly adventurer who will not threaten her innocence. He is looking for a pure mistress, and she wants him to be a reformed sinner so that she can gratify her forbidden impulses through him retrospectively. Rochester, however, is planning to commit bigamy; once his intentions are revealed, Jane has no choice but to flee.

The event that seems to end Jane's chances for happiness actually contributes to both the education and the vindication patterns and prepares the way for a much more satisfactory resolution than if Rochester had been free to marry her. When Helen Burns chastises her for thinking "too much of the love of human beings" and urges her to live for the approval of her conscience, Jane says that she would "rather die" than live without love (60; ch. 8). When Rochester pleads with her to remain at Thornfield, Jane demonstrates her spiritual growth by forsaking love and risking death in the name of conscience. She also proves that Rochester was right to have regarded her as a "unique" person who was not "liable to take infection" from him (126; ch. 15). She shows once and for all that she does not have "a wicked heart" (28; ch. 4), as Brocklehurst had said, but that she is a supremely religious person. In the happy days of courtship, she had been in danger of losing sight of God for Rochester, "of whom [she] had made an idol" (241; ch. 24). In her flight from Thornfield, Jane lives only for God and the heavenly reward of virtue.

Unlike Helen Burns, however, Jane cannot really be satisfied without human love. She has a chance to live for religion alone by joining St. John as a missionary, but she longs for the affirmation of her desirability as a woman that only Rochester can give. Without the intervention of the author, Jane would have been paralyzed by her conflicting needs; but when Bertha is removed and Rochester's misfortunes make him humble and religious, Jane's needs for love and for righteousness can both be fulfilled.

Indeed, by the end of the novel all Jane's needs are met without her having had to outgrow her anxiety and defensiveness. When Miss Temple leaves Lowood, Jane's aggressive energies rise to the surface, and she longs to go forth into the world "to seek real knowledge of life amidst its perils" (74; ch. 10). But despite her appearance of boldness, Jane is afraid of exposing herself to reproach; she wants, "above all things," the result of her "endeavours to be respectable, proper, en règle" (77; ch. 10). Through Rochester she can vicariously experience life and its perils while keeping the real thing at a distance. She wants him *to have lived* an exciting life, to be a nearly extinct volcano whose occasional modest eruptions frighten inferior beings but involve no real danger to her. After Rochester proposes, Jane is apprehensive about being his wife. She feels inferior because of her lack of "fortune, beauty, [and] connections" (247; ch. 25). Although she likes to hear about his travels, she is not keen on accompanying him as a fine lady and strenuously resists his efforts to adorn her. Her conquest of Rochester at once compensates for and exacerbates her sense of inadequacy. She could not have been happy had they married at this point, even had Rochester been free.

When Jane marries Rochester, she is no longer poor, she has connections, and, since he is maimed and blind, her looks no longer matter. "[F]ine clothes and jewels" are "not worth a fillip" now (393; ch. 37). Jane won't have to be a fine lady or encounter life "amidst its perils." Rochester is as dependent on her as she is on him and just as content to lead a reclusive existence. Jane needs at once to be great and small, and her relation with Rochester satisfies both requirements. He is a "royal eagle, chained to a perch" and she is the "sparrow" who will "become [his] purveyor" (387; ch. 37). The relationship with Rochester that Jane so romanticizes is, in Horneyan terms, a mutual morbid dependency (see *Neurosis* 239–58) in which she has no existence of her own; but the ending of the novel is such a perfect wish-fulfillment fantasy that it obscures her psychological problems.

In teaching *Jane Eyre*, I emphasize the contrast between the rhetorical presentation of Jane as an inherently noble person who outgrows her desire for vengeance and lives up to the highest religious and moral ideals and the mimetic portrait of Jane as a severely damaged child who neither outgrows her difficulties nor seems to suffer their likely consequences. She tries to compensate for her lack of self-esteem by disproving the despised version of her identity to which she was constantly exposed at Gateshead and by actualizing the idealized version of herself that she derives from Helen and Rochester. Jane succeeds in her project through the magic of the plot, which has been tailored to her rigid and often contradictory needs. Before we examine the contrivances by which Jane's portrayal is obscured, my students tend to be under the spell of the rhetoric and to see Jane as both vindicated and educated. By the time we are finished, however, they find Jane's life with Rochester to be a narrow existence that serves her neurosis but leaves little room for self-fulfillment. They say that her exultation in being "absolutely bone of his bone and flesh of his flesh" (397; ch. 38) gives them "the creeps."

Jane Eyre and Family Systems Therapy

Jerome Bump

When we teach *Jane Eyre* in the context of literary history, we often stress the differences between the Victorian era and our own, especially the increase in the heterogeneity of readers (which makes the assumption of a common religion or even spirituality difficult); the decline of repression today, particularly in sexuality; and the gains made by feminism (which may make Jane seem too weak to be a protofeminist heroine). Indeed, if we approach the novel from the perspective of current varieties of feminism, Marxism, or social construction theory, we might argue that the essentialist conception of the family, which the Victorians seemed to take for granted, merely masks difference, inequality, and injustice.

Nevertheless, we have the option of emphasizing similarities between the Victorians and ourselves. Contemporary American fiction, for example, like Victorian fiction, seems obsessed with the dynamics of dysfunctional families. While many Americans pay less lip service to reverence for "home and family life" and are less likely to regard the family as the "cornerstone" of civilization (Wohl 9–10), families today also have conflicting values. Anthony Wohl, in his collection of essays, *The Victorian Family*, explores "some of the domestic roots" of the "contradictory forces, of self-confidence and inner doubts, of dogma and unbelief, of sexual repression and exploitation, of intimacy and alienation, of deference to authority and revolt" (14) that people in the nineteenth and the twentieth centuries have experienced. While today's culture may be characterized more, say, by sexual exploitation than by sexual repression, the basic theme of Victorian fiction remains dominant: "escape from the family" (Wohl 15). Hence, even from the point of view of literary history, we may feel free to identify with aspects of Jane's struggle.

In many varieties of psychological and reader-centered criticism we are invited to identify with Jane. In the 1950s, Lesser demonstrated that

> one can scarcely discuss many literary issues without making some use of psychology. In particular, it is difficult to disregard psychology in intensive analysis of individual works . . . without some knowledge or assumptions about what affects human beings more and what less. Thus the real issue which confronts students of literature today is not *whether* to use psychology but what *kind* of psychology to use.
>
> (296–97)

I describe, in this essay, how a new reader-centered psychological approach to literature, combined with awareness of sexism, classism, and racism, has made reading *Jane Eyre* a powerful, deeply relevant personal experience for me and many of my students. The most successful teaching method for me is to adapt some of the principles of group psychotherapy as it is practiced today. A popular approach now (Kerr), as we see in John Bradshaw's series on PBS (since published as books), is based on family systems theory. In the 1950s, general systems theory and human ecology revealed new aspects of individuals as members of social groups. The off-spring of these schools of thought, family systems theory (Foley 39–45; Kerr; Bradshaw, *Family* 27), identifies the interactions and feedback loops that connect the individuals in families. Though family therapy can trace its roots back to Harry Stack Sullivan and Alfred Adler (Christensen) and ulti-mately to Freud's treatment of young Hans, family systems theory is asso-ciated with Murray Bowen's work at the Menninger Clinic in the 1950s and apparently originated in 1954 when D. D. Jackson applied the term *family homeostasis* to the way families behave as units. The specific goal was to help families in which individuals suffer from schizophrenia, chemical de-pendence, or psychosomatic illness such as anorexia nervosa, but family sys-tems theory has been found to be applicable to many dysfunctional families.

Literature, the repository of thousands of years of stories and emotions about families, has been used in psychotherapy so often that the term *biblio-therapy* was coined for this form of art therapy (Bump, "Reader-Centered Criticism"; "Innovative Bibliotherapy"). Thus one would expect that litera-ture would be valuable in the exemplification and exploration of this new theory of family systems and that the field in turn can make a significant contribution to literary criticism and theory. Family psychologists have, in fact, written about literature—Jackson, for example, analyzed Albee's *Who's Afraid of Virginia Woolf* in detail (Watzlawick et al. 149–86), and Vincent D. Foley focused on Williams's *The Glass Menagerie* (40–41, 114, 158)—while literary critics have probed family systems theory and literature (Bump; Cohen; Mashberg; Morral).

In the classroom, I combine this approach with feminist psychology, often assigning Jean Baker Miller's *Toward a New Psychology of Women*, which examines domination-subordination, vulnerability, emotions, relationships, and cooperation in women's experience. The literary texts we read, along with Miller and Bradshaw, in my course Family in the Victorian Novel are primarily *Jane Eyre*, *Wuthering Heights*, *The Tenant of Wildfell Hall* (Anne Brontë), *Wide Sargasso Sea* (Rhys), and *The Mayor of Casterbridge*. In the second semester of my freshman course World Literature and Composition, we use *The Norton Anthology of Literature by Women*, edited by Sandra M. Gilbert and Susan Gubar, which includes *Jane Eyre*. As they respond to the texts, students are encouraged to develop their emotional literacy and awareness of roles they unconsciously adopted in their families of origin. By "emotional literacy" I mean the ability to identify and communicate emotion, as in "I felt [emotion] when I read [passage]." In my teaching I regard the class as a family and adopt the techniques some psychiatrists have identified in functional, as opposed to dysfunctional, families (Lewis and Looney; Bradshaw, *Family* 41–85).

For information about family systems theory, I introduce the videotapes of John Bradshaw and Terry Kellogg, along with Bradshaw's books on the family and on shame. To gain access to their feelings students write every day in their journals about the passages and characters, in the novels they are reading, that triggered the most significant emotions. I ask students to identify their emotions, to explain, if they can, why they responded as they did, and to consider especially the relevance of *Jane Eyre*, or another literary text, to their families and other memories. With their journals in hand, students meet in groups of four to six, either face to face or in a computer network, to examine their responses to the novel. The computerized discussion method (Bump, "Radical Changes") generates transcripts, from which I have taken the quotes in this essay to illustrate reader response. Initially, students are grouped according to their families of origin, as determined by the Moos and Moos Family Environment Scale, which measures family cohesion, expressiveness, conflict, independence, organization, and control. Later they are placed in alternative "family" groupings, often based on sex roles and Jungian personality types (determined by the Keirsey version of the Myers-Briggs personality inventory).

Before the students work in small groups, however, the class as a whole usually meets several times. Here I often model the kind of reading process I am encouraging, by explaining my emotional responses to various passages and the relevance these have to my family memories. In the beginning of the book, for example, I discuss my identification with Jane's sense of "physical inferiority" (5; ch. 1), especially her plainness compared with the blond Georgiana's beauty (12; ch. 2), and I focus on the result: because she is considered not pretty or handsome, she is not loved. Indeed, she is identified as an "interloper not of [their] race" (13; ch. 2). Richard J. Dunn adds a footnote translating "race" as "particular family," but for me Brontë's use of the word provides an opportunity to discuss racism. If we trace the change in the original meaning of *race* as the offspring of a common ancestor to the word's modern sense of a basic division of humanity based on similar physical characteristics, we can liken racism to enmity between closed family systems. We also see how judging and being judged by physical appearance, especially in mate selection, is related to racism, sexism, and classism. My memories, or Jane's, of being judged by looks sometimes trigger students' own memories. One man observed that Jane "felt a great deal of physical inadequacy that was easy for me to relate to." In this regard, Jane elicits responses from readers somewhat like those produced by Pecola, the heroine of Toni Morrison's *The Bluest Eye*. Students discuss how stereotyping on the basis of appearance leads to social injustice, and they may recall their personal experiences of unfairness. One said, "For me, *Jane Eyre* just brought up a lot of feelings of frustration and anger at the inequality and injustice in the novel, especially class inequality."

After class members discuss their emotional reactions, we explore some family dynamics in the novel, especially the way Jane's acquisition of shame in the Reed family affected her search for self-esteem. I present three stages of her development with which students can identify: family, school, and mate selection. First of all, we discuss the loss of what many addiction therapists call the "true self," the "real self," the inner child buried under all the dependency behaviors and all the false selves adopted because of family and other social pressures. There are, of course, many alternative models of multiple selves; transactional analysis, for instance, posits an adult ego state, a parent ego state, and a child ego state within each of us. Family systems theory focuses primarily on the child ego or, rather, child egos, for there are many within us: "Hypnotic age regression work clearly suggests that each of these developmental stages remains intact. There are an infant, a toddler, a pre-school and a school-age child in each of us, who feel and experience just as we did when we were children. There is an adolescent in us who feels and thinks just like we did in adolescence" (Bradshaw, *Family* 217). At these various stages most of us were not given all the nurturing and opportunities for emotional expression we needed. As a result of certain events, any one of these wounded child selves may surface in adults and make them act like dysfunctional children. Then we experience ourselves as shameful, as if we had a hole in our soul where our self-esteem should be.

In tracing how this process begins in Jane, we notice Mrs. Reed's possessiveness about her son, the son's eating disorder, and especially his sadism toward Jane (ch. 1) and animals (12; ch. 2). We then define the Reeds as a closed family system, identifying such basic rules of the system as racism, classism, and lying. We can easily see that Jane, like Heathcliff in *Wuthering Heights*, is an alien force threatening this system, which adjusts by assigning her two of its rigid roles. Jane is the scapegoat, and when she retreats to the nursery or to literature, she becomes the lost child (chs. 2–4). The scapegoat, or problem child, feeling excluded, tends to be defiant and is perceived as destructive, while the lost child is simply forgotten, left to her own devices, her own fantasy world; her family seems better off without her (Wegscheider 42–47).

According to family systems therapy, we must penetrate the layers of defense guarding this hurt and lonely inner child in order to "grieve the loss of our childhood self" (Bradshaw, *Family* 212). Reading *Jane Eyre* helps students become aware of the hurt inner child within each one of them. One man recalled, "I *really* related to the loss of true self in *Jane Eyre*, especially in the line '[W]here was the Jane Eyre of yesterday?' [260; ch. 26]. It was powerful for me. I keep wondering what ever happened to the [me] of yesterday. I miss being a child, being free, being happy." Even students who find no parallels between their families and the Reed family can identify with some aspect of Jane's school experience or her mate selection process. One student admitted, "I can identify with loss of true self as a child. I think that recently

I've started to realize that in my childhood there were a lot of things that I would have liked to forget. A lot of humiliations not so much in family relations as in school relations." One woman said, "I do relate to the lost self, but again it is not because of my family but rather my peers. No one asked me out in high school really."

Jane's love of literature, developed in her role as the lost child, also invites discussion, both of her modeling of reader response and of the therapeutic function of writing. This aspect of her character usually triggers recognition by some students — not all of them English majors: "I can recognize the lost child theory, because I read a lot when I was at home. Even now when I visit either my parents or my in-laws, I always make sure I have something to read or do where I can be alone"; "I can relate very much to Jane's role as the lost child. As a young man, I grew up alone, away from close communication with family members, hovering on the fringe of the action and decisions, never feeling a part or being a part, too stupid (so I thought) to count. I used to spend hours reading."

How this family system undermined Jane's self-esteem, beginning with the effect on her of deprivation of parental love, becomes the focus of our discussion. We consider her exclusion from the group surrounding their "mamma" (5; ch. 1) and the tension between her identification as "a strange child [the mother] could not love" (13; ch. 2) and Jane's belief that she could not live without love and kindness (24; ch. 4). Besides a sense of physical inferiority, we acknowledge that she is excluded by class and money. Constantly reminded, "[Y]ou are a dependent" (8; ch. 1), she is forced to become a servant to Bessie, herself a servant. Yet, like many victims, Jane becomes infected by this attitude, choosing not to seek out poor relations who might be kind to her: "I was not heroic enough to purchase liberty at the price of caste" (20; ch. 3).

A valuable feature of a family systems approach to the early chapters is that it acquaints students with, and gives them labels for, many forms of child abuse: not only child labor but also the isolation and terror of the Red Room, Jane's primal scene, which seems to drive her "mad" (9; ch. 2), as well as physical and verbal degradation by mother and son. The verbal attacks by Bessie, Brocklehurst, and others often take the form of religious abuse, as in Miss Abbot's comment "God will punish her: He might strike her dead" (10; ch. 2). By verifying some of this as mistreatment (33; ch. 4), Bessie helps Jane preserve her sanity. Similarly, merely identifying as abuse some of what happens to Jane can shed light, for some students, on events in their own childhood.

Most victims are not aware that they internalize their abuse. In *Jane Eyre*, however, the process is fairly evident. Students can easily discern how Jane's lowered self-esteem becomes self-perpetuating, especially in the Red Room, exchanges with Brocklehurst, and even with her surrogate mother, Bessie. For example, Bessie tells her she is "the most wicked and abandoned child ever reared," and Jane thinks, "I half believed her; for I felt indeed only bad feelings surging in my breast" (23; ch. 4). We perceive clearly how such negative beliefs and "mind talk" result in her habitual mood of self-doubt and her death wishes, including her desire to starve to death.

Of course, Jane's situation is that of the orphan in search of a family. Yet many students can relate to this typically Victorian plot by exploring the possibility that at some point they may have wished to belong to a "perfect" family that offered unconditional love; they may even be searching for such a family now, in life as well as in literature. Jane obviously seeks a loving father in Mr. Reed and finds consolation in the thought of him and her father and mother in heaven acknowledging her mistreatment. She finds a surrogate father in Mr. Lloyd, who, as an apothecary, is analogous to doctors today who intervene in cases of child abuse. From Jane's point of view, however, his brief first visit represents an abandonment, until, on his return, he suggests school as a way out of the dysfunctional family. Though that alternative also proves dangerous for Jane, an acknowledgment that education was an important outlet for me and many students is useful. Students are invited, during these discussions, to identify ways they have been seeking father figures and others who can help them with unfinished family business and to examine the role of school as escape in their lives.

Memories of searches for mother figures are usually triggered by the Bessie-Jane interchanges. Obviously, Bessie sometimes fulfills Jane's need for a surrogate mother. She embraces Jane and gives her motherly advice (33–34; ch. 4), with the result that Jane clings to Bessie's neck when she leaves the Reeds. Bessie is also a storyteller; like the Jane who speaks to us, she has a "remarkable knack of narrative" (24; ch. 4). Indeed, one of the most important gifts Bessie gives Jane is the song of the orphan child who found a loving parent in God (18; ch. 3). Though the song is infected with the death wish, the sense of a higher power who loves her for her own sake becomes a vital resource for Jane in her struggles with her dependence on Rochester.

Space does not permit discussion here of all the stages of Jane's development, but in the mate selection process we examine how sexism and Jane's fundamental need for a functional family contribute to her dependence. We focus on her discovery that she had made a god of Rochester and must achieve deeper personal spirituality in the usual Victorian pattern of conversion before she can replace such dependence with an equal, interdependent relationship. This struggle is foreshadowed in the early incident of her "cherishing a faded graven image," her doll (24; ch. 4). Later she will come to identify her love for Rochester as idolatry. Students may have had similar responses to people they love. One student said, "I have made a god out of a lot of the people I have dated, and that is what suffocated what I thought was a strong relationship." Such experiences encourage some students to relate to John Reed's accusation "you are a dependent" in terms of emotional rather than economic subjection.

Because many students are neither as religious as the Victorian reader was assumed to be, nor perhaps even sympathetic to Bradshaw's broad definition of spirituality, they usually understand the problem of "idolatry" better when it is identified as "codependence," or addiction to an individual. However, I try to retain a sense of the importance the Victorians placed on access to a higher power. Some students recognize this as a stage of personal empowerment and thus of functional behavior; they can benefit from the therapy models developed in treatment programs for addiction and enmeshment that are open to transpersonal psychology and personal spirituality, or to twelve-step groups modeled on Alcoholics Anonymous. Such programs are usually based not so much on the secular, "scientific" variation of family systems theory used in the treatment of schizophrenics (Kerr and Bowen) as on the more spiritual version summarized by Bradshaw and others who work with alcoholics and codependents (Bradshaw, *Family* 179–81, 226, 228–29, 234–36). Bradshaw labeled the third stage of recovery "spiritual awakening and empowerment" (225) because "to find our true self we have to transcend our ordinary ego consciousness" (230). One student affirmed, "Like Jane, I want to strive to be the kind of person that I think God wants me to be all the time," but another admitted, "You just hit on a topic that I am struggling with — God. I have this aversion to anything religious. I need to find a 'higher power' because I want to find one, not because my mother says it is the right (only) thing to do." Many students' concepts of God are indeed influenced by their images of their parents. One recalled that "I didn't turn to God; I couldn't because He was my parents' defense." Hence some students must explore their inability to distinguish between their parents and a higher power before they can relate to Jane's pattern of conversion.

Nevertheless, virtually all readers find some aspects of Jane's behavior healthy, especially her remarkable ability as a child to stand up to a cruel parent. When Mrs. Reed tells her children not to associate with Jane, Jane retaliates, "They are not fit to associate with me" (22; ch. 4). In a more important incident, Jane, accused of being a liar, defends herself by correctly identifying the lying with the Reed family, primarily Mrs. Reed, whom she describes honestly as her enemy rather than her friend. In other words, Jane makes the kind of statements many abused students wish they had made as children. Such courageous honesty in a family system devoted to lying is a "new way of talking" (34; ch. 4) that students admire. Jane also demonstrates another version of the "talking cure" — namely, that painful emotions can be relieved by telling a confidante about them, as when she tells Mr. Lloyd of her grief. Such incidents lead us to discussions of reading and writing as therapy; the novel itself is apparently therapy for the narrator, as she contacts and loves her own inner child, and potentially for the reader.

However, I have to agree with one woman who said, "Female students will probably have an easier time in relating to Jane because of the critical representation of the recurring male dominance in the book." For many readers, gender does seem to determine the degree of identification with the central character. To make the novel more relevant to male students, who rarely see themselves as victims of sexism, we discuss how Rochester's mate selection process illustrates the hold his family system had on him. With the help of O. Christene Moore's essay and Jean Rhys's *Wide Sargasso Sea*, which I also assign, we observe that he asserts his family's emphasis on money and deception in his selection of Bertha, Céline, and Blanche (see chs. 15, 24, and 27). For information about Rochester's family of origin, we look to Mrs. Fairfax's comments (ch. 13) as well as Rochester's (ch. 27).

According to Moore, Jane is trained by the Reeds, another family obsessed with money and deception, to be the complement to Rochester in this process. While Jane is not as impressed by externals as they are, she rejects the idea of living with her relatives, the Eyres, because, for her, poverty "was synonymous with degradation" (20; ch. 3). She is deceived about them, of course, but in this and many other incidents in the novel, especially those concerning Bertha's identity, she seems remarkably willing to be deceived. Hence, Jane acts out her family drama as Rochester acts out his (chs. 1–4, 10, 16, 21, and 27). We also note that Rochester idealizes Jane as he makes Bertha his scapegoat. As Moore points out, Bertha becomes the vehicle for his antilibidinal ego (chs. 26–27), enabling him to relive his family's betrayal and rejection. Meanwhile, Jane carries out his libidinal projections (chs. 13, 15, 22, 24–25), dramatizing his dependent, unrequited love. Seeing Jane as a younger version of himself (ch. 14), he lures her into a marriage just as tainted by treachery as was his marriage to Bertha. Rochester thus re-enacts the family crimes, with Jane playing Rochester and Rochester playing Bertha: just as his family and Bertha's deceived him about Bertha's madness, he keeps the family secret from Jane. One man responded, "I agree completely that if we don't become aware of our propensities in seeking a mate, we will be doomed to repeat the cycles."

Finally, we discuss how recovery comes only as the individual faces the inner conflict: Rochester, for example, is reborn by feeling his grief, his "ceaseless sorrow" over his loss of Jane (385; ch. 37), Thornfield Hall, and all it stands for. In this light, he too becomes an important role model for all students. One student wrote, "The inner conflict *must* be faced before recovery can begin. I think that now we can do this without becoming beggars or blind and maimed, but still we must be able to face the pain and work through it alone before any real, long-lasting progress can be made."

Of course, there are limitations to a family systems approach to this book. One student commented, "Though I felt as if I had a lot of emotional reaction to *Jane Eyre*, it didn't trigger any family memories for me." Another said, "For me, the use of feminist psychology was more helpful in *Jane Eyre* than was family systems, partially because Jane had no real family for much of the book." Even when family memories are evoked, some students, especially freshmen, want to continue their denial: they simply do not want to hear much about emotions or family dysfunction if it might be too personally relevant. Hence there is considerable minimizing, as students assert that they don't have to deal with their emotions because someone else's family situation is more dramatic. One freshman became aware of this tendency in himself: "I never went through anything like Jane did at Gateshead. You know, I seem to always say that—I never had as powerful an experience as so-and-so did—that bugs me." Moreover, when the novel does stir up feelings in readers, Jane herself does not often model healthy expressions of emotion to others. Students identify with her repression. One said, "I often hold back my feelings and don't show people my emotions, mainly because I'm scared or I don't think it's 'right,' and it upsets me to see someone else doing the same thing." Another responded, "I saw myself in her, being so inexpressive. While I got angry at Jane, I also got angry and ashamed at myself for being this way." Of course, like the acknowledgments of minimizing, these reactions themselves are therapeutic.

There are also problems with a feminist approach to the novel. In the light of modern ideals, not all students find Jane a protofeminist heroine. Unless a teacher makes the point very clear, students may fail to recognize how pioneering this novel was for its day. Students see Jane as a martyr or as too sexually repressed to be a model for students today. One acknowledged that "the very fact that she desires autonomy makes her a feminist advocate," but he couldn't call her a real feminist because "she eventually subjugates herself to Rochester and loses sight of her own identity"; another added that she too easily "forgets Rochester's deceit and manipulation."

For some of the same reasons, many students dislike the ending; as one put it, "Brontë spent an entire novel picturing Jane as the intellectual and moral equal of any woman or man (including the wealthy ones considered her 'betters'). I saw indictments of classism and sexism throughout the novel as well as advertisements for education as a liberating and equalizing force. Then Brontë succumbed to the status quo and maimed the hero and dropped an inheritance in the heroine's lap so they would be a couple acceptable to society." Hence one optional assignment is to allow students to revise the ending; they often rewrite the relationship between Jane and Rochester.

More important, this novel—despite its limitations—encourages students to revise themselves, to discover or create the selves they feel they were meant to be. One woman affirmed, "Jane is a good role model in that she is victimized but refuses to play the role of victim. Most of her low morale in the novel is attributed to external considerations—appearance, wealth, etc. She rarely feels worthless regarding *real* qualities—intelligence, kindness, character, etc. I see her esteem problems to be society-based. She is physically dependent at some stages of her life, but she is generally independent emotionally and certainly intellectually."

Rediscovering *Jane Eyre*
through Its Adaptations

Donna Marie Nudd

Less than four months after *Jane Eyre* was published, W. S. Williams wrote to Charlotte Brontë and told her that her novel was being produced in a minor theater in London. Brontë immediately expressed her concern that "all would be woefully exaggerated and painfully vulgarized by the actors and actresses." Brontë contemplated:

> What, I cannot help asking myself, would they make of Mr. Rochester? And the picture my fancy conjures up by way of reply is a somewhat humiliating one. What would they make of Jane Eyre? I see something very pert and very affected as an answer to that query. Still were it in my power, I should certainly make a point of being myself a witness of the exhibition.   (Shorter 394–95)

Brontë, of course, did not witness the exhibition, though her publisher kindly supplied her with a vivid description of *Jane Eyre* — The Melodrama. Brontë thanked him for revealing "a corner of [his] great world — [his] London." "You . . . have shown me a glimpse of what I might call loathsome, but which I prefer calling *strange*. Such, then, is a sample of what amuses the metropolitan populace!" (Shorter 396).

Since that first production, adaptations of *Jane Eyre* have proliferated. In fact, plays based on Brontë works or on the Brontë family were so popular at one point that "Wilella Waldorf" wrote a witty editorial calling for a National Society for the Suppression of Plays about the Brontës (Clipping file, NYPL). In researching *Jane Eyre* adaptations in particular, I found references to forty dramas, nine television versions, and nine movies (see the appendix below). The plays include melodramas, musicals, realistic dramas, narrative productions, and even a parody. The television versions range from one-hour specials to the five-episode BBC production; the films include silent, black-and-white movies as well as the famous film versions directed by Robert Stevenson in 1944 and Delbert Mann in 1970.

There can be no denying that many great works of world literature reach the public today through adaptation. In fact, it came as no surprise to me to learn, from an article in my local newspaper, that students no longer rely on Cliff notes to circumvent reading the classics but go to the video store and rent *Great Expectations, Little Women, The Grapes of Wrath, Native Son, Wuthering Heights,* and so on. Perhaps one way teachers of Brontë can combat this clandestine practice is to teach *Jane Eyre* in conjunction with adaptations. The object, of course, would be for students to gain an understanding and appreciation not only of Brontë's original work but of the ways her novel has been transformed by adapters for particular audiences in a specific time period.

I teach *Jane Eyre* in my Performance of Literature course to approximately twenty-five upper-level students majoring in communication at Florida State University. The students spend over one-third of the semester working with Brontë's novel and several of its adaptations. Students first read the book, participate in class discussions on *Jane Eyre*, and then watch and communally criticize the Stevenson film. Afterward the students are placed in groups and assigned a play version of *Jane Eyre*. They rehearse and later perform an eight-minute scene from one of the plays and write a comparison-and-contrast paper.

After the students have first read *Jane Eyre*, I begin my lecture with some of the basic tenets of reader-response criticism — especially the claim, by advocates of the theory, that readers actively participate in creating literary meaning (Tompkins). I introduce John Dewey's description of the role of the beholder of a work of art: "Without the act of recreation the object is not perceived as a work of art. The artist selected, simplified, clarified, abridged and condensed according to his interest. The beholder must go through these operations according to his point of view and interest" (54). The class then discusses the notion that all readers, literary critics, and adapters actively re-create *Jane Eyre* by selecting, simplifying, clarifying, abridging, and condensing according to their own interests. I provide students with a general overview of the ways that literary critics have re-created *Jane Eyre* from various perspectives: biographical, Christian, psychoanalytical, Marxist, New Critical, and feminist. At the end of the lecture, I present my view of Brontë's novel as primarily a feminist romance (Nudd, "*Jane Eyre*" 12–34). Their assignment, before the next class period, is to think about two quotations: Adrienne Rich's argument that "we believe in the erotic and intellectual sympathy of [Jane and Rochester's] marriage because it has been prepared by [Jane's] refusal to accept it under circumstances which were mythic, romantic or sexually oppressive" and a prominent contemporary romance writer's assertion that "*Jane Eyre* is one of the most passionate of romantic novels; it throbs with the sensuality of a woman's growing love for a man; there is the deep longing of the lonely heart in its every line" (Rich [1979 ed.] 105; Falk 25).

During the next class period I briefly explain why I consider the novel to be a feminist romance. On the one hand, Brontë rewrites the Cinderella myth and, by doing so, exposes some of the sexual politics of that familiar tale; on the other hand, while Brontë is redefining the nature of love, she endorses a traditional view of romance. After a class discussion on ways in which Brontë's tale parallels the Cinderella myth, the chalkboard is filled with students' views on whether *Jane Eyre* is (or is not) a revision of *Cinderella*.

I add to the chalkboard any points students have missed — my own insights as well as those of Charles Burkhart, Karen Rowe, Rachel Blau DuPlessis, and Adrienne Rich.

In introducing students to the film we will view for the next two class periods — the 1944 black-and-white rendering of *Jane Eyre*, starring Orson Welles and Joan Fontaine — I point out that three men wrote the adaptation: Robert Stevenson, Aldous Huxley, and John Houseman. While watching the movie, students consider how these filmmakers "selected, simplified, clarified, abridged, and condensed" Brontë's novel according to their own interests — more specifically, whether the filmmakers' gender might have affected their choices. After the students have seen the entire film, they reread, in class, one of several scenes from Brontë's novel: Jane and Rochester's first meeting on the moors, Jane's first interview with Rochester at Thornfield, the fire scene, the proposal scene, the engagement period, Jane's leave-taking, or the couple's reunion. My intention is for the students to have Brontë's narrative fresh in mind before we review the same incident in the Stevenson film. Although virtually any scene with Joan Fontaine and Orson Welles will serve to demonstrate the filmmakers' androcentric biases, my favorite is the horse scene.

We first discuss the ways Brontë's horse scene is both typically romantic and undeniably feminist. Rochester, we note, wears a "riding cloak, fur collared, and steel clasped" and has a "dark face, with stern features and a heavy brow" (99; ch. 12). Yet Brontë's romantic hero, far from being a beautiful young gentleman of fancy, is more a middle-aged grump; and his first action is to fall from the horse and swear (98; ch. 12). We explore Sandra M. Gilbert and Susan Gubar's view that Brontë uses the fairy-tale paradigm in this initial scene between Jane and Rochester to establish the couple as "spiritual equals" (*Madwoman* 352).

After our discussion, I replay the two-minute film clip of the horse scene. The students realize immediately that the filmmakers have emphasized the Gothic, romanticized images while censoring Brontë's radical notion of Jane and Rochester as "spiritual equals." Indeed, virtually every sound or image in the scene serves to underscore Rochester's power: the bell tolls an eerie warning, the horns blare as if announcing a king's arrival, the horse's hooves thunder. Moreover, we never actually *see* Rochester fall down; instead, a magnificent steed is reined up an instant before its hooves would have crushed the hapless governess. And then the wayward steed rises from the mist — a herald, as it were, of the caped figure, her savior, who shoots up from the dry ice like Thor from the thundering clouds. We note the differences between the novel's Rochester, who moves haltingly to the stile and sits through the initial conversation, and the film's hero, who looms over the diminutive Jane. The clip ends with Rochester easily mounting his horse and galloping into the night; whereas, in the novel, Rochester leans "with some stress" on Jane's shoulder, limps to his horse, and then springs to his saddle "grimacing grimly as he made the effort, for it wrenched his sprain" (101; ch. 12).

In the end, the students discover how systematically the filmmakers have edited out the adult Jane Eyre's feminism in this scene and chosen instead to highlight only the Gothic romance (Nudd, "*Jane Eyre*" 80–93; Higashi; Ellis and Kaplan). We then discuss other scenes in the film version and contrast them with our own views of Brontë's original. Once the students have become aware of the androcentric biases in the film, I point out that Stevenson's *Jane Eyre* was shown on Tallahassee's cable television no less than thirty-one times in 1990. Is it possible, I ask, that as many people in America saw Stevenson's *Jane Eyre* on Cinemax, Disney, and other movie channels as read Brontë's original that year? The students leave the class with the sobering realization that for millions of Americans, Stevenson's *Jane Eyre* is Brontë's *Jane Eyre*.

When we meet again, the students are given their next performance and paper assignments. I divide the students into six groups and ask each group to read one of three stage adaptations of *Jane Eyre* on reserve at the library—John Brougham's 1856 melodrama, Helen Jerome's 1937 realistic play, and a typescript of James Prideaux's 1980 musical parody of both Charlotte's and Emily Brontë's classics, called *Jane Heights*. The students assigned to the melodrama are encouraged to read at least one book on nineteenth-century British melodrama (E. Bentley, Booth, Cross, Davies, or Smith). The students working with the Jerome version are encouraged to read her article on her experience in bringing *Jane Eyre* to the stage ("Return"), to glance over her book *The Secret of Woman*, and to look at some of the changes she made in different published versions of her adaptation. Finally, the students who are working on Prideaux's parody are expected to read *Wuthering Heights*.

The students have two choices for their paper assignment. The first option is to take one character from Brontë's novel and compare the levels of characterization—physical, social, dispositional, psychological, and moral—with the counterpart in the stage adaptation (Long and HopKins 125). The second is to compare one scene from the novel with its equivalent in the stage adaptation. In both paper assignments, the students are encouraged to speculate as to *why* the adapter made the changes. Are the changes justified by being inherently more melodramatic? realistic? parodic? Are they based on the playwright's conception of the audience's expectations? Do the differences in the novel and the play reflect the idiosyncratic views of the playwright? Did the gender of the playwright affect adaptation choices? Does the adaptation reflect the playwright's particular time period?

The students, of course, research and write their papers outside of class. During class, each group chooses a scene from its stage adaptation and prepares to perform it. My teaching assistant and I work with different groups offering practical suggestions for improvement. During the rehearsal process, we encourage the students to create their characters as the individual play-wrights rendered them. The students come to realize that each stage adaptation offers particular challenges.

For example, the students tackling Brougham's work often have to struggle to memorize and deliver the highly elevated rhetoric in a truly melodramatic fashion. Consider this soliloquy of Jane's, which occurs in the play before Jane has met Rochester and after she has had a disagreeable episode with the Ingrams:

> Shame, shame upon their cruelty; the pride that blazed within me is quenched in the flood of my great disappointment. Is this the pleasant change which I had pictured? This is the hard sterile rock my distant hope had tinted over with the softest moonlight. Better, a thousand times better, my solitary cell once more, than be gibed and mocked at by the vulgar-wealthy; to have the badge of servitude engraved upon my very heart, and know that tyrant circumstance has placed me in a world all prison, where every human being is a watchful jailor, and where you must endure the unceasing lash of insolence, the certain punishment of the statuteless but unforgiven crime, poverty.
>
> (13)

Through performance, students come to appreciate, as Robertson Davies once claimed, that heroes and heroines of melodramas "are splendid speakers, positive Roman candles of simile and metaphor" (51). They also realize that the "humble nineteenth-century playgoer went to the theatre to hear people like himself talking not as he talked but rather as he would like to talk if it lay within his power" (14).

When we reassemble to watch the final performances from the melodrama, the realistic play, and the musical parody, the students have the unique opportunity to see various ways that Brontë's novel has been interpreted by three very different playwrights. Moreover, the students' performances carry us full circle back to a discussion of the novel.

After viewing the scene from Brougham, for instance, we discuss what characteristics of Brontë's novel are particularly melodramatic. Students, of course, are quick to point out the villainous Reed family, who get their comeuppance; the theatrical interruption of the wedding scene; the numerous scenes of recognition; and Brontë's heavy reliance on fortuitous circumstances and coincidence. I present other aspects of Victorian melodrama inherent in *Jane Eyre*. For example, Peter Brooks's claim that melodrama is "the dramaturgy of virtue misprized and eventually recognized" leads into an exploration of the ways in which so many characters in the novel—the Reeds, Brocklehurst, and the Ingrams—fail to recognize, in the poor, obscure, plain little Jane Eyre, her intelligence, passion, wit, and soul (27). We also discuss the histrionic, melodramatic acting style, and I read aloud a prime example from the novel — Brontë's description of Rochester's response when he learns that Richard Mason is waiting to see him (179; ch. 19). Michael Booth's observation that characters in melodrama "are true to their surface appearances and always think and behave in the way these appearances dictate" encourages students to notice that Brontë's physical descriptions of characters like Blanche Ingram (ch. 17) and Richard Mason (ch. 18) are perfectly in keeping with their personalities (Booth, *English Melodrama* 14; Roberts 140–43). And finally, explaining that one of Brontë's admirers, George Henry Lewes, criticized *Jane Eyre* for having "too much melodrama and improbability," I read aloud her response to Lewes's comment (qtd. in Linder 3; Dunn [1987 ed.] 437–38; Gaskell 335–36).

Our discussions following the students' performances from Jerome's realistic play are usually closely tied to the scenes we saw in class. In one memorable student performance, the adult Jane Eyre, in the drawing room with Rochester, recounts and acts out in vivid detail her experiences with Brocklehurst at Lowood (Jerome [1937 ed.] 45–52). We interpret Jerome's scene as a twentieth-century commentary on repressed Victorian sexuality. Students observe, for example, that although there is no evidence in the novel that Brocklehurst wet his lips constantly or fingered the orphans' hair lasciviously, such gestures are strongly implied in the adaptation. Jerome's script clearly suggests that Brocklehurst denounced the lusts of the flesh while secretly driven by them. Moreover, the students notice that in the dramatic rendition, Rochester converses seriously with Jane while continually fighting off his physical attraction to her. In class, we discuss the scene's psychological complexity, recognizing that Jerome could not have written this scene without some knowledge of Freud.

Students who have performed and written papers on Prideaux's musical parody are eager to share their insights on other scenes not performed in class. For example, we often talk about the ways Prideaux illuminates certain characteristics of Brontë's writing in his portrayal of the protagonist. After discussing the ways in which Prideaux successfully parodies Jane's outspokenness, the formality of her dialogue, her vehement social consciousness, her "blindness" to the mysterious happenings at Thornfield, and her chauvinistic attitudes, we conclude that Prideaux had a great deal of affection for the subject of his satire.

To my mind, it is a good thing that Wilella Waldorf's National Society for the Suppression of Plays about the Brontës never came into being, for *Jane Eyre* continues to be adapted. Indeed, I was delighted to discover in the *Brontë Newsletter* that Fay Weldon's *Jane Eyre* adaptation — in which Charlotte, Branwell, Emily, and Anne "watch the action from the sidelines and also take on minor roles" — was produced in 1988 in Leeds (Barker 2). My experience in teaching Brontë's novel in conjunction with adaptations suggests that students not only gain a sense of "what amuses the metropolitan populace" but also come to a profound understanding of the ways an adapter's interpretation is influenced by a number of factors, including the adapter's gender, race, nationality, politics, knowledge of the medium, and, of course, the particular period in which the adapter wrote. In an age when so many celebrated works of world literature reach the public through adaptation, it seems of utmost importance for students to develop a healthy skepticism as well as a genuine appreciation for this technique—and its art.

Appendix: Selected Stage, Television, and Film Adaptations

All the adaptations listed here were produced in Britain, Canada, or the United States. This annotated compilation focuses on full-length stage plays of *Jane Eyre* as well as the television and film adaptations that can be rented or purchased. The stage adaptations are divided into two sections. The first section lists plays that are available in university libraries or through interlibrary loan. The second section includes manuscripts or typescripts that I found intriguing; these unpublished adaptations are housed in special theater collections or are available through the courtesy of the adapters or their agents. For additional citations of unpublished stage adaptations of *Jane Eyre*, television and film versions that are not easily accessible, and information on nineteenth-century plagiarized stage scripts, see my "Bibliography of Film, Television and Stage Adaptations of Charlotte Brontë's *Jane Eyre*."

Published Stage Adaptations

Birch-Pfeiffer, Charlotte, adapter. *Jane Eyre; or, The Orphan of Lowood*. New York: Fourteenth Street Theatre, 1870. Birch-Pfeiffer's melodrama, in which the mad woman in the attic turns out to be Rochester's sister-in-law, was the most popular stage adaptation of the nineteenth century.

Brougham, John, adapter. *Jane Eyre*. New York: French, 1856. Typical of nineteenth-century melodrama, Brougham's play alternates between scenes of desperate emotion and comic relief.

Carleton, Marjorie, adapter. *Jane Eyre*. Boston: Baker's, 1936. Carleton's adaptation is the least episodic of the realistic plays, as she casts many characters in her Thornfield scenes.

Cox, Constance, adapter. *Jane Eyre*. London: Miller, 1959. In this realistic play detailing Jane and Rochester's relationship, Rochester most admires Jane for her honesty, candor, and truth, while Jane realizes that though Rochester can be harsh, he is never unjust or unkind.

Jerome, Helen, adapter. *Jane Eyre*. Garden City: Doubleday, 1937; London: French, 1938; New York: French, 1943, 1961. Played by Katharine Hepburn in a United States touring production, Jerome's Jane Eyre has greater depth than her counterparts in most mid-twentieth-century plays. Jerome describes Rochester's character as "the first genuine caveman of literature" whose "sudden unexpected flashes of tenderness" make him approach "the hidden ideal in most women" (xiii [1937 ed.]).

Kendall, Jane [Anne Martens], adapter. *Jane Eyre*. Chicago: Dramatic, 1945.
Kendall's uninspired realistic play takes place, like so many others, entirely
at Thornfield. Jane, who starts out as a rather strong individual, turns into
a stereotypical romantic heroine.

Phelps, Pauline, adapter. *Jane Eyre*. Sioux City: Wetmore Declamation Bureau,
1941. Phelps's play is the most consistently sexist of the realistic adaptations.
In it, Bertha—not Rochester—turns out to be the bigamist.

Unpublished Stage Adaptations

Birkett, Phyllis, adapter. *Jane Eyre*. Ms. 1929, box 52. British Library. Licensed
by the Lord Chamberlain's Office, 1929. Birkett's play was originally sub-
titled "The Mystery of the Locked Room." The most fascinating aspect of the
script is the complex portrayal of Bertha Mason.

Coe, Peter, adapter. *Jane Eyre*. Rev. ts. Courtesy of Chichester Festival Theatre.
Produced in Chichester, England, 1986. Violating the novel's chronological
order, Coe's cinematic play moves freely from present tense to flashback scenes
from Jane's childhood. The montage structure is exciting and the juxtapositions enlightening.

Hartford, Huntington, adapter. *Jane Eyre*. Ts. Performing Arts Research Center,
New York Public Library, 1956. At the time, Hartford's adaptation was the
most expensive production of a realistic play ever staged in New York City.
The androcentric play centers more on Rochester than on Jane.

Haughey, Sheila, adapter. *Jane Eyre*. Ts. Courtesy of Harvest Arts Group, Chelten-
ham, England. Produced 1985. Disenchanted by the other adaptations,
Haughey and her church group produced a version that emphasizes "the novel's
decidedly Christian outlook."

Leffingwell, Miron, adapter. *Jane Eyre*. Morton Collection. Ts. 316. Univ. of
Chicago, 1909. This turn-of-the-century melodrama includes a "seduction
scene" in the first act, in which an adult Jane fights off John Reed's attempts
to make her his mistress. In the last act, a detective snaps handcuffs on Brocklehurst and carts him away for a conversion of funds belonging to Lowood
school.

Marten, Annette, adapter and dir. *Jane Eyre*. Ts. Courtesy of the adapter. Eastern
Michigan Univ. Theatre. Produced in Ypsilanti, 1989. A three-and-a-half-
hour narrative production that dramatizes Jane's passionate story of rebellion, revolt, and quest for self-fulfillment.

Prideaux, James, adapter. *Jane Heights*. Music by Arthur B. Rubinstein. Lyrics by
James Prideaux. Ts. Courtesy of William Morris Agency, Beverly Hills, Calif.
Produced in Los Angeles, 1980. Prideaux has written a delightful musical
parody of *Jane Eyre* and *Wuthering Heights*. Rochester's Byronic nature,
Catherine's resurrection, the Brontë sisters' symbolism are just some of the
aspects of the novels that Prideaux successfully satirizes.

Shaper, Hal, and Roy Harley Lewis, adapters. *Jane Eyre*. Music by Monty Stevens.
Lyrics by Hal Shaper. Ts. Courtesy of Confederation Centre of the Arts,
Charlottetown, Prince Edward Island, Canada. Produced in London, 1966,

and in Canada, 1970–71. The characters in Rochester's household continually sing of love, marriage, and sex in this elaborately produced musical. Rochester's character is the most fully and comically developed, while the audience comes to know many of the minor characters as superficially as they know the governess.

Weldon, Fay, adapter. *Jane Eyre*. Ts. Brontë Parsonage, Haworth, England, 1988. Weldon juxtaposes scenes to highlight the ways Jane's childhood experiences resonate in her adult life. Charlotte, Emily, Anne, and Branwell also narrate, occasionally perform in, comment on, and bridge scenes in Weldon's evocative adaptation.

Wills, W. G., adapter. *Jane Eyre*. Ms. 53285E. British Library. Licensed by the Lord Chamberlain's Office, 1882. In Wills's adaptation, Rochester's villainous side is shown, in contrast to other Victorian melodramas that tend to whitewash Rochester's character and intensify the depravity of the Reeds, the Ingrams, Richard Mason, or Brocklehurst.

Yordon, Judy, adapter and dir. *Jane Eyre*. Ts. Courtesy of the adapter. Ball State Univ. Theatre. Produced in Muncie, Indiana, 1989. In this occasionally melodramatic adaptation, there are three Janes: Jane in the Present tells her story, Jane in the Past relives it, while Jane the Dancer symbolizes Jane's passionate inner life.

Television and Film Adaptations

Baron, Alexander, adapter. *Jane Eyre*. Dir. Julian Aymes. With Zelah Clarke and Timothy Dalton. BBC, 1983. CBS Fox video, 1985. Color. The popularity of this four-hour BBC production stems, in part, from the fact that the adapter, director, and performers had the time to develop the complex characterizations of the novel.

Cavanaugh, James P., adapter. *Jane Eyre*. Prod. Worthington Miner. Dir. Paul Nickell. With Katharine Bard and Kevin McCarthy. Westinghouse Studio One, CBS. 4 Aug. 1952. B/W. Limited sets and a small budget may explain why this one-hour television special comes across as a poorly taped theater production. The sweet, appreciative, nurturing Jane Eyre is everything you would expect a Westinghouse-sponsored 1950s heroine to be.

Pulman, Jack, adapter. *Jane Eyre*. Dir. Delbert Mann. Prod. Frederick H. Brogger. With George C. Scott and Susannah York. Released in England and the Continent as a feature film by British Lion, 1970. Shortened version shown on NBC, 24 Mar. 1971. 16 mm, color. In this androcentric work, the equality of Jane and Rochester's relationship comes not so much from the filmmakers' perceiving the strengths of Jane's character as from their recognizing Rochester's vulnerabilities.

Stevenson, Robert, Aldous Huxley, and John Houseman, adapters. *Jane Eyre*. Dir. Stevenson. Prod. William Goetz. With Orson Welles and Joan Fontaine. Twentieth Century–Fox, 1944. B/W. Stevenson's stark, Gothic depictions of Jane's years at Gateshead and Lowood are particularly poignant. Once we arrive at Thornfield, the story becomes Orson Welles's.

Taking a Walk; or, Setting Forth from Gateshead

Robert L. Patten

"There was no possibility of taking a walk that day" (5; ch. 1). Students who have not "taken a walk" on the first day of class come to *Jane Eyre* near the midpoint of the semester, having already studied *Emma*, *Vanity Fair*, and *Wuthering Heights*. Since the course is both an introduction to fiction and a survey of Victorian novels for undergraduates and graduates, we explore ways of interrogating these books. My aim is to enable students to read in many different ways (from biographical and New Critical to semiotic and cultural) and to discover how what matters to them can be amplified and articulated. Students are therefore required to keep journals in which they set down their thoughts about three Aristotelian categories: What is a beginning? Why is a particular location the midpoint? What kind of closure is effected at the end? The journals disclose to students their own synchronic and diachronic reading processes. Students discover their recurrent interests and the way their expectations alter in the course of going from beginning to end, reflecting, and comparing stories.

Out of these journals, and our one-on-one discussions about them, usually come the topics and approaches of the term papers. Class discussions, designed to complement and extend students' individual interpretations, are organized around as many kinds of questions about the novels as we can muster. I use this method not to achieve a "school solution" or a composite reading, but to increase the students' awareness of the complexity of the evidence and the multiple ways in which texts signify — both within themselves and with respect to their cultural moment, literary context, and verbal matrix. With *Jane Eyre* we concentrate on the *journey* as paradigm for the discovery and constitution of self by the narrated subject, the narrator, the editor (Currer Bell), the author, the text, and the reader.

The first question concerns the opening. How can a novel begin with "no possibility"? Why is *not* being able to take a walk worthy of remark? One set of considerations involves the confluence of genre, narrative, and setting. When we reflect on the bildungsroman's modifications of the picaresque, we notice that the eighteenth-century picaro's journey through society modulates into the nineteenth-century protagonist's more internalized journey toward selfhood. Thus while Victorian fictional settings retain social and aesthetic significance, they also generate and are generated out of psychological and interpretive crises. The first sentence may imply that *Jane Eyre* is a novel about places, spaces, and the possibility of moving toward, away from, and within them physically or mentally. That notion of journey can be compared with the "progress" of previous heroines: Emma's restricted physical motion but fundamental reeducation (learning the language of her own head and heart); Becky's and Amelia's European peregrinations, which signify little moral or spiritual improvement; and all the conflicts between confinement and freedom at Wuthering Heights and Thrushcross Grange. Does the trope of a journey suggest some sort of growth? Does it imply growth differently for male and for female characters? Are men given freedom to roam while women are told to stay home? Jane's first declaration might be prelude to a bildungsroman about blocked motion (psychic, moral, and spiritual as well as physical), it might lead into a story about overcoming impediments, or it could prepare for an unresolvable tension between an uncongenial outside and a comforting but denied inside (to reverse some of the polarities of Emily Brontë's myth). In short, the first sentence declares that this story has at stake some kind of walk — impossible, enforced, deliberate, inadvertent — and suggests that the origin, quality, direction, and accomplishment of that ambulation by character, narrator, and reader will figure a story about Jane's development.

These budding issues flower as the novel continues. Our five classes are themselves journeys to the five principal settings: Gateshead, Lowood, Thornfield, Marsh End or Moor House, and Ferndean. What does each place incarnate? What is Jane's relation to each, and how does that connection change? What impels her to and away from each home? We discern in embryo at the beginning a pattern of exile and return that organizes Jane's quest for identity and place; her exposition of ontological, epistemological, and gender "truths"; and the very narrative strategies of her account.

We then look further at the consequences of not being able to walk. Jane doesn't seem to belong anywhere: she is exiled from the hearth by the family and from the landscape by a constitutional frailty and the rawness of the elements. Culture and nature seem equally to deny her a place; so she makes one for herself, between inside and outside, between the white mist obscuring nature on the other side of the breakfast room windows and the red curtain that screens her from society. She even seats herself "cross-legged like a Turk" (5; ch. 1) in another defiant gesture against the gender and cultural inscriptions the Reeds attempt to impose. Is this, then, the alternative to taking a walk, to make a "bubble" space, neither interior nor exterior, that Jane as Turk can then populate by taking the words and images in Thomas Bewick's *History of British Birds* and projecting them imaginatively into her own cosmos?

Jane is "profoundly" interested in migratory British birds and their solitary "haunts" in "forlorn regions of dreary space." Or, rather, in a more precisely faithful reading of the text's information, she engages in imagining, from letterpress and picture, about those "strangely impressive" and terrifying places. She interprets those images by bringing to bear a hermeneutic that is uncannily prescient as well as romantically Gothic. Her affiliations connect the shadowy notions she infers from these pictures to supernatural manifestations of "marine phantoms" and fiends (6; ch. 1). Is the deadliness of these images to be understood psychologically as a projection of her loneliness or guilt, or as a sign of her crippled imagination (she hungers equally for Bessie's tales of "love and adventure" [7; ch. 1])? Or does she here commit an act of metaphysical hubris, canceling the world as it is to fashion one responsive to her fantasies? There is nothing conventionally Edenic about "death-white realms" (6; ch. 1) and sinking wrecks, yet roaming this terrain like Frankenstein's monster in search of a mate entails a freedom to move, imagine, and create that may be imbricated in Jane's subsequent homes. Thus not taking a walk enables Jane to embark on other trips.

With her "undeveloped understanding" and "imperfect feelings" Jane finds it hard to gain more than a "shadowy" notion of these "mysterious" story-telling pictures (6; ch. 1). This narratorial observation raises other problems that students are often eager to address: it might imply that in this novel there is a "right" reading of stories, of one's relation to society and nature, that depends on developed understanding and perfected feeling. If so, is that "right" reading embedded in the narrative, in the first-person narrator, in the authority of Currer Bell, who "edited" this autobiography, in Charlotte Brontë, whose life is partly rewritten as Jane's, or in the reader before or after experiencing this story? For Jane and her narrative, clearly, "reading" pictures and text, and traveling, are figures for each other.

The Reed children break into Jane's constructed physical and mental nest. Eliza tells where Jane is hiding, while John makes grotesque faces at her and beats her. The different actions may signal the mode of aggression each gender practices throughout the novel — girls tell tales, boys enforce their rule through physical means. The Reeds violate Jane's sanctuary and reassert an imperial order in which they are superior, Jane dependent, "less than a servant," an "uncongenial alien" of a different "race" though a cousin, a "rat," a "mad cat," and a "noxious thing" (8-13; chs. 1-2). (The epithets prepare for Bertha Mason and Jane's affinity with violent bestial rebels of both sexes.) Inexorably through the opening chapter, Jane's place and identity are both erased and asserted; her strategy of dissimulated passivity is challenged, exposed as aggressive, and redirected against herself and against others. Why, students ask, does this happen? Is Jane so treated because of the peculiar pathology of the Reed offspring? Is their treatment of her sanctioned by more substantial authority, by Mrs. Reed because of her neuroses, by deceased regulators such as her husband or Jane's parents, by a patriarchal society that constructs (or in this case seems to deconstruct) Jane's identity as person, gendered subject, economic unit, and human potential? Jane's subjection appears to be enforced by even more remote patriarchal powers, "the Roman emperors" (8; ch. 1) and spiritual forces that intervene from time to time to admonish. It could be that Jane, who after all is justifying her existence, really is a violent, "repulsive" child who must learn to discipline her passion (14; ch. 2). Tyranny might even be validated on the grounds that Jane is a little "rebel slave" (9; ch. 2), declaring herself in opposition to the unwelcome restraints of culture and nature.

Sent to the Red Room, Jane shores up her psychic defenses against a notion of supernatural justice (Mr. Reed's return) that, however "consolatory in theory," "would be terrible if realised" (13; ch. 2). Jane involuntarily travels from her exile in the margin of the breakfast room (itself a peripheral space between the kitchens and nursery occupied by servants and the public spaces inhabited by the family) to incarceration in a bedroom that is a secretive female place in which Mrs. Reed keeps parchments and jewel case and the material relict ("miniature") of her husband's body and spirit (11; ch. 2). Terrified that this uncongenial, unchosen site will be reanimated, penetrated by some male "vision from another world" (14; ch. 2), Jane faints. At a simple but essential level, such a collapse is entirely plausible. Need we say anything more about it? Is her loss of consciousness an indication that taking away her mental space enciphers her, stops imagination and the production of any meaning for her? (She does not remember the prefigurative vision of Rochester as the ghost of Mr. Reed with a "great black dog behind him" [16; ch. 3] that evidently she narrates to Bessie as she recovers consciousness.) Has she been figuratively raped? And if so, does she put on the rapist's knowledge with his power, as Yeats asks of Leda's violation by patriarchal power?

At this point, we might take up some of the ways in which the novel structures apparently antithetical polarities: reason versus passion, white versus red, outside versus inside, male versus female, nature versus culture, spirit versus flesh (or letter), future versus past. We notice that the Red Room is furnished with contrasting colors, red-curtained bed with snowy counterpane standing like a tabernacle, and white "cushioned easy-chair" looking "like a pale throne" (11; ch. 2). Does this imagery initiate an association between passion and religion versus reason and earthly dominion, or will the novel progressively undercut and problematize binaries, so that religion is also associated with white and reason (e.g., Maria Temple), temporal domination with lust and blood? Should we read Jane's faint as a sign that irreconcilable opposites not of her own devising and control enforce insupportable tensions? Is the room's psychic power a projection of Jane's ire, or Mrs. Reed's, or a ghost's — like Hamlet's father, back from the dead to demand justice for his neglected child?

When Jane awakens from her second fit, the kindly apothecary Mr. Lloyd tries to determine her condition by asking her, "Well, who am I?" (15; ch. 3). Ascertaining the patient's state of awareness is still one of the first things to be done when someone is emerging into consciousness. Should we think anything more about Mr. Lloyd's question than that it is a mimetic incident in a tale purporting to be about "real" people and situations? What authorizes us to interpret further? It may be significant that Mr. Lloyd asks Jane not to indicate *where she* is or *who she* is, but *who he* is. His diagnostic implicitly registers the truth that Jane's competency depends on her recognizing not her own place but the place of others, especially males.

How has this interrelated set of experiences, from not taking a walk to recovering after the Red Room, been the opening of a novel about Jane Eyre, evidently narrated by a surviving, remembering, and reconstructing Jane? Why should the beginning of her life, and the novel as a product and projection of that life, start when she is ten? Such a late beginning would seem to foreclose the possibility of showing what psychologists conceive to be the formative stages of identity, transpiring much earlier. Maybe this passage opens the narrative because it constitutes Jane's first, most consequential insurrection, "a new thing for me" (9; ch. 2). Perhaps she founds her autobiography on this incident because it marks the dead end of one set of oppositions, an irremediable vice of conflicting forces that compress her into nullity. Then might not taking a walk—the blocked emotion, repeated and elaborated in everything that occurs subsequently during this initial event—be the necessary spur to some sort of change?

The Gateshead chapters adumbrate a pattern of enforced stasis and rebellion, loss and victory, and exile and new beginning. Jane resolves to run away or die. Has she (or the "editor" or author) found a way of telling a story, writing an identity, by overturning the generic and narratorial paradigms of bildungsroman that seemed to conflate growth and progress with motion? *Pilgrim's Progress* is as governing a pre-text here as for *Vanity Fair*, yet Brontë's novel works against many of John Bunyan's assumptions and verities. Is the textual constitution of Jane's identity a secular inscription of a spiritual paradigm or a Satanic verse? And how are Gulliver's "desolate wander[ings]" (17; ch. 3) and Pamela's trials (7; ch. 1) alternatives for protagonist and novel?

Jane's childish efforts to control her temper occasion the adult charge that she is deceitful; both "ire" and "liar" are homophones of the patronym that it is one project of the novel to unpack. Others, as we see in later classes, identify her as a wanderer (*eyre* is a circuit—that is, itinerant—court), a judge ("justices in eyre"), one who seeks or is a nest (eyrie or aerie), and an heir. Counseled against falsehood by Brocklehurst, Jane, before she starts a long journey commencing "an entrance into a new life" (21; ch. 3), tells Mrs. Reed her truths: "*Speak* I must" (30; ch. 4). Just as Eliza did, Jane uses tale-telling to expose. Jane's opening vacillates between enforced silence, involuntary exclamations, overheard conversations, and her first deliberate articulation of her character and consanguinity vis-à-vis Mrs. Reed: "*You* are deceitful!" In other words, in this founding act of rebellion, Jane for the first time commands language and wins a double victory: her soul bursts an invisible bond into "unhoped-for liberty," and her audience is cowed into submission and supplication. "Is there anything else you wish for, Jane?" Mrs. Reed asks (31; ch. 4). That dual achievement may tell us something about Jane's autobiography: it is a discourse articulating her sense of things, and it is powerfully intimidating and self-serving. Coming to Jane's narrative after the unreliableness of Austen's *Emma*, and Lockwood and Nelly in *Wuthering Heights*, some students bring an initial suspicion of Jane's veracity; the majority, however, are compelled into sympathy by Jane's rhetoric.

Another point often raised in our first class: before Jane leaves Gateshead, she tells Mr. Lloyd what she had heard from her aunt about her "poor, low relations" (20; ch. 3). If we have not hitherto considered the customary strategies of biography, we might now. Whereas most "lives" start with the subject's birth and parentage, little concerning Jane's origins is given in her opening, already displaced in time ten years. As adult narrator she withholds such information about her ancestry as she then lacked. But the novel is also structured on a double pattern of recovery: at every stage of Jane's "forward" progress toward identity as person, economic unit, mate, and member of constructed as well as inherited familial and social groups, often just as she is losing much of her hard-fought gains she learns more about her past. Those two processes — constituting an identity in the present and recovering her heritage — both define and empower Jane in paradoxical ways. The novel never lets her gain a part of her family and legacy until in other terms she has made her own self. Were she to have come into her property and power in the opening chapter, for instance, as Emma in effect does, it would have been hard for Jane or Charlotte Brontë or the novel to keep *Jane Eyre* from conforming to the system against which it is the foundation of her text to revolt. The withholding of Jane's inheritance does as much to liberate her as it does to define her.

It may not be clear whether Jane arrives at paradise as well as Ferndean, but it is clear that she intends to forge, on her own terms, a place — in the world and in the text — in which she is not a thing or discord or animal, not a slave, not a subject constructed by others, not a gender subordinated by a patriarchy. Jane wants the results of constituting her self through retrospectively narrating her journey into being, and wants those results to be ratified by her readers. The problematics of that constituting are replicated in the manifold undecidabilities of the text. For not only Jane is forced to cope with the impossibility of taking a walk that originating day; so too is every reader who with Jane derives an understanding of the implication of journeying through life and story from that uncongenial opening at Gateshead.

A Kristevan Reading of the Marriage Plot in *Jane Eyre*

David Rosenwasser

In that curious scene in which Rochester, incognito as a Gypsy crone, tells the fortunes of the unmarried women assembled at his posh house party, he proceeds to question Jane about her observations of the guests:

> "But do you never single one from the rest — or it may be, two?"
> "I do frequently; when the gestures or looks of a pair seem telling a tale: it amuses me to watch them."
> "What tale do you like best to hear?"
> "Oh, I have not much choice! They generally run on the same theme — courtship; and promise to end in the same catastrophe — marriage."
> "And do you like that monotonous theme?"
> "Positively, I don't care about it: it is nothing to me."
>
> (174–75; ch. 19)

Jane's replies to the Gypsy's questions are vague and vaguely contradictory: not only does Jane formulate her observation of the social event as a "tale" but she claims to find this tale of courtship and marriage amusing, catastrophic, and unaffecting. Moreover, her own tale, which she at different times refers to as "never ended" and "half told" (95–96, 386; chs. 12, 37), in fact offers two extended courtships and ends with marriage and maternity.

In another sense, though, Jane's assertion that the story lacks an ending is accurate, for *Jane Eyre*, like other nineteenth-century fictional works, offers us remarkable women characters seeking a place within a society in which they "have not much choice." As students focus on the treatment of courtship and marriage, they find not a "monotonous theme" but a persistent ambiguity and ambivalence toward the marriage plot that can define an entire course in the nineteenth-century English novel.

This ambiguity is explicit in the Gypsy scene not only in Rochester's cross-dressing but also in his fortune-telling. He says to Jane, "Your fortune is yet doubtful: when I examined your face, one trait contradicted another" (176; ch. 19). St. John Rivers gives one version of this contradiction in conventional gendered terms: "[T]hough you have a man's vigorous brain," he tells Jane, "you have a woman's heart" (359; ch. 34). Jane's blend of the conventional male brain and the female heart renders her simultaneously attractive and threatening to her suitors, for it empowers her to assume equality with them.

This blurring of the heroine's gender is a common feature of nineteenth-century English novels that rely on the marriage plot. In many of these novels, figures of male authority are attracted to heroines who have a trait associated with men — an intelligence that is assertive, rational, and undeferential. In Austen's *Pride and Prejudice*, Mr. Bennet describes Elizabeth as having "something more of quickness than her sisters" (52), evident in her forceful rejection of Darcy's first proposal. Maggie in Eliot's *The Mill on the Floss* is introduced with her father's misgiving that she, instead of her brother, Tom, has "the right sort o' brains for a smart fellow" (59), brains that will torture her into rejecting Stephen Guest. And Jude in Hardy's *Jude the Obscure* professes his attraction to Sue's "curious unconsciousness of gender" (203).

In short, *Jane Eyre* and the other novels I have mentioned problematize the conceptualization of gender — for characters within the novels and for readers who interpret these narratives. Yet many — perhaps most — students miss or oversimplify this element. My desire to expand the range of the discussion has led me to explore the pedagogical possibilities of literary theory.

In the 1930s Louise M. Rosenblatt understood that "it is often hard for the student to realize in a vivid or personal way that the ideas and behaviors he accepts most unquestioningly derive their hold upon him from the fact that they have been unconsciously absorbed from the society about him" (253). In considering the marriage plot, evident in *Jane Eyre* and many other nineteenth-century novels, students tend to lack critical distance. They are happy when Jane wins Rochester's love, pity him when Bertha is revealed, and feel relieved when Jane and Rochester reunite in socially sanctioned matrimony at the novel's end.

While it is not surprising that students "unquestioningly" accept normative views of gender, I try to prevent such perceptions from blinding students to the complex treatment of gender in the works we read. My aim, then, is to allow students to see, in the novels, a debate about culturally determined, formulaic readings of romantic love, which their attitudes might prevent them from noticing or taking seriously. The conventional interpretation further resists change because it corroborates another culturally sanctioned conviction — that individuals can easily escape the effects of gender construction. Thus students want to read in novels such as *Jane Eyre* the celebration of the growth and ultimate victory of all that is "individual" in Jane and Rochester.

A possible first step in producing a more complex understanding of these works is, then, to complicate the ways that students think about the construction of gender. But the attempt to estrange students from their gut reactions to the marriage plot so that they can gain critical distance may seem to be an authoritarian silencing of their feelings as naive and wrong. This unwanted result is especially likely if students feel that they are competing with sophisticated professional assessments assigned as secondary reading.

One way out of this predicament is to share with students a theory of gender that provides a vocabulary for performing their own distanced readings. Contemporary proponents of literary theory in fact assert its key role in teaching students because it promotes critical distance. Theory, according to Jonathan Culler, has the "power to make strange the familiar and to make readers conceive of their own thinking, behavior, and institutions in new ways" (9).

I find the work of the feminist psychoanalytic theorist Julia Kristeva pedagogically useful for this purpose because her focus on issues of gender blurs the conventional concepts of masculine and feminine without inverting or polarizing the old valuations. She offers students a flexible framework that challenges their preconceptions but allows them to experiment with their readings of the novels and link their findings with larger cultural, philosophical, and linguistic concerns. I introduce Kristeva by distributing the following two paragraphs as a handout on the second day of class discussion, after students have read the first twelve chapters of *Jane Eyre*:

> The literary theorist Julia Kristeva uses gender to talk about the ways we try to make sense of experience. She posits two modes, the *symbolic* and the *semiotic*, which she variously describes as "signifying processes," "realms," and "dispositions" [e.g., "Revolution" 102; *Desire* 18, 134]. The symbolic she associates with paternalistic authority. The symbolic is a code of fixed and often rigid meanings of God, the father, the state, the law, property, class, and so forth. Put another way, the symbolic refers to the social and cultural forces embodied in language that serve to establish and maintain order. The semiotic is fluid and plural, characterized by a creative excess over precise meaning that often delights in negating the symbolic [Eagleton, *Literary Theory* 188–89]. Kristeva associates the semiotic with the feminine, specifically the infant's relationship with its mother; she sees the semiotic realm as preverbal, a disposition to the world that is later submerged by the child's acquisition of language and consequent entry into the (symbolic) system of society [*Desire* 136].
>
> It is important not to oversimplify as we use these terms. Kristeva does not formulate actual differences in the ways that men and women view the world; rather, she reformulates ways of being and thinking that have been conventionally associated with the concepts of "masculine" and "feminine." Because, as Kristeva makes clear, "the subject is always *both* semiotic *and* symbolic," his or her speech can never "be either 'exclusively' semiotic or 'exclusively' symbolic, and is instead marked by an indebtedness to both" ["Revolution" 93]. "Inseparable" from the symbolic, the semiotic exists within society, "erupting" as "influxes" that "remodel the symbolic order," renewing the way that we understand our habitation in the patriarchal realm ["Revolution" 113;

Desire 134]. According to one scholar, Kristeva sees the woman as "both 'inside' and 'outside' male society, both a romantically idealized member of it and a victimized outcast. She is sometimes what stands between man and chaos, and sometimes the embodiment of chaos itself. That is why she troubles the neat categories of such a [symbolic] regime, blurring its well-defined boundaries. Women are represented within male-governed society, fixed by sign, image, and meaning; yet because they are also the 'negative' of that social order, there is always in them something which is left over, superfluous, unrepresentable, which refuses to be figured there." The semiotic is not, then, a synonym for "female": it is a mode of being and of discourse, a force within society that yet opposes it [Eagleton, *Literary Theory* 190].

Working from this brief handout, I encourage students to locate passages in *Jane Eyre* that display the tension between the symbolic and the semiotic — for example, in the doublings and oppositions that Brontë constructs between and within characters. Jane herself offers a polarized version of this scheme when she confesses to us:

I never in my life have known any medium in my dealings with positive, hard characters, antagonistic to my own, between absolute submission and determined revolt. I have always faithfully observed the one, up to the very moment of bursting, sometimes with volcanic vehemence, into the other. (352; ch. 34)

On the one hand, she conforms to the symbolic, telling the patriarchal Rochester, "I like to serve you, sir, and to obey you in all that is right" (190; ch. 20). On the other hand, as many scholars have suggested, Jane bears strong affinities to the mad and murderous Bertha, whose low peal of laughter has "thrilled" her as she espouses her feminist critique atop the third story at Thornfield:

Women are supposed to be very calm generally: but women feel just as men feel; they need exercise for their faculties and a field for their efforts as much as their brothers do; they suffer from too rigid a restraint, too absolute a stagnation, precisely as men would suffer. (96; ch. 12)

And it is Bertha's face that Jane sees in the mirror when her wedding veil — a symbol of the "bashaw" Rochester's desire to dress Jane "like a doll" (236–37; ch. 24) — is ripped (247; ch. 25).

After students have identified both a symbolic and a semiotic Jane, I caution them against overemphasizing the latter, since Brontë is not espousing the conventional associations of the head with male and the heart with female but complicating such associations. When Rochester pleads with Jane to "transgress a mere human law" and accompany him abroad, Jane resists: "I will hold to the principles received by me when I was sane, and not mad — as I am now" (279; ch. 27). And later, a symbolic Jane confesses to us, "I feel now that I was right when I adhered to principle and law, and scorned and crushed the insane promptings of a frenzied moment. God directed me to a correct choice: I thank His providence for the guidance" (316; ch. 31). But a semiotic Jane scorns St. John when he argues that providence has selected her to serve as his missionary wife (359; ch. 34). And so forth. As I attempt to show my students, the novel vacillates with "volcanic vehemence" between Kristeva's extremes. In its many voices, it gives support to feminism and to passion (Jane's "revolt") as well as to piety and obedience to law (Jane's "submission").

In the days following discussion of the handout, I focus on Brontë's use of forms of the word *conventionality* and ultimately on her ambivalence toward prevailing narrative conventions: the author, like the heroine, is confined by and attempting to disrupt — as well as attracted to and attempting to preserve — the marriage plot. First, however, we remain closer to the story, beginning with Rochester's use of *conventional* to imply a set of repressed and oppressed behaviors. He tells Jane:

> The Lowood constraint still clings to you somewhat; controlling your features, muffling your voice, and restricting your limbs; and you fear in the presence of a man and a brother — or father, or master, or what you will — to smile too gaily, speak too freely, or move too quickly; but, in time, I think you will learn to be natural with me, as I find it impossible to be conventional with you.

Rochester's professed aim here is to release Jane, the "curious sort of bird," from the "cage" in which she is "a resolute captive" (122; ch. 14) — that is, to free her from her confinement within the symbolic, within patriarchal convention and all of the class and gender stereotyping associated with Lowood. Although it is impossible to determine how ironic Brontë is in this scene, we can read the passage another way, interpreting Rochester's anticonventional perspective as a ploy to deceive Jane. Does his version of the "natural," opposed to convention, also include lying to Jane about Bertha? Or is Rochester responding semiotically to his love for Jane, trying to overcome his own symbolic limitations, as he argues for "overleaping an obstacle of custom — a mere conventional impediment, which neither your conscience sanctifies nor your judgment approves"? (192; ch. 20). Such questions provide rich material for discussion.

Jane's use of *conventionality* is similarly rich in ambiguity and ambivalence. In both key scenes in which Jane uses the term, we can see the novel struggling against its own limited choices. Both times Jane (like Rochester) sees the conventional as an impediment; she aims to get beyond it, to establish her semiotic revolt; but, paradoxically, such revolt tends to summon its opposite, some form of symbolic containment.

On first seeing Rochester after returning from her aunt's funeral, Jane blurts out ("something in me said for me, and in spite of me"), "[W]herever you are is my home — my only home" (216; ch. 22). Later, in the garden, having been "roused to something like passion," she tells Rochester, "I am not talking to you now through the medium of custom, conventionalities, nor even of mortal flesh — it is my spirit that addresses your spirit; just as if both had passed through the grave, and we stood at God's feet, equal, — as we are!" (222; ch. 23). During this semiotic eruption, Jane uses language suggestive of a visionary new order. Ironically, this captivating vision propels Rochester to the conventional symbolic ending: he proposes. Whether Jane goes beyond "conventionalities" only to arrive at conventionality is a question that prepares students for a fruitful discussion of the marriage at the end of the novel.

This discussion can build on the difference between Jane's impulsively articulated vision and Rochester's response, as they are crystallized in their competing semiotic and symbolic definitions of "home." Jane explicitly yokes "home" and the "conventional" when she confronts St. John Rivers about his covert passion for Rosamond:

> Again the surprised expression crossed his face. He had not imagined that a woman would dare to speak so to a man. For me, I felt at home in this sort of discourse. I could never rest in communication with strong, discreet, and refined minds, whether male or female, till I had passed the outworks of conventional reserve, and crossed the threshold of confidence, and won a place by their heart's very hearthstone.
>
> (330; ch. 32)

Unlike the previous passage, here Jane the narrator delivers a meditated declaration of principles. Yet we can see, in her imagery of inside and outside, the contradictions that reveal Brontë's unsettled attempt to synthesize the two realms, semiotic and symbolic, here manifested as free open space and solid (stone) enclosed space. Jane speaks of a place where she can engage in that "sort of discourse" in which she feels "at home." But the home she gets is not this visionary way of being in the world, a semiotic fluidity, but the structured, symbolic space of matrimony. Jane locates the semiotic home of "discourse" outside ("outworks") convention but ends by housing it at the hearth, the conventional icon of sentimental domesticity.

Jane Eyre's problem is that she is trapped in a plot like the one that she dismisses during her interview with the Gypsy-Rochester. When St. John reveals that she is an heiress, many students are surprised by her cool response: "[T]here are other chances in life far more thrilling and rapture-giving; *this*

is solid, an affair of the actual world" (336; ch. 33). The conventional heroine
would be thrilled with money, students say, so why not Jane? A comparison
of her response to the inheritance with Rochester's compels students to interpret why his language — "Ah, this is practical — this is real!" (382; ch. 37) —
strikingly resembles hers in its emphasis on fitting into the "real" world.
They must confront the fact that Jane (like Rochester) has come finally to
situate herself within a symbolic view of the world. "Thrilling" is clearly
a semiotic tag for Jane (see 96; ch. 12, e.g.), but only symbolic money makes
her "real."

It would appear that at the end of the novel the thrill is gone. Brontë
gives us the "perfect concord" (397; ch. 38) of traditional closed form: we
learn about the fates of the other characters, and the sometimes demonic
Rochester submits to God the father and then asserts his own literal patriarchy, giving Jane a son. Like Elizabeth Bennet, Jane has sacrificed her
aggressive spirit to domestic quietude, while the pressing social problems
that the novels have raised remain unresolved. In the secluded green world
of Ferndean, we do not hear Jane railing against patriarchy, as she had
atop the third story at Thornfield, that it is

> narrow-minded in [women's] more privileged fellow-creatures to say
> that they ought to confine themselves to making puddings and knitting
> stockings, to playing on the piano and embroidering bags. It is thought-
> less to condemn them, or laugh at them, if they seek to do more or
> learn more than custom has pronounced necessary for their sex.
>
> (96; ch. 12)

That voice has gone, vanished into a pastoral romance.

Indeed, I believe that all the works I have mentioned in this essay offer
problematic resolutions of the marriage plot. In work after work, contraction
counters expansion; the symbolic form counters the semiotic eruption within
that form. In the fairy land of Pemberley, secure from intrusions by what the
narrator terms her "vulgar" relations (391), Elizabeth Bennet need not worry
about the laws of entail that victimize women economically — and that gave
rise to the plot of *Pride and Prejudice*. Instead, we glimpse her protecting
Darcy from indecorousness, "anxious to keep him to herself, and to those
of her family with whom he might converse without mortification" (391).

The two endings of *Great Expectations* suggest Dickens's ambivalence
toward closure, with even the published ending, in which Pip and Estella
leave the garden hand and hand, offering a scene of enervation rather than
passion. Estella confesses, "I have been bent and broken, but — I hope —
into a better shape," to which Pip replies vaguely, "We are friends."
And while he foresees "no shadow of another parting from her" (493), this
eventuality is not confirmed by the retrospective narrator Pip within the
tale itself.

Similarly, the endings of *The Mill on the Floss* and *Jude the Obscure* evade these novels' own critiques of marriage and the marriage plot. Unable to resolve the dilemma facing Maggie — whether to allow her to marry Stephen, obey her brother, or reunite with Philip — George Eliot escapes from the book with the flood that kills her heroine, who never enters into gendered adulthood. And Hardy, caught up in a diatribe against marriage, fails to envision a means of accommodating the semiotic for Sue Bridehead, who burns her nightgown as she leaves the husband she loves for the one who disgusts her.

The dilemmas that Brontë and Jane face offer us useful insights into a dominant predicament that novelists and heroines face in the nineteenth-century novel: how to imagine a workable social identity and home for passionate, intelligent women within the world of the novel and the society it depicts — while still operating within the conventions of the marriage plot. The problem, in Terry Eagleton's terms, is to integrate the semiotic "something . . . left over" in Jane and the other heroines that "refuses to be figured" in the symbolic conventional world. While exploring how social conventions define and circumscribe the place of women, the novels critique narrative conventions as well. The works are themselves concerned with placing their heroines; they explore how novelistic tradition and the society that surrounds the novels' heroines at once spur and frustrate efforts to locate a new place for women. In the straining — or failure? — of these attempts lies their interest.

CONTRIBUTORS AND SURVEY PARTICIPANTS

The following scholars and teachers helped in the preparation of this book by contributing essays, responding to the survey of approaches to teaching *Jane Eyre*, or participating in both activities. Their assistance made the volume possible.

Dennis W. Allen, *West Virginia University*
Orphia Jane Allen, *New Mexico State University*
Sue Ann Betsinger, *Aledo, TX*
Bege K. Bowers, *Youngstown State University*
Robert Bray, *Illinois Wesleyan University*
Jerome Bump, *University of Texas, Austin*
Mary Burgan, *Indiana University, Bloomington*
Cynthia Carlton-Ford, *University of Cincinnati*
James Diedrick, *Albion College*
Margery S. Durham, *University of Minnesota, Twin Cities*
Lynette Felber, *New Mexico State University*
Benjamin F. Fisher, *University of Mississippi*
Janet H. Freeman, *Denison University*
Susan VanZanten Gallagher, *Calvin College*
Margaret Goscilo, *Moorhead State University*
A. Waller Hastings, *Northern State College*
Tamar Heller, *Williams College*
Mark M. Hennelly, Jr., *California State University, Sacramento*
Diane Long Hoeveler, *Marquette University*
Thomas L. Jeffers, *Marquette University*
Keith A. Jenkins, *Rice University*
John O. Jordan, *University of California, Santa Cruz*
John Kucich, *University of Michigan, Ann Arbor*
Beth Lau, *California State University, Long Beach*
David J. Leigh, *Seattle University*
Donna Marie Nudd, *Florida State University*
Bernard J. Paris, *University of Florida*
Robert L. Patten, *Rice University*
Mary Poovey, *Johns Hopkins University*
Phyllis C. Ralph, *University of Kansas*
David Rosenwasser, *Muhlenberg College*
Lorie Roth, *Armstrong State College*
Kathleen G. Rousseau, *West Virginia University*
Yoshiaki Shirai, *Shinshu University*
Shirley A. Stave, *Emory University*
Robert Wellisch, *College of Saint Thomas*

WORKS CITED

Editions of *Jane Eyre*

Brontë, Charlotte. *Jane Eyre. The Norton Anthology of Literature by Women: The Tradition in English*. Ed. Sandra M. Gilbert and Susan Gubar. New York: Norton, 1985. 347–735.

——. *Jane Eyre*. Signet Classics edition. New York: NAL, 1960.

Dunn, Richard J., ed. *Jane Eyre*. By Charlotte Brontë. Norton Critical Edition. New York: Norton, 1971.

——, ed. *Jane Eyre*. By Charlotte Brontë. Norton Critical Edition. 2nd ed. New York: Norton, 1987.

Jack, Jane, and Margaret Smith, eds. *Jane Eyre*. By Charlotte Brontë. Oxford: Clarendon–Oxford UP, 1969; rpt. with corrections, 1975.

Leavis, Q. D., ed. *Jane Eyre*. By Charlotte Brontë. Harmondsworth: Penguin, 1966.

Schorer, Mark, ed. *Jane Eyre*. By Charlotte Brontë. Riverside edition. Boston: Houghton, 1959.

Smith, Margaret, ed. *Jane Eyre*. By Charlotte Brontë. World's Classics edition. Oxford: Oxford UP, 1975.

Books and Articles

Abel, Elizabeth, Marianne Hirsch, and Elizabeth Langland, eds. *The Voyage In: Fictions of Female Development*. Hanover: UP of New England, 1983.

Abrams, M. H., et al., eds. *The Norton Anthology of English Literature*. 5th ed. 2 vols. New York: Norton, 1986.

Adams, Maurianne. "Family Disintegration and Creative Reintegration: The Case of Charlotte Brontë and *Jane Eyre*." Wohl 148–79.

——. "*Jane Eyre*: Woman's Estate." *The Authority of Experience: Essays in Feminist Criticism*. Ed. Arlyn Diamond and Lee R. Edwards. Amherst: U of Massachusetts P, 1977. 137–59.

Alexander, Christine. *A Bibliography of the Manuscripts of Charlotte Brontë*. Haworth: Brontë Soc.–Meckler, 1982.

——. *The Early Writings of Charlotte Brontë*. Oxford: Blackwell, 1983.

——, ed. *The Glass Town Saga, 1826–1832*. Oxford: Blackwell, 1987. Vol. 1 of *An Edition of the Early Writings of Charlotte Brontë*. 3 vols. to date.

——, ed. *The Rise of Angria, 1833–1834*. Oxford: Blackwell, 1991. Vol. 2, pt. 1, of *An Edition of the Early Writings of Charlotte Brontë*. 3 vols. to date.

———, ed. *The Rise of Angria, 1834–1835.* Oxford: Blackwell, 1991. Vol. 2, pt. 2, of *An Edition of the Early Writings of Charlotte Brontë.* 3 vols. to date.

Allen, Walter. *The English Novel: A Short Critical History.* New York: Dutton, 1954.

Allott, Miriam, ed. *The Brontës: The Critical Heritage.* London: Routledge, 1974.

———, ed. *Charlotte Brontë: Jane Eyre and Villette: A Casebook.* London: Macmillan, 1973.

Altick, Richard D. *The English Common Reader: A Social History of the Mass Reading Public: 1800–1900.* Chicago: U of Chicago P, 1957.

———. *Victorian People and Ideas.* New York: Norton, 1973.

Antal, Frederick. *Fuseli Studies.* London: Routledge, 1956.

Armstrong, Nancy. *Desire and Domestic Fiction: A Political History of the Novel.* New York: Oxford UP, 1987.

Auerbach, Nina. "Charlotte Brontë: The Two Countries." *University of Toronto Quarterly* 42 (1973): 328–42. Rpt. in *Romantic Imprisonment: Women and Other Glorified Outcasts.* By Auerbach. New York: Columbia UP, 1985. 195–211.

———. *Woman and the Demon: The Life of a Victorian Myth.* Cambridge: Harvard UP, 1982.

Austen, Jane. *Pride and Prejudice.* Ed. Tony Tanner. New York: Penguin, 1972.

Bachelard, Gaston. *The Flame of a Candle.* Trans. Joni Caldwell. 1964. Dallas: Dallas Inst., 1989.

———. *The Psychoanalysis of Fire.* Trans. Alan C. M. Ross. 1938. Boston: Beacon, 1964.

Baer, Elizabeth. "The Sisterhood of Jane Eyre and Antoinette Cosway." Abel, Hirsch, and Langland 131–48.

Bakhtin, M. M. *The Dialogic Imagination: Four Essays.* Ed. Michael Holquist. Trans. Caryl Emerson and Michael Holquist. Austin: U of Texas P, 1981.

———. *Rabelais and His World.* Trans. Helena Iswolsky. Cambridge: Cambridge UP, 1968.

Banks, J. A. *Prosperity and Parenthood: A Study of Family Planning among the Victorian Middle Class.* London: Routledge, 1954.

Barker, Juliet. "An Interview with Fay Weldon." *Brontë Newsletter* 7 (1988): 1–2.

Barthes, Roland. *Mythologies.* Trans. Annette Lavers. New York: Hill, 1972.

Baudrillard, Jean. "For a Critique of the Political Economy of the Sign." *Selected Writings.* Ed. Mark Poster. Stanford: Stanford UP, 1988. 57–97.

———. "Sign Function and Class Logic." *For a Critique of the Political Economy of the Sign.* Trans. Charles Levin. St. Louis: Telos, 1981. 29–62.

Beaty, Jerome. "*Jane Eyre* and Genre." *Genre* 10 (1977): 619–54.

Beer, Patricia. *Reader, I Married Him: A Study of the Women Characters of Jane Austen, Charlotte Brontë, Elizabeth Gaskell, and George Eliot.* New York: Harper, 1974.

Bellis, Peter. "In the Window-Seat: Vision and Power in *Jane Eyre.*" *ELH* 54 (1987): 639–52.

Bentley, Eric. "Melodrama." *The Life of the Drama*. New York: Atheneum, 1964. 195–218.

Bentley, Phyllis. *The Brontës*. London: Thames, 1986.

———. *The Brontës and Their World*. New York: Viking, 1969.

Benveniste, Emile. "The Nature of Pronouns." *Problems* 217–22.

———. *Problems in General Linguistics*. Trans. Mary Elizabeth Meek. Coral Gables: U of Miami P, 1971.

———. "Subjectivity in Language." *Problems* 223–30.

Benvenuto, Richard. "The Child of Nature, the Child of Grace, and the Unresolved Conflict in *Jane Eyre*." *ELH* 39 (1972): 620–38.

Berg, Maggie. *Jane Eyre: Portrait of a Life*. Boston: Twayne, 1987.

Berman, Ronald. "The Innocent Observer." *Children's Literature* 9 (1981): 40–50.

Bernstein, Susan D. "Madam Mope: The Bereaved Child in Brontë's *Jane Eyre*." *Adolescents, Literature, and Work with Youth*. Ed. J. Pamela Weiner and Ruth M. Stein. New York: Haworth, 1985. 117–29.

Bettelheim, Bruno. *The Uses of Enchantment: The Meaning and Importance of Fairy Tales*. New York: Knopf, 1976.

Bjork, Harriet. *The Language of Truth: Charlotte Brontë, the Woman Question, and the Novel*. Lund: Gleerup, 1974.

Blom, Margaret Howard. *Charlotte Brontë*. Boston: Twayne, 1977.

Bloom, Harold, ed. *Modern Critical Interpretations: Charlotte Brontë's* Jane Eyre. New York: Chelsea, 1987.

———. *Modern Critical Views: The Brontës*. New York: Chelsea, 1987.

Blos, Peter. *On Adolescence: A Psychoanalytic Interpretation*. New York: Free, 1962.

Bodenheimer, Rosemarie. "Jane Eyre in Search of Her Story." *Papers on Language and Literature* 16 (1980): 387–402. Rpt. in Bloom, *Modern Critical Views* 97–112.

Boos, Florence, ed. With Lynn Miller. *Bibliography of Women and Literature*. 2 vols. to date. New York: Holmes, 1989–.

Booth, Michael. *English Melodrama*. London: Jenkins, 1965.

———. Introduction. *Hiss the Villain: Six English and American Melodramas*. New York: Blom, 1964. 9–40.

Borsch-Supan, Helmut. *Caspar David Friedrich*. Trans. Sarah Twohig. New York: Braziller, 1974.

Boumelha, Penny. "'And What Do the Women Do?' Jane Eyre, Jamaica, and the Gentleman's House." *Southern Review* 21 (1988): 111–22.

Bradshaw, John. *Bradshaw On: The Family, a Revolutionary Way of Self-Discovery*. Pampano Beach: Health Communications, 1988.

———. *Homecoming: Reclaiming and Championing Your Inner Child*. New York: Bantam, 1990.

Brontë, Anne. *Agnes Grey*. London: Dent, 1985.

———. *The Tenant of Wildfell Hall*. Ed. Herbert Rosengarten. Oxford: Clarendon–Oxford UP, 1991.

Brontë, Charlotte. "Caroline Vernon." *Five Novelettes* 273–358.

——. *Five Novelettes*. Ed. Winifred Gérin. London: Folio, 1971.

——. *The Professor*. Ed. Herbert Rosengarten and Margaret Smith. Oxford: Clarendon–Oxford UP, 1987.

——. *The Professor*. Ed. Margaret Lane. London: Dent, 1974.

——. *"The Secret" and "Lily Hart": Two Tales by Charlotte Brontë*. Ed. William Holtz. Columbia: U of Missouri P, 1979.

——. *Shirley*. Ed. Andrew Hook and Judith Hook. London: Penguin, 1974.

——. *Shirley*. Ed. Herbert Rosengarten and Margaret Smith. Oxford: Clarendon–Oxford UP, 1979.

——. *Something about Arthur*. Ed. Christine Alexander. Austin: Humanities Research Center, U of Texas P, 1981.

——. *Villette*. Ed. Herbert Rosengarten and Margaret Smith. Oxford: Clarendon–Oxford UP, 1984.

Brontë, Emily. *Wuthering Heights*. Ed. William M. Sale, Jr. New York: Norton, 1972.

Brooks, Peter. *The Melodramatic Imagination*. New Haven: Yale UP, 1976.

Brougham, John, adapter. *Jane Eyre*. New York: French, 1856.

Buckley, Jerome Hamilton. *Season of Youth: The Bildungsroman from Dickens to Golding*. Cambridge: Harvard UP, 1974.

——. *The Victorian Temper: A Study in Literary Culture*. 1951. New York: Vintage-Random, 1964.

Bump, Jerome. "D. H. Lawrence and Family Systems Theory." *Renascence* 44 (1991): 61–80.

——. "Innovative Bibliotherapy Approaches to Substance Abuse." *Arts in Psychotherapy* 17 (1990): 355–62.

——. "Radical Changes in Class Discussion Using Networked Computers." *Computers and the Humanities* 24 (1990): 49–65.

——. "Reader-Centered Criticism and Bibliotherapy: Hopkins and Selving." *Renascence* 42 (1989–90): 65–86.

Burgan, William M. "Masonic Symbolism in *The Moonstone* and *The Mystery of Edwin Drood*." *Dickens Studies Annual* 16 (1987): 257–303.

Burkhart, Charles. *Charlotte Brontë: A Psychosexual Study of Her Novels*. London: Gollancz, 1973.

Butery, Karen Ann. "The Contributions of Horneyan Psychology to the Study of Literature." *American Journal of Psychoanalysis* 42 (1982): 39–50.

——. "Jane Eyre's Flight from Decision." *Literary Review* 24 (1981): 222–51. Rpt. in Paris, *Third Force* 114–35.

Buttlin, Martin, and Evelyn Joll. *The Paintings of J. M. W. Turner*. Vol 1: *Plates*. New Haven: Yale UP, 1977.

Campbell, Joseph. *The Power of Myth*. With Bill Moyers. Ed. Betty Sue Flowers. New York: Doubleday, 1988.

Caskey, Noelle. "Interpreting Anorexia Nervosa." *The Female Body in Western Culture: Contemporary Perspectives*. Ed. Susan Rubin Suleiman. Cambridge: Harvard UP, 1986.

Chase, Karen. *Eros and Psyche: The Representation of Personality in Charlotte Brontë, Charles Dickens, and George Eliot.* New York: Methuen, 1984.

Chase, Richard. "The Brontës; or, Myth Domesticated." *Forms of Modern Fiction.* Ed. William V. O'Connor. Minneapolis: U of Minnesota P, 1948. 102–13. Rpt. in Dunn, *Jane Eyre* (1971 ed.) 462–71.

Checkland, S. G. *The Rise of Industrial Society in England 1815–1885.* London: Longmans, 1964.

Christensen, Oscar. "Family Counseling: An Adlerian Orientation." *Proceedings of a Symposium on Family Counseling and Therapy.* Ed. G. Gasda. Athens: U of Georgia School of Educ., 1971.

Cirker, Blanche, ed. *1800 Woodcuts by Thomas Bewick and His School.* Introd. Robert Hutchinson. New York: Dover, 1962.

Clipping file on *Jane Eyre.* Theater and Drama Collection. Performing Arts Research Center, New York Public Library.

Cockshut, A. O. J. *Man and Woman: A Study of Love and the Novel, 1740–1940.* New York: Oxford UP, 1978.

Cohen, Paula Marantz. *The Daughter's Dilemma: Family Process and the Nineteenth-Century Domestic Novel.* Ann Arbor: U of Michigan P, 1991.

———. "Stabilizing the Family System at *Mansfield Park.*" *ELH* 54 (1987): 669–93.

Cohn, Jan. *Romance and the Erotics of Property: Mass-Market Fiction for Women.* Durham: Duke UP, 1988.

Cowart, David. "Oedipal Dynamics in *Jane Eyre.*" *Literature and Psychology* 31 (1981): 33–38.

Craik, W. A. *The Brontë Novels.* London: Methuen, 1968.

Cross, Gilbert B. *Next Week — East Lynne: Domestic Drama in Performance.* London: Associated UP, 1977.

Crump, Rebecca W. *Charlotte and Emily Brontë: A Reference Guide.* 3 vols. Boston: Hall, 1982–86.

Culler, Jonathan. *On Deconstruction: Theory and Criticism after Structuralism.* Ithaca: Cornell UP, 1982.

Daiches, David, and John Flower. *Literary Landscapes of the British Isles: A Narrative Atlas.* New York: Paddington, 1979.

Dale, Peter Allan. "Charlotte Brontë's 'Tale Half-Told': The Disruption of Narrative Structure in *Jane Eyre.*" *Modern Language Quarterly* 47 (1986): 108–29.

Davies, Robertson. *The Mirror of Nature.* Toronto: U of Toronto P, 1983.

DeLamotte, Eugenia C. *Perils of the Night: A Feminist Study of Nineteenth-Century Gothic.* New York: Oxford UP, 1990.

Derrida, Jacques. "Différance." *Margins of Philosophy.* Trans. Alan Bass. Chicago: U of Chicago P, 1982. 1–27.

Dessner, Lawrence J. *The Homely Web of Truth: A Study of Charlotte Brontë's Novels.* The Hague: Mouton, 1975.

Dewey, John. *Art as Experience.* 1934. New York: Capricorn, 1958.

Dickens, Charles. *Great Expectations.* Ed. Angus Calder. New York: Penguin, 1985.

———. *The Old Curiosity Shop.* Ed. Angus Easson. London: Penguin, 1972.

Dijkstra, Bram. *Idols of Perversity: Fantasies of Feminine Evil in Fin-de-Siècle Culture*. New York: Oxford UP, 1986.

Donaldson, Laura E. "The Miranda Complex: Colonialism and the Question of Feminist Reading." *Diacritics* 18 (1988): 65–77.

Dry, Florence Swinton. *The Sources of* Jane Eyre. Cambridge: Heffer, 1940.

du Maurier, Daphne. *Rebecca*. 1938. New York: Avon, 1979.

Dunn, Richard. "The Natural Heart: Jane Eyre's Romanticism." *Wordsworth Circle* 10 (1979): 197–204.

DuPlessis, Rachel Blau. "Endings and Contradictions." *Writing beyond the Ending: Narrative Strategies of Twentieth-Century Women Writers*. Bloomington: Indiana UP, 1985. 1–19.

Duthie, Enid Lowry. *The Brontës and Nature*. New York: St. Martin's, 1986.

———. *The Foreign Vision of Charlotte Brontë*. New York: Barnes, 1975.

Eagleton, Terry. *Literary Theory: An Introduction*. Minneapolis: U of Minnesota P, 1983.

———. *Myths of Power: A Marxist Study of the Brontës*. London: Macmillan, 1975.

Elias, Norbert. *The History of Manners*. Trans. Edmund Jephcott. New York: Pantheon, 1982.

Eliot, George. *The Mill on the Floss*. Ed. A. S. Byatt. New York: Penguin, 1979.

Ellis, Kate, and Ann Kaplan. "Feminism in Brontë's Novel and Its Film Versions." *The English Novel and the Movies*. Ed. Michael Klein and Gillian Parker. New York: Ungar, 1981. 83–94.

Ewbank, Inga-Stina. *Their Proper Sphere: A Study of the Brontë Sisters as Early-Victorian Female Novelists*. Cambridge: Harvard UP, 1966.

Falk, Kathryn. *How to Write a Romance and Get It Published*. New York: Signet, 1984.

Fielding, Henry. *Tom Jones*. Introd. George Sherburn. New York: Modern Library–Random, 1950.

Foley, Vincent D. *An Introduction to Family Therapy*. 2nd ed. Orlando: Grune, 1986.

Forster, E. M. *Aspects of the Novel*. 1927. London: Arnold, 1949.

Foucault, Michel. *Discipline and Punish: The Birth of the Prison*. Trans. Alan Sheridan. New York: Vintage, 1977.

———. *The History of Sexuality: An Introduction*. Trans. Robert Hurley. Vol. 1. New York: Random, 1980.

———. *Madness and Civilization*. Trans. Richard Howard. London: Tavistock, 1961.

Fraser, Rebecca. *The Brontës: Charlotte Brontë and Her Family*. New York: Crown, 1988.

Freeman, Janet. "Speech and Silence in *Jane Eyre*." *Studies in English Literature* 24 (1984): 683–700.

Freud, Sigmund. "Analysis of Phobia in a Five-Year-Old Boy." *The Complete Works of Sigmund Freud*. Ed. J. Strachey. Vol. 10. London: Hogarth, 1964. 5–148.

Frye, Northrop. *The Secular Scripture: A Study of the Structure of Romance.* Cambridge: Harvard UP, 1976.

Gaskell, Elizabeth. *The Life of Charlotte Brontë.* 1857. Ed. and introd. Alan Shelston. Harmondsworth: Penguin, 1975.

Gates, Barbara T. " 'Visionary Woe' and Its Revisions: Another Look at Jane Eyre's Pictures." *Ariel* 7.4 (1976): 36–49.

Gay, Peter. *The Education of the Senses.* Vol. 1 of *The Bourgeois Experience: Victoria to Freud.* 2 vols. New York: Oxford UP, 1984.

Genette, Gérard. *Narrative Discourse: An Essay in Method.* Trans. Jane E. Lewin. Ithaca: Cornell UP, 1980.

Gennep, Arnold van. *The Rites of Passage.* Trans. Monika Vizedom and Gabrielle L. Caffee. Chicago: U of Chicago P, 1960.

Gérin, Winifred. *The Brontës: The Creative Work.* Writers and Their Work 236. Harlow: Longman, 1974.

———. *The Brontës: The Formative Years.* Writers and Their Work 232. Harlow: Longman, 1973.

———. "Byron's Influence on the Brontës." *Keats-Shelley Memorial Bulletin* 17 (1966): 1–19.

———. *Charlotte Brontë: The Evolution of Genius.* New York: Oxford UP, 1967.

Gilbert, Sandra M., and Susan Gubar. *The Madwoman in the Attic: The Woman Writer and the Nineteenth-Century Literary Imagination.* New Haven: Yale UP, 1979.

Gilead, Sarah. "Liminality and Antiliminality in Charlotte Brontë's Novels: *Shirley* Reads *Jane Eyre.*" *Texas Studies in Literature and Language* 29 (1987): 302–22.

Godwin, William. *A Memoir of the Author of A* Vindication of the Rights of Woman. 1798. New York: Garland, 1974.

Gregor, Ian, ed. *The Brontës: A Collection of Critical Essays.* Englewood Cliffs: Prentice, 1970.

Griffin, Gail B. "The Humanization of Edward Rochester." *Women and Literature* 2 (1982): 118–29.

Hagstrum, Jean. *Sex and Sensibility: Ideal and Erotic Love from Milton to Mozart.* Chicago: U of Chicago P, 1982.

Hannah, Barbara. *Striving towards Wholeness.* New York: Putnam, 1971.

Hardy, Barbara. *The Appropriate Form: An Essay on the Novel.* London: Athlone, 1964.

Hardy, Thomas. *Jude the Obscure.* Ed. C. H. Sisson. New York: Penguin, 1978.

Heilman, Robert B. "Charlotte Brontë, Reason, and the Moon." *Nineteenth-Century Fiction* 14 (1960): 283–302.

———. "Charlotte Brontë's 'New' Gothic." *From Jane Austen to Joseph Conrad.* Ed. Robert Rathburn and Martin Steinmann, Jr. Minneapolis: U of Minnesota P, 1958. 118–32. Rpt. in O'Neill 32–35; Gregor 96–109; Dunn, *Jane Eyre* (1971 ed.) 457–62; Dunn, *Jane Eyre* (1987 ed.) 458–62; Allott, *Charlotte Brontë* 195–204.

Hennelly, Mark M., Jr. " 'In a State Between': A Reading of Liminality in *Jane Eyre.*" *Victorian Literature and Culture* (forthcoming).

———. "*Jane Eyre*'s Reading Lesson." *ELH* 51 (1984): 693–717.

Heuscher, Julius E. *A Psychiatric Study of Fairy Tales*. Springfield: Thomas, 1963.

Higashi, Sumiko. *"Jane Eyre*: Charlotte Brontë vs. the Hollywood Myth of Romance." *Journal of Popular Film* 6 (1977): 13–31.

"Hints on the Modern Governess System." *Fraser's Magazine* Nov. 1844: 571–83.

Horney, Karen. *Neurosis and Human Growth: The Struggle toward Self-Realization*. New York: Norton, 1950.

———. *Our Inner Conflicts*. New York: Norton, 1945.

Houghton, Walter E. *The Victorian Frame of Mind, 1830–1870*. New Haven: Yale UP, 1957.

Hughes, R. E. *"Jane Eyre*: The Unbaptized Dionysos." *Nineteenth-Century Fiction* 18 (1964): 347–64.

Hylson-Smith, Kenneth. *Evangelicals in the Church of England: 1734–1984*. Edinburgh: Clark, 1988.

Ironside, Robin. *Pre-Raphaelite Painters*. London: Phaidon, 1948.

Jackson, D. D. "The Question of Family Homeostasis." *Psychiatric Quarterly Supplement* 31 (1957): 79–90.

Jay, Elisabeth. *The Religion of the Heart: Anglican Evangelicalism and the Nineteenth-Century Novel*. Oxford: Clarendon–Oxford UP, 1979.

Jerome, Helen, adapter. *Jane Eyre*. Garden City: Doubleday, 1937; London: French, 1938; New York: French, 1943, 1961.

———. "Return to Innocence." *Stage* 14 (1937): 45–46.

———. *The Secret of Woman*. London: Chapman, 1923.

Johnstone, Christopher. *John Martin*. New York: St. Martin's, 1974.

Kalikoff, Beth. "The Falling Woman in Three Victorian Novels." *Studies in the Novel* 19 (1987): 357–67.

Kaplan, Cora. " 'Like Any Other Rebel Slave': Gender, Race, and Nation in *Jane Eyre*." U of Michigan, 26 Jan. 1990.

Keefe, Robert. *Charlotte Brontë's World of Death*. Austin: U of Texas P, 1979.

Kerr, Michael E. "Chronic Anxiety and Defining a Self." *Atlantic* Sept. 1988: 35–58.

Kerr, Michael E., and Murray Bowen. *Family Evaluation: The Role of the Family as an Emotional Unit That Governs Individual Behavior and Development*. New York: Norton, 1988.

Knies, Earl. *The Art of Charlotte Brontë*. Athens: Ohio UP, 1969.

Kristeva, Julia. *Desire in Language: A Semiotic Approach to Literature and Art*. Ed. Leon S. Roudiez. Trans. Thomas Gora, Alice Jardine, and Leon S. Roudiez. New York: Columbia UP, 1980.

———. "Revolution in Poetic Language: The Semiotic and the Symbolic." *Revolution in Poetic Language*. Trans. Margaret Waller. New York: Columbia UP, 1984. 19–106. Rpt. in *The Kristeva Reader*. Ed. Toril Moi. New York: Columbia UP, 1986. 89–136.

Kroeber, Karl. *Styles in Fictional Structure: The Art of Jane Austen, Charlotte Brontë, and George Eliot*. Princeton: Princeton UP, 1971.

Kucich, John. *Repression in Victorian Fiction: Charlotte Brontë, George Eliot, and Charles Dickens*. Berkeley: U of California P, 1988.

Landow, George P. *Victorian Types, Victorian Shadows: Biblical Typology in Victorian Literature, Art, and Thought.* London: Routledge, 1980.

Lane, Margaret. *The Brontë Story: A Reconsideration of Mrs. Gaskell's Life of Charlotte Brontë.* London: Heinemann, 1953.

Leavis, F. R., and Q. D. Leavis. *Dickens the Novelist.* London: Chatto, 1970.

Leavis, L. R. "*David Copperfield* and *Jane Eyre.*" *English Studies* 67 (1986): 167–73.

Leavis, Q. D. Introduction. Leavis, *Jane Eyre* 7–29.

Lerner, Laurence. "Bertha and the Critics." *Nineteenth-Century Literature* 44 (1989): 273–300.

Lesser, Simon O. *Fiction and the Unconscious.* Boston: Beacon, 1957.

Lessing, Doris. *The Four-Gated City.* New York: Knopf, 1969.

Lewis, Jerry M., and John G. Looney. *The Long Struggle: Well-Functioning Working Class Black Families.* New York: Brunner, 1983.

Linder, Cynthia. *Romantic Imagery in the Novels of Charlotte Brontë.* New York: Barnes, 1978.

Lodge, David. "Fire and Eyre: Charlotte Brontë's War of Earthly Elements." *The Language of Fiction.* London: Routledge, 1966. 114–43.

Long, Beverly Whitaker, and Mary Frances HopKins. *Performing Literature: An Introduction to Oral Interpretation.* Englewood Cliffs: Prentice-Hall, 1982.

Macaulay, Catharine. *Letters on Education.* London: Dilley, 1790.

Martin, Robert B. *The Accents of Persuasion: Charlotte Brontë's Novels.* New York: Norton, 1966.

Martin, Robert K. "*Jane Eyre* and the World of Faery." *Mosaic* 10 (1977): 85–95.

Mashberg, Amy L. "Co-dependence and Obsession in *Madame Bovary.*" *Dionysos* 2.1 (1990): 28–40.

Maynard, John. *Charlotte Brontë and Sexuality.* Cambridge: Cambridge UP, 1984.

Miller, D. A. "*Cage aux Folles*: Sensation and Gender in Wilkie Collins's *The Woman in White.*" *Representations* 14 (1986): 107–36.

Miller, Jane. *Women Writing about Men.* New York: Pantheon, 1986.

Miller, Jean Baker. *Toward a New Psychology of Women.* Boston: Beacon, 1976.

Miller, J. Hillis. *The Disappearance of God: Five Nineteenth-Century Writers.* Cambridge: Belknap–Harvard UP, 1963.

———. *The Form of Victorian Fiction: Thackeray, Dickens, Trollope, George Eliot, Meredith, and Hardy.* Notre Dame: U of Notre Dame P, 1968.

Miller, Nancy K. "Emphasis Added: Plots and Plausibilities in Women's Fiction." *PMLA* 96 (1981): 36–48.

Millgate, Jane. "Jane Eyre's Progress." *English Studies, Anglo-American Supplement* 50 (1969): xxi–xxix.

———. "Narrative Distance in *Jane Eyre*: The Relevance of the Pictures." *Modern Language Review* 63 (1968): 315–19.

Milton, John. *Paradise Lost.* Ed. Merritt Y. Hughes. New York: Odyssey, 1962.

Modleski, Tania. *Loving with a Vengeance: Mass-Produced Fantasies for Women.* 1982. New York: Methuen, 1984.

Moers, Ellen. *Literary Women: The Great Writers.* 1976. New York: Oxford UP, 1985.

Moglen, Helene. *Charlotte Brontë: The Self Conceived*. New York: Norton, 1976.

Monahan, Melodie. "Heading Out Is Not Going Home: *Jane Eyre*." *Studies in English Literature* 28 (1988): 589–608.

Moore, O. Christene. "Family Patterns in *Jane Eyre* and *Wide Sargasso Sea*." Master's thesis. U of Texas, Austin, 1990.

Morral, Frank. "Engendering Relationships in Shakespeare's Comedies and Tragedies." *Systematic Therapist* 1 (1990): 55–79.

Nead, Lynda. *Myths of Sexuality: Representations of Women in Victorian Britain*. Oxford: Blackwell, 1990.

Nestor, Pauline. *Charlotte Brontë*. Totowa: Barnes, 1987.

———. *Female Friendships and Communities: Charlotte Brontë, George Eliot, Elizabeth Gaskell*. Oxford: Clarendon–Oxford UP, 1985.

Neufeldt, Victor A., ed. *The Poems of Charlotte Brontë: A New Text and Commentary*. Garland English Texts 9. New York: Garland, 1985.

Nudd, Donna Marie. "Bibliography of Film, Television, and Stage Adaptations of Charlotte Brontë's *Jane Eyre*." *Brontë Society Transactions* 20 (1991): 169–72.

———. "*Jane Eyre* and What Adapters Have Done to Her." Diss. U of Texas, Austin, 1989.

Oates, Joyce Carol. "Romance and Anti-romance: From Brontë's *Jane Eyre* to Rhys's *Wide Sargasso Sea*." *Virginia Quarterly Review* 61 (1985): 44–58.

O'Neill, Judith, ed. *Critics on Charlotte and Emily Brontë*. Coral Gables: U of Miami P, 1968.

Opie, Iona, and Peter Opie. *The Classic Fairy Tales*. New York: Oxford UP, 1974.

Paris, Bernard J. *A Psychological Approach to Fiction: Studies in Thackeray, Stendhal, George Eliot, Dostoevsky, and Conrad*. Bloomington: Indiana UP, 1974.

———, ed. *Third Force Psychology and the Study of Literature*. Rutherford: Fairleigh Dickinson UP, 1986.

Passel, Anne. *Charlotte and Emily Brontë: An Annotated Bibliography*. New York: Garland, 1979.

Pell, Nancy. "Resistance, Rebellion, and Marriage: The Economics of *Jane Eyre*." *Nineteenth-Century Fiction* 31 (1977): 397–420.

Peters, Margot. *Charlotte Brontë: Style in the Novel*. Madison: U of Wisconsin P, 1973.

———. *Unquiet Soul: A Biography of Charlotte Brontë*. Garden City: Doubleday, 1975.

Peterson, M. Jeanne. "The Victorian Governess: Status Incongruence in Family and Society." *Suffer and Be Still: Woman in the Victorian Age*. Ed. Martha Vicinus. Bloomington: Indiana UP, 1972. 3–19.

Pickrel, Paul. "*Jane Eyre*: The Apocalypse of the Body." *ELH* 53 (1986): 165–82.

Pinion, Francis B. *A Brontë Companion: Literary Assessment, Background, and Reference*. New York: Barnes, 1975.

Politi, Jina. "*Jane Eyre* Class-ified." *Literature and History* 8 (1982): 55–66.

Pollard, Arthur. With photographs by Simon McBride. *The Landscape of the Brontës*. Exeter: Webb, 1988.

Poovey, Mary. *Uneven Developments: The Ideological Work of Gender in Mid-Victorian England*. Chicago: U of Chicago P, 1988.

———. "*A Vindication of the Rights of Woman* and Female Sexuality." Wollstonecraft, *Vindication* 343–55.

Prideaux, James, adapter. *Jane Heights*. Music by Arthur B. Rubinstein. Lyrics by Prideaux. Ts. Produced 1980.

Qualls, Barry. *The Secular Pilgrims of Victorian Fiction: The Novel as Book of Life*. Cambridge: Cambridge UP, 1982.

Quennell, Peter. *Romantic England: Writing and Painting 1717–1851*. New York: Macmillan, 1970.

Radcliffe, Ann. *The Mysteries of Udolpho: A Romance, Interspersed with Some Pieces of Poetry*. 1794. Ed. Bonamy Dobrée. Oxford: Oxford UP, 1980.

Ralph, Phyllis C. *Victorian Transformations: Fairy Tales, Adolescence, and the Novel of Female Development*. New York: Lang, 1989.

Ratchford, Fannie E. *The Brontës' Web of Childhood*. New York: Russell, 1941.

Ratchford, Fannie E., and William C. DeVane, eds. *Legends of Angria: Compiled from the Early Writings of Charlotte Brontë*. New Haven: Yale UP, 1933.

Reynolds, Graham. *Victorian Painting*. New York: Macmillan, 1966.

Rhys, Jean. *Wide Sargasso Sea*. 1966. New York: Penguin, 1968.

Rich, Adrienne. "Jane Eyre: The Temptations of a Motherless Woman." *Ms.* Oct. 1973: 68 +. Rpt. in *On Lies, Secrets, and Silence: Selected Prose, 1966–1978*. By Rich. New York: Norton, 1979. 89–106. Rpt. in Dunn, *Jane Eyre* (1987 ed.) 462–75.

Rigby, Elizabeth. Rev. of *Jane Eyre*, by Charlotte Brontë. *Quarterly Review* Dec. 1848. Rpt. in Dunn, *Jane Eyre* (1987 ed.) 440–43.

Rigney, Barbara. *Madness and Sexual Politics in the Feminist Novel*. Madison: U of Wisconsin P, 1978.

Riley, Michael. "Gothic Melodrama and Spiritual Romance: Vision and Fidelity in Two Versions of *Jane Eyre*." *Literature/Film Quarterly* 3 (1975): 145–59.

Roberts, Doreen. "*Jane Eyre* and 'The Warped System of Things.' " *Reading the Victorian Novel: Detail into Form*. Ed. Ian Gregor. Totowa: Barnes, 1980. 131–49.

Rodolff, Rebecca. "From the Ending of *The Professor* to the Conception of *Jane Eyre*." *Philological Quarterly* 61 (1982): 71–89.

Rosenblatt, Louise M. *Literature as Exploration*. 1938. Rev. ed. New York: Noble, 1968.

Rosengarten, Herbert J. "The Brontës." *Victorian Fiction: A Second Guide to Research*. Ed. George H. Ford. New York: MLA, 1978. 172–203.

Rousseau, Jean Jacques. *Emile*. Trans. Barbara Foley. New York: Dutton-Everyman, 1974.

Rowe, Karen E. " 'Fairy Born and Human Bred': Jane Eyre's Education in Romance." Abel, Hirsch, and Langland 69–89.

Russ, Joanna. "Somebody's Trying to Kill Me and I Think It's My Husband: The Modern Gothic." *The Female Gothic.* Ed. Juliann E. Fleenor. Montreal: Eden, 1983. 31–56.

Sabol, C. Ruth, and Todd K. Bender. *A Concordance to Brontë's* Jane Eyre. New York: Garland, 1981.

Sadoff, Dianne F. *Monsters of Affection: Dickens, Eliot, and Brontë on Fatherhood.* Baltimore: Johns Hopkins UP, 1982.

Said, Edward. *Orientalism.* New York: Pantheon, 1978.

Scarry, Elaine. *The Body in Pain: The Making and Unmaking of the World.* New York: Oxford UP, 1985.

Schivelbusch, Wolfgang. *Disenchanted Night: The Industrialization of Light in the Nineteenth Century.* Trans. Angela Davis. 1983. Berkeley: U of California P, 1988.

Schmidt, Helen von. "The Dark Abyss, the Broad Expanse: Versions of the Self in *Jane Eyre* and *Great Expectations.*" *Dickens Quarterly* 2 (1985): 84–92.

Schwartz, Narda Lacey. *Articles on Women Writers: A Bibliography.* Vol. 1: *1960–1975.* Vol. 2: *1976–1984.* Santa Barbara: ABC-Clio, 1977, 1986.

Sheridan, Alan. *Michel Foucault: The Will to Truth.* London: Tavistock, 1980.

Shorter, Clement, ed. *The Brontës: Life and Letters.* Vol. 1. New York: Haskell, 1969.

Showalter, Elaine. *The Female Malady: Women, Madness, and Culture in England, 1830–1980.* New York: Pantheon, 1985.

———. *A Literature of Their Own: British Women Novelists from Brontë to Lessing.* Princeton: Princeton UP, 1977.

Silverman, Kaja. *The Subject of Semiotics.* New York: Oxford UP, 1983.

Smith, James. *Melodrama.* London: Methuen, 1973.

Spacks, Patricia Meyer. *The Female Imagination.* New York: Knopf, 1975.

Spivak, Gayatri Chakravorty. "Three Women's Texts and a Critique of Imperialism." *Critical Inquiry* 12 (1985): 243–61.

Spring, David. *The English Landed Estate in the Nineteenth Century: Its Administration.* Baltimore: Johns Hopkins UP, 1963.

Stevenson, Lionel. *The English Novel: A Panorama.* Boston: Houghton, 1960.

Stewart, Garrett. "Teaching Prose Fiction: Some 'Instructive' Styles." *College English* 37 (1975): 383–401.

Stone, Donald D. *The Romantic Impulse in Victorian Fiction.* Cambridge: Harvard UP, 1980.

Stone, Lawrence. *Family, Sex, and Marriage in England, 1500–1800.* New York: Harper, 1979.

Sullivan, Paula. "Fairy Tale Elements in *Jane Eyre.*" *Journal of Popular Culture* 12 (1978): 61–74.

Tayler, Irene. *Holy Ghosts: The Male Muses of Emily and Charlotte Brontë.* New York: Columbia UP, 1990.

Thackeray, William Makepeace. *The Letters and Private Papers of William Makepeace Thackeray.* Ed. Gordon N. Ray. 4 vols. Cambridge: Harvard UP, 1946.

Thompson, E. P. *The Making of the English Working Class*. New York: Pantheon, 1964.

Thorpe, Michael. " 'The Other Side': *Wide Sargasso Sea* and *Jane Eyre*." *Ariel* 8.3 (1977): 99–110.

Thurman, Judith. "Reader, I Married Him." *New Yorker* 20 Mar. 1989: 109–14.

Thwing, Leroy. *Flickering Flames: A History of Domestic Lighting through the Ages*. Rutland: Ruslight, 1958.

Tillotson, Kathleen. *Novels of the Eighteen-Forties*. Oxford: Clarendon–Oxford UP, 1954.

Tomory, Peter. *The Life and Art of Henry Fuseli*. New York: Praeger, 1972.

Tompkins, Jane P., ed. *Reader-Response Criticism*. Baltimore: Johns Hopkins UP, 1980.

Traeger, Jorg, ed. *Caspar David Friedrich*. New York: Rizzoli, n.d.

Turner, Victor. "Betwixt and Between: The Liminal Period in *Rites de Passage*." *The Forest of Symbols: Aspects of Ndembu Ritual*. Ithaca: Cornell UP, 1967. 93–111.

———. "Liminal to Liminoid, in Play, Flow, Ritual: An Essay in Comparative Symbology." *From Ritual to Theatre: The Human Seriousness of Play*. New York: Performing Arts Journal Pub., 1982. 20–60.

Twitchell, James B. *Romantic Horizons: Aspects of the Sublime in English Poetry and Painting, 1770–1850*. Columbia: U of Missouri P, 1983.

Vargish, Thomas. *The Providential Aesthetic in Victorian Fiction*. Charlottesville: UP of Virginia, 1985.

Watt, Ian. *The Rise of the Novel*. Berkeley: U of California P, 1957.

Watzlawick, Paul, et al. *Pragmatics of Human Communication: A Study of Interactional Patterns, Pathologies, and Paradoxes*. New York: Norton, 1967.

Wegscheider, Don. *If Only My Family Understood Me*. Minneapolis: Compcare, 1979.

Wilks, Brian. *The Brontës*. New York: Viking, 1976.

Williams, Ioan. *The Realist Novel in England: A Study in Development*. London: Macmillan, 1974.

Williams, Judith. *Perception and Expression in the Novels of Charlotte Brontë*. Ann Arbor: UMI, 1988.

Wilson, F. A. C. "The Primrose Wreath: The Heroes of the Brontë Novels." *Nineteenth-Century Fiction* 29 (1974–75): 40–57.

Winnifrith, Tom. *The Brontës*. London: Macmillan, 1977.

———. *The Brontës and Their Background: Romance and Reality*. New York: Barnes, 1973.

Wise, Thomas James, and John Alexander Symington, eds. *The Brontës: Their Lives, Friendships and Correspondence*. The Shakespeare Head Brontë. 4 vols. Oxford: Blackwell, 1932.

———. *The Miscellaneous and Unpublished Writings of Charlotte and Patrick Branwell Brontë*. The Shakespeare Head Brontë. 2 vols. Oxford: Blackwell, 1936, 1938.

Wohl, Anthony, ed. *The Victorian Family: Structure and Stresses*. London: Croon Helm, 1978.

Wollstonecraft, Mary. *Collected Letters of Mary Wollstonecraft*. Ed. Ralph M. Wardle. Ithaca: Cornell UP, 1979.

———. *A Vindication of the Rights of Woman*. 1792. 2nd ed. Ed. Carol Poston. New York: Norton, 1988.

Wood, Christopher. *Panorama: Paintings of Victorian Life*. London: Faber, 1976.

———. *The Pre-Raphaelites*. New York: Viking, 1981.

Woolf, Virginia. "*Jane Eyre* and *Wuthering Heights*." *The Common Reader*. New York: Harcourt, 1925. 219–27. Rpt. in Dunn, *Jane Eyre* (1971 ed.) 454–57; Dunn, *Jane Eyre* (1987 ed.) 455–57.

———. *A Room of One's Own*. 1929. New York: Harcourt, 1963.

Wyatt, Jean. *Reconstructing Desire: The Role of the Unconscious in Women's Reading and Writing*. Chapel Hill: U of North Carolina P, 1990.

Yeazell, Ruth. "More True than Real: Jane Eyre's 'Mysterious Summons.'" *Nineteenth-Century Fiction* 29 (1974–75): 127–43.

Films and Filmstrips

The Brontës: Fantasy and Reality. Two sound filmstrips. Guidance-Harcourt, 1985.

The Brontës of Haworth. Prod. Christopher Fry. Films for the Humanities, 1991. 4 hr., 9 min. Color.

Jane Eyre. Dir. Julian Aymes. With Zelah Clarke and Timothy Dalton. BBC, 1983.

Jane Eyre. Dir. Delbert Mann. Prod. Frederick H. Brogger. With Susannah York and George C. Scott. British Lion, 1970.

Jane Eyre. Prod. Worthington Miner. With Katherine Bard and Kevin McCarthy. Westinghouse Studio One, CBS, 1952.

Jane Eyre. Dir. Robert Stevenson. Prod. William Goetz. With Joan Fontaine and Orson Welles. Twentieth Century–Fox, 1944.

Kellogg, Terry, screenwriter. *Family, Codependency, and Recovery*. Series of six videocassettes. Lifeworks, 1988.

The Nineteenth-Century Novel. Filmstrip 1: *Austen, the Brontës, and George Eliot*. Filmstrip 2: *Dickens and Thackeray*. Sound filmstrips. Films for the Humanities, 1981.

The Yorkshire of the Brontë Sisters. Videocassette (VHS or Beta). Films for the Humanities, 1988. 15 min. Color.

Recordings

Bloom, Claire, Anthony Quayle, et al. *Jane Eyre: An Abridgement of the Novel*. 3 LPs. Caedmon, LC 75-750930, 1969.

Colby, Vineta. *Jane Eyre*. Audiotape. Everett/Edwards 3872. Gould, 1976.

INDEX

Abrams, M. H., 28
Adams, Maurianne, 9, 10, 77
Adler, Alfred, 131
Albee, Edward, 131
Alexander, Christine, 6, 16
Allen, Dennis W., 10, 11, 21
Allen, Walter, 8, 13
Allott, Miriam, 8, 14, 29
Altick, Richard D., 8, 83
Antal, Frederick, 98, 100, 103
Armstrong, Nancy, 10, 107, 119
Auerbach, Nina, 10, 101, 103
Austen, Jane, 21, 23, 27, 52, 89, 153, 155

Bachelard, Gaston, 84, 86
Baer, Elizabeth, 13
Bakhtin, M. M., 87, 120
Banks, J. A., 43
Bard, Katharine, 15
Barker, Juliet, 144
Barthes, Roland, 119
Baudrillard, Jean, 21, 111–12, 113
Beaty, Jerome, 12, 67
Beer, Patricia, 9, 13
Bellis, Peter, 11
Bender, Todd K., 8
Bentley, Eric, 142
Bentley, Phyllis, 7, 15, 30
Benveniste, Emile, 77
Benvenuto, Richard, 11
Berg, Maggie, 67
Berman, Ronald, 13
Bernstein, Susan D., 10, 91
Bettelheim, Bruno, 56, 58, 90
Bewick, Thomas, 15, 20, 83, 98, 100, 149
Bible, 12, 20, 62, 63, 64, 66, 69, 70, 72, 73, 74
Bjork, Harriet, 9
Blom, Margaret Howard, 7, 13, 29, 32
Bloom, Claire, 15
Bloom, Harold, 14, 67
Blos, Peter, 56
Bodenheimer, Rosemarie, 11, 14
Boos, Florence, 16
Booth, Michael, 142, 144
Borsch-Supan, Helmut, 100, 103
Boumelha, Penny, 77
Bowen, Murray, 131, 136
Bowkett, Jane Maria, 101
Bradshaw, John, 21, 131, 132, 133, 136

Branwell, Elizabeth, 63
Brontë, Anne, 5, 13, 31, 33, 98, 102, 131, 144
Brontë, Branwell, 32, 33, 36, 99, 102, 144
Brontë, Elizabeth, 38
Brontë, Emily, 13, 15, 30, 31, 33, 36, 102, 142, 144, 149
Brontë, Patrick, 13, 29, 63
Brontës, the, 6, 7, 12, 15, 16, 23, 37, 99, 139, 144
Brooks, Peter, 143
Brougham, John, 142, 143
Brown, Ford Madox, 101, 102
Buckley, Jerome H., 8
Bump, Jerome, 10, 21, 131, 132
Bunyan, John, 12, 91, 152
Burgan, Mary, 11, 20
Burgan, William M., 88
Burkhart, Charles, 10, 141
Burney, Fanny, 23
Butery, Karen Ann, 10, 13
Buttlin, Martin, 100, 103
Byron, George Gordan, Lord, 12, 38, 98, 99

Campbell, Joseph, 89
Caskey, Noelle, 117
Cecil, David, 14
Chase, Karen, 9, 13, 80
Chase, Richard, 9–10, 14
Checkland, S. G., 43
Christensen, Oscar, 131
Cirker, Blanche, 98, 103
Clarke, Zelah, 15
Cockshut, A. O. J., 8
Cohen, Paula Marantz, 131
Cohn, Jan, 121
Colby, Vineta, 15
Coleridge, Samuel Taylor, 12, 100
Collins, Charles Alston, 101
Collins, Wilkie, 50
Cowart, David, 92
Craig, G. Armour, 14
Craik, W. A., 9, 14
Crompton, David, 14
Cross, Gilbert B., 142
Crump, Rebecca W., 16
Culler, Jonathan, 156

Daiches, David, 15
Dale, Peter Allan, 11

Dalton, Timothy, 15
Davies, Robertson, 142, 143
DeLamotte, Eugenia C., 12, 50
Derrida, Jacques, 87, 88, 91
Dessner, Lawrence J., 12
DeVane, William C., 6
Dewey, John, 140
Dicey, Cluer, 90
Dickens, Charles, 12, 13, 21, 87, 160
Diedrick, James, 12, 19
Dijkstra, Bram, 101, 103
Disney, Walt, 56, 90, 142
Donaldson, Laura E., 109
Dry, Florence Swinton, 12
du Maurier, Daphne, 52
Dunn, Richard J., 4, 12, 16, 28, 63, 79,
   82, 83, 108, 115, 132, 144
DuPlessis, Rachel Blau, 11, 141
Duthie, Enid Lowry, 10, 12, 13

Eagleton, Terry, 4, 10, 14, 156, 157,
   161
Edgeworth, Maria, 23
Egg, Augustus, 101
Elias, Norbert, 120
Eliot, George, 13, 42, 155, 161
Ellis, Kate, 14, 142
Ewbank, Inga-Stina, 9, 14

Falk, Kathryn, 140
Fielding, Henry, 87
Flower, John, 15
Foley, Vincent D., 131
Fontaine, Joan, 14, 141
Forster, E. M., 124
Foucault, Michel, 83, 116, 117, 118–19,
   120
Fraser, Rebecca, 6–7, 99, 102, 103
Freeman, Janet H., 7, 19, 30
Freud, Sigmund, 131, 144
Friedrich, Caspar David, 99, 100
Frith, William Powell, 101
Frye, Northrop, 89
Fuseli, Henry, 98, 100

Gallagher, Susan VanZanten, 11, 20
Gaskell, Elizabeth, 4, 6, 7, 29, 31,
   36–37, 38, 42, 83, 144
Gates, Barbara T., 11
Gay, Peter, 112
Genette, Gérard, 76
Gennep, Arnold van, 92
Gérin, Winifred, 6, 7, 12, 13, 36, 63
Gilbert, Sandra M., 4, 5, 8, 9, 13, 14,
   22, 28, 50, 53, 54, 66, 67, 77, 100,
   106, 112, 131, 141
Gilead, Sarah, 92
Godwin, William, 23, 26

Goscilo, Margaret, 15, 20
Graefle, Albert, 101
Gregor, Ian, 14
Griffin, Gail B., 10
Gubar, Susan, 5, 8, 9, 13, 14, 22, 28, 50,
   53, 54, 66, 67, 77, 100, 106, 112, 131, 141

Hagstrum, Jean, 117
Hannah, Barbara, 10
Hardy, Barbara, 11, 14
Hardy, Thomas, 155, 161
Héger, Constantin, 36, 37, 38, 102
Heilman, Robert B., 4, 10, 12, 14
Heller, Tamar, 12, 20
Hennelly, Mark M., Jr., 11, 20, 92
Heuscher, Julius E., 56
Hicks, George Elgar, 101
Higashi, Sumiko, 14, 142
Hoeveler, Diane Long, 10, 21
Holtz, William, 6
Homans, Margaret, 14
HopKins, Mary Frances, 142
Horney, Karen, 126
Houghton, Walter E., 8
Houseman, John, 141
Hughes, R. E., 11
Hunt, William Holman, 101
Huxley, Aldous, 141
Hylson-Smith, Kenneth, 62

Imlay, Gilbert, 26
Ironside, Robin, 101, 102, 103

Jack, Jane, 4, 5
Jackson, D. D., 131
Jay, Elisabeth, 62, 63
Jeffers, Thomas L., 7, 19–20
Jenkins, Keith A., 11, 12, 20
Jerome, Helen, 142, 144
Johnson, Samuel, 91
Johnstone, Christopher, 99, 103
Joll, Evelyn, 100, 103
Jordan, John O., 11, 20
Julian of Norwich, 67

Kalikoff, Beth, 13
Kaplan, Ann, 14, 142
Kaplan, Cora, 105, 108
Keefe, Robert, 10, 12
Kellogg, Terry, 132
Kerr, Michael E., 131, 136
Kilburne, George Goodwin, 101
Kingsley, Charles, 37
Kinkead-Weekes, Mark, 14
Knies, Earl, 9, 11
Kristeva, Julia, 21, 156–57, 158
Kroeber, Karl, 11, 13
Kucich, John, 10, 20, 119

Landow, George P., 69, 75
Lane, Margaret, 7, 33
Leavis, F. R., 4, 13
Leavis, L. R., 13
Leavis, Q. D., 4, 13, 27, 39
Lerner, Laurence, 90
Lesser, Simon O., 130
Lessing, Doris, 91
Lewes, George Henry, 82, 144
Lewis, Jerry M., 132
Linder, Cynthia, 10, 144
Lodge, David, 10, 14, 88
Long, Beverly Whitaker, 142
Looney, John G., 132

Macaulay, Catharine, 23
Mann, Delbert, 14, 139
Marshall, Richard, 90
Martineau, Harriet, 41
Martineau, Robert Braithwaite, 101
Martin, John, 38, 99
Martin, Robert B., 9, 14
Martin, Robert K., 12
Marx, Karl, 111
Mashberg, Amy L., 131
Maynard, John, 9, 10, 122
McBride, Simon, 7, 15
McCarthy, Kevin, 15
Meredith, George, 39
Miller, D. A., 50
Miller, Jane, 10
Miller, Jean Baker, 131
Miller, J. Hillis, 8, 62
Miller, Lynn, 16
Miller, Nancy K., 49
Millgate, Jane, 11, 12
Mill, John Stuart, 41
Milton, John, 99
Modleski, Tania, 50, 52
Moers, Ellen, 50
Moglen, Helene, 4, 6, 9, 12, 14, 22, 28
Monahan, Melodie, 121, 122
Monod, Sylvère, 14
Montagu, Mary Wortley, Lady, 23
Moore, O. Christene, 137
Morral, Frank, 131
Morrison, Toni, 132

Nead, Lynda, 101, 103
Nestor, Pauline, 7, 9, 13
Neufeldt, Victor A., 6
Nichols, Arthur Bell, 6
Nudd, Donna Marie, 14, 15, 21, 140, 142
Nussey, Ellen, 36

Oates, Joyce Carol, 13
O'Neill, Judith, 14

Opie, Iona, 56, 58, 59, 60
Opie, Peter, 56, 58, 59, 60

Paris, Bernard J., 10, 13, 21, 126
Passel, Anne, 15
Patten, Robert L., 13, 21
Peel, Thomas, 101
Pell, Nancy, 9
Perrault, Charles, 56, 90
Peters, Margot, 6, 11, 36, 41
Peterson, M. Jeanne, 8, 30, 43
Pickrel, Paul, 10, 11
Pinion, Francis B., 7, 12, 15
Plath, Sylvia, 109
Politi, Jina, 10, 77, 78
Pollard, Arthur, 7, 15
Poovey, Mary, 8, 20, 27, 45
Poston, Carol, 28
Prideaux, James, 142, 144

Qualls, Barry, 12
Quayle, Anthony, 15
Quennell, Peter, 100

Radcliffe, Ann, 50, 51
Ralph, Phyllis C., 12, 20
Rankley, Alfred, 101
Ratchford, Fannie E., 6, 34
Redgrave, Richard, 102
Reynolds, Graham, 101, 103
Rhys, Jean, 13, 91, 106, 131, 137
Rich, Adrienne, 4, 9, 22, 28, 140, 141
Rigby, Elizabeth, 79, 82, 108
Rigney, Barbara, 9
Riley, Michael, 14
Roberts, Doreen, 11, 144
Robinson, Lydia, 36
Rodolff, Rebecca, 34
Rosenblatt, Louise M., 155
Rosengarten, Herbert J., 5, 12, 15
Rosenwasser, David, 11, 13, 21
Rousseau, Jean Jacques, 24, 26
Rowe, Karen E., 12, 141
Russ, Joanna, 52, 53

Sabol, C. Ruth, 8
Sadoff, Dianne F., 10, 13
Said, Edward, 107
Scargill, M. H., 14
Scarry, Elaine, 84
Schiller, Friedrich von, 91
Schivelbusch, Wolfgang, 83
Schmidt, Helen von, 13
Schorer, Mark, 5, 8
Schwartz, Narda Lacey, 16
Scott, George C., 14
Scott, Walter, Sir, 12, 91, 98

Sexton, Anne, 109
Shakespeare, William, 98
Sheridan, Alan, 122
Shorter, Clement, 139
Showalter, Elaine, 8, 9, 10, 13
Silverman, Kaja, 77
Smith, James, 142
Smith, Margaret, 4–5, 12
Southey, Robert, 102
Spacks, Patricia Meyer, 8
Spivak, Gayatri Chakravorty, 10, 13,
    78, 107, 109
Spring, David, 83
Stevenson, Lionel, 8, 13
Stevenson, Robert, 14, 21, 139, 140,
    141, 142
Stewart, Garrett, 11
Stone, Donald D., 12
Stone, Lawrence, 117
Sullivan, Harry Stack, 131
Sullivan, Paula, 12
Symington, John Alexander, 6, 36, 37,
    41, 108

Tayler, Irene, 122
Taylor, Harriet, 41
Taylor, Mary, 36, 37, 41
Tennyson, Alfred, Lord, 62
Thackeray, William Makepeace, 4, 29,
    38, 39
Thompson, E. P., 25
Thorpe, Michael, 13, 106
Thurman, Judith, 38
Thwing, Leroy, 83
Tillotson, Kathleen, 9, 13, 14
Tomory, Peter, 98, 100, 103

Tompkins, Jane P., 140
Traeger, Jorg, 100, 103
Turner, J. M. W., 38, 99
Turner, Victor, 88, 92–95
Twitchell, James B., 99, 103

Vargish, Thomas, 11, 13

Watt, Ian, 111
Watzlawick, Paul, 131
Wegscheider, Don, 133
Weldon, Fay, 144
Welles, Orson, 14, 141
Wesley, Charles, 62
Wesley, John, 62
Whitefield, George, 62
Wilks, Brian, 7, 15, 98, 102, 103
Williams, Ioan, 8
Williams, Judith, 11
Williams, Raymond, 14
Williams, Tennessee, 131
Williams, W. S., 29, 41, 139
Wilson, F. A. C., 10
Wilson, William Carus, 38
Winnifrith, Tom, 7, 8, 11, 12, 13, 63
Wise, Thomas James, 6, 36, 37, 41,
    108
Wohl, Anthony, 130
Wollstonecraft, Mary, 19, 22–24, 25–27
Wood, Christopher, 101, 102, 103
Woolf, Virginia, 4, 8, 9, 14, 51, 109
Wordsworth, William, 12
Wyatt, Jean, 122

Yeazell, Ruth, 12
York, Susannah, 14